Sunderland
Player of the Year
1976–2011

Sunderland
Player of the Year
1976–2011

Rob Mason

First published in Great Britain in 2011 by The Derby Books Publishing Company Limited, 3 The Parker Centre, Derby, DE21 4SZ.

This paperback edition published in Great Britain in 2013 by DB Publishing, an imprint of JMD Media Ltd

ISBN 978-1-78091-340-7

Printed and bound in the UK by Copytech (UK) Ltd Peterborough

Contents

Dedication

This celebration of Sunderland Players of the Year is dedicated not to a player but a supporter. Now chairman of the Sunderland AFC Supporters' Association (SAFCSA), George Forster has been a stalwart of the association since just a few months after its 1965 formation. A true gentleman who represents all that is good in football, George is a friend to all and a brilliant ambassador for SAFC.

Introduction

It was Sunderland's all time record League goalscorer Charlie Buchan who came up with the idea of the Footballer of the Year award. The national accolade, first won by the legendary Stanley Matthews in 1947–48, is to this day the major individual award in the game. No player has ever won it while with Sunderland although two have been runners-up. In 1964, promotion-winning skipper Charlie Hurley missed out to England's future World Cup-winning captain Bobby Moore, who in '64 won the FA Cup with West Ham. Twenty-six years later Kevin Phillips came second in the season, he was Europe's top scorer, to future Sunderland manager Roy Keane who became the Football Writers' Association (FWA) Footballer of the Year.

Having been instrumental in the creation of the FWA, Buchan – who played for Sunderland either side of World War One – was the brains behind the country's leading football magazine *Charles Buchan's Football Monthly*, and an instigator of the Football Writers' Association and thus the Footballer of the Year award was born.

Many clubs began their own awards several years before Sunderland. It was the Sunderland Supporters' Association who started a Player of the Year award. Perhaps buoyed by Bob Stokoe leading the Lads back into the top flight in 1976 three years after the famous Cup win, the fans decided to commence the Sunderland Player of the Year award in the 1976–77 season. Consequently the inaugural winner of the trophy – Joe Bolton – did so in a relegation campaign. 'The first Player of the Year sponsor was a tailor called Joe Hind,' remembers Ann Howe of the SAFCSA, who also recalls: 'The first winner was Joe Bolton who got a suit and he was over the moon. The players received something for their award from the sponsor. Ian Atkins got a beautiful coffee table from Majestic computers when they sponsored the award for example.'

Eventually in 1980–81 the club decided to add an official award to the SAFCSA honour. As 1991–92 winner John Byrne says, 'It's a bit like the different belts in boxing.' In that Cup Final season Byrne took the official title while the original Supporters' Association trophy went to cult hero John Kay, who missed his big day at Wembley through injury.

In most years since the two awards have run concurrently the same player has taken both. For the purposes of this book the SAFCSA winner has been featured for the first few years but in the years where two awards have been made the official winner is the player who has been discussed, although both winners have been acknowledged in each chapter's introductory details of the season. In both 2002–03 and 2005–06, when Sunderland were relegated with record low points totals, the Supporters' Association did not have an award ceremony, although they did in 1986–87 despite the side being relegated to Division Three. 'One year it was booked and everything. We had the tickets printed but we just couldn't sell them so it was cancelled,' explains Ann Howe. In contrast in 2007–08 when Derby County thankfully took away Sunderland's unwanted record of gathering the lowest number of points in a top-flight season, the Rams gave their Player of the Year award to their fans.

For many years the official award was decided upon based on votes submitted to the local paper, the *Sunderland Echo*, and the club's own match programme. In 1994–95 for one season only three main awards were made. The club made its own award via its programme in addition to what was a separate *Echo* award with the SAFCSA trophy completing the trio. Polish right-back Dariusz Kubicki won the club's official programme award that year and is the player focused on for that season here. In recent years the official club award has been won based on votes submitted via their own website, safc.com.

In 2010–11 SAFC held their first ever awards dinner. This was a glittering occasion that saw numerous awards including goal and save of the season with the major prize being the Player of the Year accolade. Phil Bardsley deservedly emerged as the winner. Bardsley is not unlike the first winner Joe Bolton. Both are hard-as-nails full-backs who chip in with the occasional spectacular goal. The fact that more defenders than forwards have been Player of the Year tells you something about the Sunderland supporters who vote for them. Strikers command the bulk of the headlines – and Sunderland have indeed had some superb strikers who have been Player of the Year – but the fans recognise the value of a player over a full season. Many of Sunderland's Players of the Year have been back four men, often the sort of stalwarts who rarely make the headlines but who do their stuff week in, week out. The Red and White Army expect their heroes to get stuck in but they expect quality as well. Anyone who has won enough votes to be judged the team's best player, not on an odd occasion when everything goes right for them, but consistently over an entire campaign, deserves to be recognised. Sunderland supporters know their football and appreciate players who give their all and make the most of the ability they have been blessed with.

The list of names featured in the chapters to follow will bring back many great memories. As well as focusing on the individual, the chapters seek to tell the story of the season – be it one of delight or disaster – in an attempt to put the Player of the Year's contribution into context.

Most of the Players of the Year have been tracked down and interviewed specifically for this book. Where individuals were impossible to locate then their contemporaries have remembered them or I have researched their thoughts of the time from programme interviews that they did with me. What was consistent in the recollections of all the players spoken to was how much being Player of the Year meant to them. Once the boots are hung up for the final time, regardless of whether the player has a cupboard full of medals and caps or none, if they have been Player of the Year it shows how much the fans have appreciated their efforts.

Enjoy the memories.

Rob Mason
SAFC publications editor and club historian
August 2011

Acknowledgements

Firstly I would like to thank all of the players who happily contributed to this book. Without exception they gave their time freely and were eager to help out. Many were interviewed on the phone. Jeff Clarke was on a bus home in Dundee after dropping his car off to be serviced: you don't expect your heroes to be on the bus but it shows they're normal. Special thanks to Julio Arca, who after hearing I was trying to get in touch with him, courtesy of James Hunter of the *Evening Chronicle*, rang me from Argentina. Gary Bennett as ever is red and white through and through and offered lots of insight on many of the Players of the Year who were his teammates in over a decade at Roker Park.

Kevin Ball won just one official accolade but a record four Sunderland AFC Supporters' Association awards and as always was generous with his time. As was the 1998–99 winner, known now as much for what he's done off the pitch as on it: chairman Niall Quinn, who kindly contributed the foreword.

Special thanks go to my wife Barbara whose SAFC knowledge from years of proof-reading means that she no longer just corrects me on typos but now picks up errors of fact too. This book only goes back to 1976 but my better half's knowledge even of the 1890s surpasses that of almost everyone I know. Do not tell me – I know we should get out more!

My thanks are also due, as they are so many times, to George Forster, chairman of the Sunderland Supporters' Association and to long-serving Supporters' Association stalwart Ann Howe. Along with their colleagues in the SAFCSA they have done so much to organise Player of the Year events since the earliest days of the award.

Foreword

Sunderland have had seasons that were either fantastic or terrible but seldom do we get dull years on Wearside – emotions are so entwined with what happens at the Stadium of Light that every kick matters enormously.

Football is a team game and whoever becomes the Player of the Year does not win it just because he has had a great season. Just as a goalscorer needs teammates to create chances for him or a defender needs to be part of a cohesive unit, one player cannot make a team successful by himself. That is why this book does not only focus on the Player of the Year but also tells the story of each season.

Since the award first came into existence there have been many worthy winners, several of whom I played with and once I was fortunate enough to be the recipient myself.

Sunderland supporters possess incredible passion and loyalty. To be voted the Player of the Year by the Red and White Army is an achievement people look back on for the rest of their lives knowing that they have been appreciated. This official SAFC book will let you relive the contributions made by the players you have voted for since Joe Bolton became the first winner in 1976–77. Enjoy the memories and look forward to more to come as we hope the competition for the accolade of being Player of the Year will be immense in the seasons ahead.

Niall Quinn

Award Winners

1976–77 Joe Bolton	**1994–95** Dariusz Kubicki
1977–78 Bobby Kerr	**1995–96** Richard Ord
1978–79 Shaun Elliott	**1996–97** Lionel Perez
1979–80 Jeff Clarke	**1997–98** Kevin Phillips
1980–81 Stan Cummins	**1998–99** Niall Quinn
1981–82 Nick Pickering	**1999–2000** Kevin Phillips
1982–83 Ian Atkins	**2000–01** Don Hutchison
1983–84 Paul Bracewell	**2001–02** Jody Craddock
1984–85 Chris Turner	**2002–03** Sean Thornton
1985–86 Mark Proctor	**2003–04** Julio Arca
1986–87 Gary Bennett	**2004–05** George McCartney
1987–88 Eric Gates	**2005–06** Dean Whitehead
1988–89 Marco Gabbiadini	**2006–07** Nyron Nosworthy
1989–90 Marco Gabbiadini	**2007–08** Kenwyne Jones
1990–91 Kevin Ball	**2008–09** Danny Collins
1991–92 John Byrne	**2009–10** Darren Bent
1992–93 Don Goodman	**2010–11** Phil Bardsley
1993–94 Gary Bennett	

Joe Bolton

Division One: 20th out of 22 – relegated
FA Cup: Third round, lost to Wrexham in a replay
League Cup: Third round, lost to Manchester United in a second replay
Top scorer: Bob Lee, 13 goals, all League
Ever present: Joe Bolton, 48 out of 48 League and Cup games, 1 goal
Player of the Year: Joe Bolton

Sunderland had been Division Two champions in 1975–76 in the last full season under the managership of Bob Stokoe and the final campaign that lacked a Player of the Year award. Had one existed there would have been plenty of candidates in a title-winning year but by the time a choice had to made as to who would become the first ever SAFC Supporters' Association Player of the Year, Sunderland were doomed to relegation. Inevitably in a season that resulted in demotion there were few contenders for the crown, despite the fact that under Stokoe's eventual successor Jimmy Adamson the Lads had staged a rousing fightback only to be denied at the death after shenanigans at an infamous Coventry City v Bristol City game.

At the start of September there was no indication of the trouble ahead. A positive pre-season had kept confidence high following promotion and the season began solidly if unspectacularly with three draws, the first two goalless, followed by a pulsating 2–2 with Arsenal before a bumper gate at Roker Park.

As the Sunderland team bus pulled away from Ashton Gate after the fourth game of the campaign, the visitors had been walloped 4–1 by a Bristol City side who had been promoted behind the Wearsiders, it effectively marked the end of one of the club's finest post-war periods. It signalled a period of upheaval. Just over six weeks later manager Bob Stokoe had left. Between the Bristol City game and Stokoe's resignation the 1973 FA Cup Final hero 'keeper Jimmy Montgomery had played his record 627th and final match, three other players had also made their final appearances for the club while another four made their bow.

By the end of the campaign Monty's fellow Cup winners Dick Malone and Billy Hughes were among a further seven players to have worn red and white for the final time. Sunderland had been dumped back into the Second Division which they had striven so hard to get out of since becoming the nation's darlings when winning the Cup in 1973.

Back then Joe Bolton was a teenager just starting out in the team. He had debuted towards the close of the previous (1971–72) season, given the final four games of the campaign by manager Alan Brown, a man famous for giving youth a chance. Joe had started the first two games of what proved to be the Cup-winning season and after missing out to fellow youngster Keith Coleman in his left-back berth was then brought back by 'Bomber' Brown for what proved to be the manager's last game. Retained by caretaker boss Billy Elliott for the former Sunderland hard man's first match in charge, Bolton then waited for another opportunity under new boss Stokoe.

That arrived in the first game of the triumphant Cup run at Notts County. Joe held his place for the replay but was then sidelined as Stokoe added experience to the side with the purchase of Newcastle left-back Ron Guthrie.

'Stokoe bought Ron to add a bit of experience – that's what he said to me, like,' remembers Bolton. 'Bob bought a lot of experienced lads from Newcastle, even later on with

Bob Moncur a few years later. When he brought in Ron Guthrie I just thought my chance would come eventually and it did. It was just a new face, it's happened at many a club, when a new manager comes in he brings people in and it just seems to lift the place. I hadn't really been into Alan Brown either. I was just a young lad at the time. I didn't know the things that were going on at the club. I was in and out of the team.' Joe recalls of his early days: 'I'd played a few games and then Keith Coleman played not long before Alan Brown left. He gave me my debut though and I'll always owe him that. A lot of people got on with him and a lot didn't.

'I remember the Notts County game in the Cup. I got a whack in the head. I didn't get stitched but I was bleeding at the back. I can remember just after the game Stokoe said we were going to have a game of golf on the Monday. I didn't think he was including me. I turned to Vic Halom and asked, "Does he mean me as well?" Vic says, "Oh yeah, because you played." I'd never done that before with Alan Brown. I thought, "Oh well, he's changing things and including the young lads and he's making it enjoyable for them as well." I got on with Bob Stokoe all right.'

Bolton developed so well under Stokoe that he had begun to force Cup winner Guthrie out of the side within a few months of the Wembley success. By the end of October 1973 Joe was beginning to be viewed as first-choice left-back, although Guthrie came back into the reckoning in 1974–75, Bolton spending most of the second half of that season in midfield. 'I played midfield when Ian Porterfield had his accident. Ron was playing left-back and I was playing midfield,' Joe explains, Cup Final goalscorer Porterfield having been very badly injured in a car crash shortly before Christmas 1974. Bolton was being brought down for a penalty in his first excursion as a midfielder at Blackpool a couple of months later.

With Guthrie released at the end of the season, Bolton reverted to his favoured left-back position, gaining a Second Division Championship medal in 1976 prior to his Player of the Year season. Little did people realise as they left Bristol City's Ashton Gate after that heavy first defeat since the return to the top flight that those two points – it was still two points for a win – would keep the Robins up and condemn Sunderland to relegation come the day of reckoning. The solid start of three draws fell away, with the Bristol game being the first of three successive losses.

Joe's only goal of the season brought a hard-fought point away to West Ham but by now the Lads were propping up the division and worse was to follow. Another three-game losing streak did not even bring a goal for the Wearsiders with two of the defeats coming on home soil, manager Bob Stokoe resigning after the second of those, a 1–0 home defeat to Aston Villa. Scottish international Alex Cropley's Villa winner signalled the 56th defeat Sunderland had suffered since Stokoe arrived a month short of four years earlier. However there had been 92 wins, 49 draws and two trophies in that spell and the resignation was something that Stokoe would come to regret. At the time though, Stokoe was suffering through ill health.

'I felt sick before, during and after the game,' Stokoe admitted. 'I had been talking to people like Matt Busby and Jackie Milburn, seeking their advice on how I felt and what I should do. They all said the same thing to me: "Get out of the game before it completely consumes and harms you." My own doctor had told me I needed to take a break, unanimously supporting the views of my family.'

After 10 games the Lads were without a win and had collected just one point from the last seven fixtures. Former Carlisle manager Ian MacFarlane had been Stokoe's number two and took over the reins at Roker Park. 'He was called the big man,' recalls Joe, 'Smashing bloke, mind.' Sunderland remained rock bottom of the League after the Scot's first match in charge, goals from ex-Arsenal skipper Frank McLintock and the man who had infamously knocked the

FA Cup off its table at Sunderland a few days after the 1973 Cup win, Stan Bowles, giving mid-table QPR a comfortable 2–0 win in London.

Still the solitary win of the season had been over Second Division Luton Town in the League Cup before Sunderland's first defeat of the campaign. There was better news though with a League win at last in MacFarlane's second game, 2–1 at Coventry. Bob Stokoe had spent £200,000 on making Bob Lee Sunderland's record buy and the former Leicester City man gave Sunderland a half-time lead with his first goal for the club. Another from Cup survivor Billy Hughes ensured a 2–1 victory and the hope that this was the kick-start to the season that the Black Cats were waiting for.

Things would get an awful lot worse before they got better for the Lads. Several acts of what was a dramatic season were yet to unfold but the denouement would come at the Highfield Road stadium where Sunderland beat Coventry at the end of October.

Defender Jackie Ashurst, having disagreed with MacFarlane over whether he should play at centre-back or right-back, was left out of the side after the caretaker manager's first game. As often happens with a struggling side, the team was chopped and changed. Sunderland used 30 players in 1976–77. Bolton was the only player to play in both the first two and last two games of the season. Indeed, come the end of the campaign no other player came near Bolton's record of appearing in every fixture. While Joe started all 42 League games – as well as all six Cup ties – only three other players managed 30 or more: new signings Barry Siddall and Bob Lee, neither of whom were at the club until October, and Jackie Ashurst, who featured in 30 games. Bolton was the constant presence in a season that brought more managers than wins until February.

Nonetheless, that first win over Coventry provided a boost and even briefly lifted the club off the foot of the table. Bolton's goal at West Ham had been the only time Sunderland had scored in the previous five League games but despite an unlucky and hard-fought 1–0 home reverse to eventual champions Liverpool, belief was returning to what was a newly promoted side with a handful of new signings who were beginning to find their feet. A fightback from two goals down to earn a thrilling 3–3 draw at a foggy Manchester United was backed up with a first home win of the season, Ray Train's first League goal for the club and Lee's fourth in as many matches continuing the fighting spirit as they overturned a half-time deficit against Tottenham.

Sadly the improvement was a flash in the pan. Sunderland would not gain another point for over two months, or even score for 10 League games after Billy Hughes' final goal for the club, a penalty in a 3–1 defeat at Bobby Robson's Ipswich a week after the victory over Spurs.

The city of Sunderland's motto is *Nil Desperandum* meaning 'Never Despair' but the football club gave *Nil Desperandum* a whole new meaning as they embarked on a run of 10 League games without scoring a goal.

MacFarlane oversaw the first blank in a defeat at Derby after which he was replaced by Jimmy Adamson. Hopes of a new manager having an immediate positive impact were wiped out as Sunderland went on what was, up to then, the worst run in the club's history. Beginning with a 2–0 defeat at Birmingham City, Adamson saw his side beaten by a goal from future Sunderland assistant manager Viv Busby in his first home game. That result dumped Sunderland back at the foot of the table ahead of their next match, a Christmas fixture away to rivals Newcastle. The score at St James' would have been worse than the Halloween horror of 2010 had it not been for superlative performances from centre-backs Jeff Clarke and Jim Holton. Aided by Joe Bolton and Dick Malone at full-back, the back four were engaged in damage limitation for 90 minutes as high-riding Newcastle stayed fifth in the table, their second goal coming from Sunderland-born future Rokerite Alan Kennedy.

The match was the 282nd and last for 1973 FA Cup winner Malone as the new manager set about making changes. The previous game had seen forward Alan Foggon make his final appearance for the club, while within a week midfielder Tommy Gibb had also pulled on a red and white shirt for the last time. Having had his football education as part of a successful young side at Burnley a decade and a half earlier, Adamson – like Stokoe's predecessor Brown, another Burnley old boy – turned to youth. Within three games of becoming Sunderland manager Adamson had handed debuts to local youngsters Alan Brown and Tim Gilbert. Speed merchant Brown was known as the 'Easington Express' and had scored goals as if they were going out of fashion in the club's minor teams but he too was blighted by bad luck in the first team. A struggling side created few chances and when one did come his way at Anfield on New Year's Day he connected perfectly only to see his effort come back off the underside of the bar as Sunderland lost against League leaders Liverpool.

It seemed as if nothing would go right and that 'world against you' feeling was reinforced when a defensive mix-up gifted fellow strugglers Coventry a last-minute winner. Unable to score, Sunderland had at least looked like taking a rare point from a goalless draw when disaster struck. No one realised just how big a disaster that late Donal Murphy goal was. The Sky Blues would finish a single point above Sunderland.

Adamson was soon to completely turn to youth. The third round of the FA Cup brought Third Division promotion chasers Wrexham to the North East. They had already knocked Spurs out of the League Cup at White Hart Lane so were not to be taken lightly and with Sunderland at rock bottom the Welsh side fancied their chances. Having not scored since mid-November, the Wearsiders at last found the net – not once but twice – but it was only enough for a draw.

The replay saw Sunderland lose 1–0 to a team two divisions lower but the match was to be a significant one as Adamson blooded starlets Shaun Elliott and Kevin Arnott. Along with Gary Rowell, who had just begun to hold down a regular starting place, the trio reinvigorated Sunderland. One more League game followed before the tide began to turn, another defeat, this time 2–0 at Leicester. The goal drought was not over but two goalless draws instilled a little belief ahead of a rare Friday night game when fellow strugglers Bristol City were the visitors. The Robins were in decent form, their only defeat in their previous four games having been away to Manchester United.

It is a football manager's job to inspire confidence and Adamson was doing his damnedest to do so despite the side having still to score a League goal going into his 10th League game as manager. 'You are going to see some fireworks soon!' he claimed boldly in his programme notes. He also pointed out that he was 'playing the stars' in answer to critics who argued he should not be casting aside senior professionals in favour of untried youngsters. Billy Hughes, Ray Train, Jim Holton and Tommy Gibb had all played what proved to be their last games since the turn of the year.

It was Mel Holden who lit the blue touchpaper to Adamson's fireworks. Ending the goal drought with a winner against Bristol City lifted a weight off the team's backs. Suddenly Sunderland were unbeaten in three games, had kept three clean sheets in a row and wonder of wonders, had actually scored a goal! What's more, the Bristol City match was the first of four home games in a row. With Holden having released the pressure, Sunderland went from not being able to score to not being able to stop scoring.

Middlesbrough, West Brom and West Ham had 16 goals put past them with just one in reply as Sunderland climbed out of the relegation zone and to the top of the 'form table'. A trip to title-chasing Manchester City brought the harshest defeat of the season, the Lads losing 1–0 to a penalty from old boy Dennis Tueart after the softest penalty award in many a year while at the other end Mel Holden had a goal disallowed for offside despite the ball seeming to be played back to him.

By now brimful of confidence with a defence boosted by the experienced Colin Waldron and still featuring Joe Bolton as a consistent and powerful presence at left-back, Sunderland were producing expansive football that belied their lowly position. With Arnott, Elliott and Rowell providing energy and style, that unjust defeat at Man City was one of only two in an astonishing 18-game run that took Sunderland into the final game of the season with a good chance of avoiding the drop having looked to have no chance.

A long season boiled down to two sets of 90 minutes which were meant to be played simultaneously on a Thursday night. Sunderland travelled to Everton knowing a point would keep them up regardless of the score in the night's other key game between Coventry City and Bristol City. A point for Sunderland would see Coventry relegated unless they won while a victory for the Sky Blues would see Bristol City go down. The only way both combatants at Highfield Road could survive was if they drew and Sunderland lost at Goodison Park. The 1976–77 season was the first played with goal difference rather than goal average used to determine placings of teams level on points and Sunderland had the best goal difference of the three sides battling to avoid joining Spurs and Stoke in going down.

Everton had nothing to play for but Sunderland had run out of steam and lost 2–0. The tank was empty after a tremendous fightback in the second half of the season, climaxed by a wonderful effort to rescue a point at Norwich the previous Saturday. At Carrow Road and at Goodison the Roker Roar was out in force. Consider the gates: 27,787 watched Sunderland at Norwich – only the Canaries' derby with Ipswich had exceeded that figure while their previous home gate had been less than 20,000 for the visit of Everton. At Everton Sunderland pulled in over 36,000 compared to the 20,102 who saw their home game the previous Saturday or the 25,208 who saw their final home game of the campaign five days later.

Despite the bumper gates featuring massive away support, Sunderland's games at Norwich and Everton kicked-off on time. In contrast, at the Coventry v Bristol City match the kick-off was delayed, reportedly due to crowd congestion. The gate was 36,903 – over a thousand less that had seen Coventry's home game with Liverpool nine days earlier which had kicked-off on schedule. The delay gave Coventry and Bristol City an advantage over Sunderland. Both would know the outcome of the Lads' game. Had Sunderland got a point or better at Everton no doubt the closing stages of the Coventry–Bristol game would have been fiercely contested – not least with Leeds old boys Norman Hunter and Terry Yorath on opposite sides, not to mention recent Sunderland man Jim Holton in the Coventry line up.

Infamously though Coventry chairman Jimmy Hill was allegedly the man responsible for instructing that the Sunderland score should be put up on the scoreboard and announced on the tannoy. With the score 2–2 at Coventry with 10 minutes to go both sides were safe providing no one else scored. Coventry were rocking. They'd let a two-goal lead slip and a draw was not enough for them. Had they not been sure of Sunderland's score at Everton they would have needed a goal against a Bristol City side who had the momentum. Comfortable in the knowledge that they were both safe if there was no further scoring, Bristol were content to let Coventry play keep-ball for the closing stages. It is worth noting that Bristol City manager Alan Dicks was a former Coventry player and had previously been assistant manager to Jimmy Hill at Highfield Road. In 1990, when he was Fulham chairman, Hill appointed Dicks as assistant manager at Craven Cottage and later promoted him to manager.

Despite all their heroic efforts, Sunderland were relegated and would not be promoted again until 1980. Having been relegated in 1970, this 1976–77 season would be the only full season

Sunderland would have in the top flight in the decade of the 1973 FA Cup win. Joe Bolton had played in the early rounds of the Cup win as a youngster and by now had developed into a key member of the team. The side changed enormously throughout the season with Joe being one of only three men who started the first game and the last. His only realistic rivals for Sunderland's inaugural Player of the Year award were the youngsters Rowell, Arnott and Elliott, but Arnott and Elliott had played less than half the games while Rowell had not started three in a row until after Christmas. In a year of upheaval, Bolton had been a solid presence, a rare model of consistency in a team that for half a season struggled and for half a season soared.

'I just got stuck in,' reasons Joe when asked why he thinks the crowd took to him as they did. 'I'll admit I wasn't the most skilful player out there but I always gave 100 per cent. I was a bit embarrassed to be made Player of the Year to be honest. I thought there were better players in the team than me. The players had their own vote for Player of the Year and I voted for Jeff Clarke even though he'd been injured.'

A naturally modest man, Joe has to be asked if Jeff Clarke won the Players' Player award before sheepishly admitting that he won that as well, quickly adding, 'I played most of the games, didn't I?' In staggering contrast to how he was on the pitch, Joe is slow in coming forward off it. The most naturally modest of people, Joe fully deserved to be the first Sunderland Player of the Year, and at a club where the fans prize honesty and integrity as well as ability, Joe Bolton is as good a name as you could want to have as a first Player of the Year.

The man who would win the second Player of the Year award at Sunderland was 1973 FA Cup-winning captain Bobby Kerr, who remembers Joe with affection.

'Joe was a young lad who didn't want to get involved,' says Bobby. 'He used to get on the bus by the AA box near the Ramside at Durham. When he first got on the bus he used to cadge the sweeties but before long he was getting on with a big bag of "ket". He'd put them on the card table, say 'Here ye are' and then go down to the back of the bus and sit eating his own. He was a magnificent lad and I don't think he realised how good a player he was. Joe was a special player. I remember one time he insisted on switching over from left-back to right-back so he could still kick the winger who he'd given a hard time and had swapped sides. He went over to the other side so he could still get him. That was Joe!'

Joe Bolton at Sunderland

Debut: 17 April 1972: Sunderland 5–0 Watford

Last game: 2 May 1981: Liverpool 0–1 Sunderland

Total appearances (all competitions): 315+10 as sub / 12 goals

Season by season

1971–72	4 games / 0 goals
1972–73	15+3 games / 1 goal
1973–74	33+4 games / 0 goals
1974–75	22+3 games / 3 goals
1975–76	43 games / 1 goal
1976–77	48 games / 1 goal
1977–78	39 games / 3 goals
1978–79	39 games / 3 goals
1979–80	29 games / 0 goals
1980–81	43 games / 0 goals

Other clubs

Middlesbrough 1981–83

Sheffield United 1983–85

Matlock Town (player-caretaker manager)

Division Two: Sixth out of 22 (pre Play-off days)
FA Cup: Third round, lost at home to Bristol Rovers
League Cup: Second round, lost to Middlesbrough in a replay
Top scorer: Gary Rowell, 19 goals, 18 League, 1 League Cup
Ever present: Barry Siddall, 45 out of 45 League and Cup games
Player of the Year: Bobby Kerr

Having been relegated by a hair's breadth after a stirring second half of the season, hopes were high that the Lads would bounce straight back, perhaps at the first time of asking, and certainly much quicker than the six years it had taken them on each of the two previous occasions they had dropped into the second tier. Two decades earlier Sunderland still held the proud boast of being the only club in the country to have never played in any division except the top one but this relegation business was becoming a habit the Wearsiders would become far too familiar with.

Bobby Kerr had captained the club to FA Cup triumph in 1973 when Sunderland became the first Second Division Cup winners since 1931. Three hard-fought seasons later the Lads belatedly won promotion only to find themselves back in Division Two a mere 12 months later. As 1977–78 kicked-off Bobby Kerr was the last remaining Cup winner still with the club.

Manager Jimmy Adamson was beginning his first full season and had lost England midfielder Tony Towers following relegation, with Sunderland-born ex-Arsenal fringe player Wilf Rostron the only notable newcomer.

A huge travelling support gave Hull what would prove to be their biggest gate of the season on the opening day of the campaign, indeed almost a third more than their second-best attendance versus Spurs. Being able to take around 10,000 fans to a Second Division away game, however, was not always an advantage. Often opponents simply raised their games as they had when facing the recent FA Cup winners and the Tigers duly mauled Sunderland 3–0.

Bobby Kerr missed the next two games with new boy Rostron taking his place and it was not until early October with the team languishing in 17th position after a dismal start that Kerr found himself beginning a run in the team. The player Bob Stokoe dubbed his 'Little General' had been a fixture in Sunderland's first-choice side throughout the decade. The tiny Scot had played a minimum of 40 games a season throughout the 1970s until 1976–77, when he had played 35 times.

Once he returned to the side, Bobby remained a fixture, missing only one of the remaining 34 games as Sunderland gradually got into their stride. The sixth-highest appearance maker in SAFC history, Bobby Kerr had better seasons than the one in which he was Player of the Year. All of those better years though were before the Player of the Year prize began. From the day he burst on to the scene with a debut winner against Manchester City on New Year's Eve going into 1967, Bobby was a special player. The 5ft 4in teenager scored seven goals in his first 11 games – including two against Newcastle – before he broke his leg in an FA Cup tie with Leeds. Bobby would break his leg again but the diminutive Scot would look down on the team he first broke his leg against when he lifted the FA Cup at Wembley in 1973. By the time 1977–78 came around all of his Wembley teammates had left the club. Only the captain had not left the ship.

Bobby is in no doubt as to who was responsible for that: manager Jimmy Adamson, who replaced Cup messiah Bob Stokoe following a brief spell under caretaker manager Ian MacFarlane.

Bobby Kerr with the trophy.

'My memory is that Jimmy Adamson was a brilliant tactician but the players who were left from the Cup Final all felt that he wanted to get rid of the last five of us. He wanted to bring his own squad in, which was Burnley's squad. To be honest, I think that what he did at Sunderland started the decline of Sunderland in the Leagues. As a tactician doing things like working out free-kicks he was brilliant but as a man we never got on very well.'

From Adamson's arrival on the last day of November 1976, Jimmy Montgomery, Dick Malone, Billy Hughes and Ian Porterfield of the Wembley winners all moved on by the time the 1977–78 season got going.

Ashington-born Burnley legend Adamson had brought in a host of players and staff from Turf Moor, not just players Mick Docherty (son of Manchester United manager Tommy Docherty), Colin Waldron and Doug Collins, but also Barley Mow-born assistant manager Dave Merrington and general manager Gordon Butterfield. In a re-run of a situation football clubs witness ad infinitum, the manager's new boys and the old regime's players were two teams within a team.

'We didn't really mix,' says Kerr, who specifies one exception. 'They came to play and they went. One or two didn't fit in, like Waldron and Collins. I lived around the corner from Mick Docherty and Mick was going through a rough time. Myself and a couple of the lads took him out to a supporters' club and once the supporters met him they liked him and Mick's attitude managed to win them round. I firmly believe that if you go and meet the supporters they realise that you're not a bad bloke anyway.'

Football fixtures, of course, specialise in quirks and who should be Sunderland's opening opponents at Roker Park but Adamson and Co's old club Burnley. With Docherty and Waldron playing, Collins on the bench but Bobby missing, Sunderland bounced back from the Hull defeat by this time winning 3–0 thanks largely to a brace from centre-forward Mel Holden. Victory over the boss's old club, however, would be the only win in the first dozen games. By mid-October Waldron and Collins had been discarded but Sunderland were in the lower reaches of the Second Division and had been dumped out of the League Cup by local top-flight rivals Middlesbrough.

A run of four wins and a draw turned things round. The improvement coincided with Bobby being back in the fold. As diminutive as England's 1966 World Cup winner Alan Ball, who played opposite Kerr for Arsenal in the 1973 FA Cup semi-final when Kerr would ultimately become only the second Sunderland captain to raise the Cup aloft at Wembley, Kerr had similar attributes to Ball, who had been labelled a player of perpetual motion when he helped England to become world champions. Having lost his place after the opening game, Kerr started just two of the next seven games, not even making the bench for three of them. Restored to the side for a home draw with Cardiff, he played in a defeat at Southampton before helping to turn things round. Lying 18th after defeat at the Dell, Sunderland climbed to seventh on the day Bobby scored his first goal of the season in a November draw at Notts County. The goal was a birthday present for Bobby, who had turned 30 three days earlier.

A week before, five different players had found the back of the net as Bristol Rovers got back on their coach at Roker Park to contemplate a lengthy journey home that suddenly seemed even

longer. Sunderland sadly lacked consistency. Only three of the next dozen games would be won, the last of them seeing Kerr open the scoring as Sunderland became the third successive side to stick five goals past Sheffield United. In the meantime Bristol Rovers had returned to Roker to knock Sunderland out of the FA Cup and had beaten the Wearsiders in the League return. To highlight the Red and Whites' ability to turn in performances that were hot or cold, a week after being sharp against the Blades they leaked five themselves at struggling Cardiff.

Despite a goal drought, two goals in six games yielded a win and three draws as the Lads plodded around in the middle of the table. Bobby's winner against Stoke lifted the Lads up to eighth in early April but the possibility of promotion had long since dropped off the agenda. A finishing flourish of five wins in the final six games put Sunderland in sixth spot, their highest placing of the season. But with the Play-offs not yet introduced, Sunderland were a dozen points away from the lowest promoted team.

That side were a Glenn Hoddle-inspired Spurs who Sunderland beat 3–2 at White Hart Lane on the penultimate Saturday of the season to knock them off the top spot they had held for three months. Spurs had been unbeaten at home all season including a sensational 9–0 thrashing of Bristol Rovers (in the previous away game before Rovers conceded five at Roker). Victory at the Lane indicated what Sunderland were capable of and while this was the first time Sunderland had managed a top-half finish in a season following relegation, a promotion charge had never got going. Adamson's side had scored more than top-of-the-table Bolton but conceded more than bottom-of-the-pile Hull.

Bobby Kerr had some great days at Sunderland. Given his debut by Ian McColl, he fought back from a twice broken leg to play all but four of the last 118 games of Alan Brown's reign before becoming Bob Stokoe's Cup-winning captain. There was no love lost though between Kerr and Adamson and by the end of August '78 the 1977–78 Player of the Season and Wembley winner had played his last game in red and white as Adamson ignored him. However, Bobby takes some satisfaction from his final season: 'Basically Jimmy Adamson had left before I left so I had the pleasure of seeing him go but I think he'd left me with a bad background with people at the top. He'd probably said too much to people at the wrong time and I was on my way out of the club,' says Bobby.

Adamson suddenly left Sunderland in October 1978 to take over at Leeds, his assistant Merrington following a few weeks later. Although he did not get back into the first team, Kerr stayed until March when he was reunited with Bob Stokoe who signed him for Blackpool where his old pal Dick Malone was already one of the leading lights and future Sunderland 'keeper Iain Hesford the last line of defence. Bobby stayed at Blackpool for another full season before returning to the North East, seeing out his playing days at Hartlepool where, according to Colin Foster's *A Century of Poolies – The Who's Who of Hartlepool United 1908–2008*: 'Bobby appeared on the outside to be nothing more than another player who turned up at Pools for a final pay day. However his performances during the 1980–1981 season after joining the club in July 1980 proved different.'

Bobby Kerr had proved his worth up the coast from Hartlepool at Sunderland on 433 occasions. As the chant of the time pointed out: 'He's here, he's there, he's every f*****g where, Bobby Kerr, Bobby Kerr.' Bobby was around long enough, though, to suffer the stick that sometimes comes a player's way as well as the support.

'Oh yes,' he says. 'It stands up to be counted that the fans have been absolutely magnificent. When they're bad they're bad and when they're good they're magnificent and I had my bad times. The stick always came from the Clock Stand. I always remember hearing someone shouting: "Kerr – get yersell off, and take Micky Henderson with you!" I'll never forget that. I always remember it and then one day around about that time I scored at the Roker End. I hit the ball and it bounced, and bounced, and bounced, and bounced, and somehow went in. I was veering towards the Clock Stand and I went over and gave them a V-sign. After the game Doug Weatherall, who wrote for the *Daily Mail*, came to me and said, "Bobby, you're gonna have to apologise." I said, "Doug, you apologise 'cos I'm not." Sure enough in Monday's paper Doug wrote that Bobby Kerr had apologised but I'll say now that I didn't.'

Asked if he minds if the truth comes out after all these years, he says emphatically: 'Why-aye! Tell it like it is.' The way it is, is that Bobby Kerr was a great servant to SAFC. Had the Player of the Year award been around in his younger years the chances are he would have won it more than once. As it is, Kerr the Cup Final captain is the only member of the Cup-winning team(s) to win a Player of the Year award. A real grafter with no little skill allied to the ability to find the back of the net, Bobby Kerr deserved to play in better teams than he did under Jimmy Adamson at Sunderland – and thankfully, five years before his Player of the Year season, he did exactly that.

Bobby Kerr at Sunderland
Debut: 31 December 1966: Sunderland 1–0 Manchester City (scored)
Last game: 30 August 1978: Sunderland 0–2 Stoke City
Total appearances (all competitions): 419+14 as sub / 69 goals

Season by season

1966–67	11 games / 7 goals
1967–68	0 games
1968–69	16+1 games / 2 goals
1969–70	26+7 games / 6 goals
1970–71	40+1 games / 10 goals
1971–72	50 games / 12 goals
1972–73	51 games / 7 goals
1973–74	51 games / 3 goals
1974–75	48 games / 8 goals
1975–76	49 games / 7 goals
1976–77	32+3 games / 2 goals
1977–78	38+2 games / 4 goals
1978–79	4 games / 0 goals

Other clubs
Blackpool 1979–80
Hartlepool United 1980–81

Shaun Elliott

Division Two: Fourth out of 22
FA Cup: Fourth round, lost to Burnley in a replay
League Cup: Second round, lost to Stoke City
Anglo-Scottish Cup: Eliminated at group stage
Top scorer: Gary Rowell, 22 goals, 21 League, 1 FA Cup
Ever present: No one
Player of the Year: Shaun Elliott

Hopes were high of a return to the top flight. Following the dramatic and controversial relegation of the season before last, a dreadful start had scuppered ambitions of an immediate return in Jimmy Adamson's first full season in charge. However a run of just one defeat in the final eight games resulted in the Lads' highest placing of the season also being their final position. A good home Anglo-Scottish Cup victory over 1977–78 Division Two champions Bolton added to the belief that Sunderland were promotion material.

The opening day visitors to Wearside were Charlton Athletic, who had been beaten 3–0 at Roker in the last game of the previous campaign. On that occasion Joe Bolton had skied a penalty that would have given the full-back an astonishing hat-trick. Spot kick specialist Gary Rowell had stepped aside to give Bolton his opportunity but still got his customary goal. Rowell was on the score sheet again as the 1978–79 campaign got under way, this time a single strike being enough for the two points that were still the reward for victory.

Missing from the side was the man who would become the Player of the Year but it would be the only game Shaun Elliott would miss for the entire season. Elliott was back in the side three days later for a trip to Orient where he replaced Jeff Clarke in partnering Jackie Ashurst in the centre of defence. Elliott had missed the run-in to the previous season having been used in midfield in his last spell in the side.

A naturally gifted player, Elliott had come into the team as a midfielder at the start of 1977 and was seen as much as a midfielder as a defender. Although Elliott and Clarke often played in the same side and Elliott had had a stint at centre-back as a replacement for the injured Clarke, it was not until September 1978 that the pair started a game as central defensive partners. They complemented each other superbly. When people recall partnerships it is most often front twos – Quinn and Phillips, Gates and Gabbiadini for instance – but the combination of Elliott and Clarke proved just as valuable to Sunderland as a pairing that might dovetail admirably up front.

'Jeff is my best friend in football,' says Shaun. 'We hit it off straight away. Nobody beat him in the air but if anybody got past him at all I was very quick and they had to get past me too. Without being too conceited you'd have to go a long way to find a better central defensive partnership than us.'

Elliott's point is unarguable. If asked to pick an all-time Sunderland XI most supporters would not have Shaun Elliott and Jeff Clarke in the reckoning although if they remember them they would no doubt agree that each was a very good player. No one would claim Clarke was as good a centre-half as Charlie Hurley or Dave Watson for instance, or insist that Elliott was better than Colin Todd. But put Clarke and Elliott together and, as Shaun says, 'You'd have to go a long way to find a better central defensive partnership.' So often managers look to find a system that accommodates the best 10 outfield players at their

disposal, rather than accepting that sometimes including a talented player is not always the best thing for the effectiveness of the team. Consider the way successive England managers have tried to play both Steven Gerrard and Frank Lampard. Indisputably both great players but might the balance of the team have been better if only one played? Perhaps it is a bit like replacing a part in the engine of a family saloon with a piece of a Rolls-Royce engine. The new part might be superb but it is not necessarily the best thing to get the engine running smoothly. Elliott and Clarke simply went together like strawberries and cream or John Lennon and Paul McCartney. Unsurprisingly, Clarke took the Player of the Year award 12 months after Elliott.

A run of just one defeat in nine games soon after Elliott and Clarke linked up in defence helped build confidence if not make an impression on the League table. Come the end of October and Sunderland were only ninth after too many draws. Moreover, by this time manager Jimmy Adamson had jumped ship and departed for Leeds United where he replaced Jock Stein.

Adamson's assistant, Dave Merrington, took the reins for eight games and did well in lifting the club from ninth to fourth before the lure of linking up with his mentor at Elland Road proved too strong.

Merrington's move meant disruption with a third man in charge before Christmas. Thankfully for Sunderland they had an ideal man to take over in Billy Elliott. No relation to Shaun, Billy had played for England, as well as over 200 games for the club in the fifties, and had been caretaker manager before. Then as now he took over from a man who had played for and managed Burnley; now as then, the man who took over the side he steered would go on to have great success.

In 1972 Billy Elliott had been responsible for switching Dave Watson from useful centre-forward to the exceptional centre-back that won the Man of the Match award in the 1973 FA Cup Final under Bob Stokoe. Now six years on from his earlier stint as caretaker, Billy Elliott would stay in charge until the end of the season, see his team go within a whisker of promotion and then, having been overlooked for the manager's post, would look on from Darlington, where he became manager, as Sunderland won promotion the following year under Ken Knighton, who had been Billy's coach.

Unfashionable Cambridge United, managed by Ron Atkinson, won their first ever game at Roker Park in Billy Elliott's opening game. Sunderland had won their previous home match 5–0 so it was an inauspicious start followed by a couple of draws.

As has so often been the case it was the FA Cup that started the ball rolling. A frosty January night brought top-flight Everton to the North East. The Toffees – who included former Sunderland favourite Colin Todd – would finish fourth that season and to date had lost just one of their 11 away games in the First Division, but they could not cope with the rampant Red and Whites. The unerring Gary Rowell gave Sunderland a first-half advantage with a trademark penalty; Bob Lee getting the goal that rendered Martin Dobson's strike for the visitors redundant.

Beating Everton gave everyone a real boost. Two solid away draws took the unbeaten run to five before Burnley were beaten with a terrific second-half fightback. The Turf Moor club played a significant role in Sunderland's season, not just because Adamson and Merrington had been Burnley men. Early in the season Sunderland had had two men sent off in the first half at Burnley with the game goalless before sensationally going on to emerge 2–1 winners with a Rowell brace. Completing the double over them at home had supporters getting ahead of themselves, anticipating a Cup run as Burnley were Sunderland's fourth-round opponents.

Bad weather caused the game at Turf Moor to be postponed several times and though the game was eventually played on an evening, huge travelling support gave the Clarets a gate bettered only by their Boxing Day derby with Blackburn. The replay was set for the following Monday night with the prize of a trip to League leaders Liverpool in the fifth round. Although the replay in front of Roker's biggest gate in almost two years proved to be a calamitous night, no one was too dispirited. Goalkeeper Ian Watson, whose only previous game was in the pre-season Anglo-Scottish Cup, conceded a soft goal early on as the visitors went on to triumph 3–0.

There was certainly disappointment at going out of the Cup but there was a promotion battle to fight and everyone of a red and white persuasion was still on 'cloud nine' following the match played 48 hours ahead of the Cup replay. On the Saturday Sunderland had gone to Newcastle and wiped the floor with their rivals, winning 4–1 on the day Gary Rowell became a legend with a hat-trick.

The victory over the Magpies was the first of four in a row in the League, extending the unbeaten League run into double figures.

Home defeat to eventual champions Crystal Palace proved a blip as just one point was dropped from the next half a dozen games which included an important 1–0 win away at promotion rivals Stoke. However, a body blow was suffered in the single-goal win over Orient that followed the visit of Palace. The winner against the O's gave Gary Rowell his 21st goal in 32 League games but it would be his last of the season as an injury sustained late in the game ruled him out for the rest of the campaign. Had the goal poacher been available for the run-in maybe the agonies still to be suffered could have been avoided.

With five games to go Sunderland sat second in the table and looked good for promotion. Two surprise home defeats would cost Billy Elliott and Sunderland dearly. Over 35,000 – a gate only so far surpassed for the Wear-Tyne derby – turned up to see the game against bottom-of-the-table Blackburn, only for Howard Kendall's experienced team to inflict a shock defeat with a penalty scored by future Newcastle coach Derek Fazackerly. Responding with a solid away win at Cambridge, Sunderland even topped the table for the only time in the campaign thanks to a thrilling 6–2 win over Sheffield United. The Lads required a four-goal winning margin against the struggling Blades to go top and managed it in the most dramatic fashion. Two goals in the final three minutes made it 6–2, Wilf Rostron having claimed his only Sunderland hat-trick with the help of two penalties. However, the visitors got a penalty of their own in injury time only for Barry Siddall to save Gary Hamson's spot kick and take Sunderland to the top.

Siddall was a great character who, like Elliott, missed just a single game that season. He remembers: 'We had people like Shaun Elliott, Gary Rowell, Kevin Arnott and Bob Lee so we were a decent side.'

With two games to go and still in the era of two points for a win, Sunderland and Stoke were in pole position with 53 points. Brighton were a point behind on 52 with Crystal Palace on 51 points, but crucially with a game in hand. Brighton and Stoke still had to play Newcastle so the Geordies were in place to do their North East neighbours a favour and similarly the other Magpies of Notts County still had to face Stoke and Palace. Sunderland could guarantee themselves promotion regardless of results elsewhere by winning both of their remaining games which consisted of a Welsh double against Cardiff and Wrexham.

With four teams chasing the three promotion spots it was a question of which side would crack. Sadly that team would be Sunderland. The home defeat to Blackburn had been survived but a slip-up in front of the biggest gate of the season saw mid-table Cardiff play with the freedom of a team with nothing to play for and they inflicted a fatal blow on Wearside promotion ambitions by beating Sunderland 2–1. On the same day Brighton and Cardiff won while Newcastle did Sunderland a good turn by holding Stoke to a draw in the Potteries, but the Roker defeat left red and white promotion hopes beyond their control.

The Roker Roar decamped en masse to north Wales, almost doubling Wrexham's average gate on the seventh anniversary of the 1973 FA Cup win. Elliott, as usual, was immaculate, as goals from Rostron and Alan Brown gave Billy Elliott's boys the result they wanted but as at Everton two years earlier supporters were hanging on for results elsewhere on their transistor radios. As at Goodison, rumours flew and some prematurely started to think promotion was won but it was not. Brighton had won 3–1 at Newcastle, where defeat for the Seagulls would have seen Sunderland go up. Stoke had similarly won at Notts County, thereby also securing promotion, and Palace had won away to Orient. Sunderland and Palace were locked on the same number of points but the Londoners had one game to play. Their opponents would be Burnley, with whom there was no love lost as far as Sunderland were concerned, but Wearside had six agonisingly long days to wait, hoping that maybe the Clarets would spring a Selhurst Park surprise to allow Sunderland to sneak up. In the event Palace won 2–0 with future Sunderland forward Dave Swindlehurst scoring for the third successive match and so Sunderland were condemned to another year out of the top flight.

The consistent Shaun Elliott would again miss just a single game as Sunderland went on to win promotion the following year and would remain a regular in the side for another six seasons, the last of which would see Shaun become the first player to win the Sunderland Player of the Year award for a second time. That 1985–86 award would come from the SAFC Supporters' Association in a year when the official award went to midfielder Mark Proctor.

1978–79 had proved to be a near miss but Elliott was a deserving winner of the individual award. Sunderland had not yet reached the top flight but in Shaun Elliott they had a player of top class calibre.

Capped by England at B level the following season, Elliott would eventually total 368 appearances in red and white, being allowed to leave by new manager Lawrie McMenemy when on the brink of a testimonial season after a year when suspension had cost him the chance to captain Sunderland at Wembley in the League Cup Final.

Man of the Match at Wembley was Norwich centre-back and future Sunderland manager Steve Bruce, who would become a teammate of Shaun's when Elliott joined him at Carrow Road. 'I became friendly with Shaun and our wives really hit it off, in fact, Shaun's wife is Godmother to my daughter but because of one reason or another Shaun didn't play an awful lot at Norwich so we didn't have a lot of games alongside each other' says Bruce.

Undoubtedly Elliott's best days were at Sunderland and like so many players he looks back on his time on Wearside with enormous affection: 'Basically I never wanted to leave but all of a sudden my move was done and dusted in two days. Lawrie just came and saw me and said, "I'm selling you", so I had very little option,' says Shaun of his abrupt departure. 'The thing about Sunderland is that if you are one of the players and the fans accept you, people really love you and it is reciprocated because as a player for this club I deeply appreciate its fantastic supporters.'

Shaun Elliott at Sunderland

Debut: 12 January 1977: Wrexham 1–0 Sunderland
Last game: 3 May 1986: Sunderland 2–0 Stoke City
Total appearances (all competitions): 363+5 as sub / 11 goals

Season by season

1976–77	20 games / 1 goal
1977–78	27+4 games / 3 goals
1978–79	45 games / 0 goals
1979–80	51 games / 4 goals
1980–81	42 games / 0 goals
1981–82	42 games / 1 goal
1982–83	25 games / 0 goals
1983–84	38 games / 0 goals
1984–85	38+1 games / 0 goals
1985–86	35 games / 2 goals

Other clubs

Seattle Sounders (loan) 1981
Norwich City 1986–88
Blackpool 1988–91
Colchester United 1991–92
Gateshead 1992–93
Bishop Auckland 1993–95
Whitley Bay 1995–96
Durham City 1996

Jeff Clarke

Division Two: Second out of 22 – promoted
FA Cup: Third round, lost at home to Bolton Wanderers
League Cup: Fourth round, lost away to West Ham United in a replay
Anglo-Scottish Cup: Eliminated at group stage
Top scorer: Bryan 'Pop' Robson, 22 goals, 20 League, 2 League Cup
Ever present: Steve Whitworth, 49 out of 49 League and Cup games
Player of the Year: Jeff Clarke

Centre-half Jeff Clarke was a stalwart of the side that won promotion in Sunderland's centenary season but was missing when promotion was won. Clarke had been stretchered off in the penultimate game at Cardiff. 'I ruptured my medial ligament,' recalls Jeff, wincing at the memory. 'It was the most painful thing I've ever had in my life. It was a crunch game that we needed to win. The ball went out for what was obviously our throw and left-back Joe Hinnigan ran forward to take it just as the referee signalled it was Cardiff's ball. They took the throw quickly to the man Joe had just left. I raced over to cover and stretched to clear just as Joe came steaming in and took both of us out. It was the only time I was ever stretchered off the pitch and I listened to updates on the rest of the game from a hospital in Cardiff.'

Victory in that final away game at Cardiff would have secured promotion but a point left Sunderland sweating on needing to take another from their remaining match at home to West Ham. Leicester, Birmingham and Chelsea were in a four-horse race with Sunderland for the three promotion spots. As Sunderland drew in Wales, Leicester and Birmingham sealed promotion while a Chelsea win featuring two goals from future Sunderland winger Clive Walker completed the Londoners' fixtures with them a point ahead of Sunderland, who still had a game to play and a far superior goal difference.

Sunderland-born Kevin Dillon, future Sunderland player and coach Keith Bertschin and Alan Curbishley – who 18 years later would manage Charlton to Play-off Final victory over Sunderland – were Birmingham's scorers in a thrilling home draw with Notts County, the Midlanders knowing that a point was enough as Chelsea would have had to have won by nine goals to overtake them on goal difference. While fans of Leicester and Birmingham popped open the champagne and looked forward to life in the top flight, just over 28,000 trooped home from Stamford Bridge knowing they were in third place with three to go up but that they needed to rely on London rivals West Ham winning at Roker Park to elevate them to Division One. For all concerned there was an agonising nine-day wait as the Hammers had their own date with destiny at Wembley against Arsenal in the FA Cup Final 48 hours before they were due at Roker Park.

Supporters' nerves were on edge. Would the Lads gain the point they required or would the weight of expectation restrict them against an expansive West Ham side freed of their own Cup pressures? Under John Lyall West Ham followed Sunderland and Southampton to become the third Second Division team to win the FA Cup in eight years after sensationally defeating Arsenal by a goal to nil. Moreover they had gone into the Cup Final on the back of a couple of handsome League victories and had already beaten Sunderland twice. The Lads had lost at the Boleyn Ground in the League and the League Cup but had drawn at Roker in the League Cup. A repeat of that 1–1 scoreline would be enough to see Sunderland promoted and Chelsea condemned to another year away from the top level. But Chelsea denied Sunderland at the

death in 1963 and older fans who recalled Tommy Harmer's 'in off his private parts' winner 17 years earlier were worried that once again 'Blue would be the Colour'.

Once the West Ham game came around Sunderland made no mistake and won 2–0. 'West Ham were still partying after winning the Cup, and although we couldn't get the ball off them for the first 20 minutes we were running on so much adrenalin that we were always going to win,' says midfielder Kevin Arnott, who opened the scoring while Clarke's successor as the following season's Player of the Year, Stan Cummins, wrapped things up.

'I was in hospital getting updates on the match from the radio,' says Jeff. 'I'd been moved to a hospital in Sunderland by then and about half past eleven some friends turned up with a bottle of champagne. It wasn't the players though – they'd have been paralytic by then!'

Had Sunderland won at Cardiff as well as beating West Ham they would have been champions ahead of Leicester but, of course, football is riddled with 'what ifs' and equally had promotion already been secured before the Cup winners came to town perhaps the same result would not have been forthcoming. What mattered was that Sunderland were promoted and while Jeff Clarke missed out on the night of nights he was far from forgotten as 'There's only one Jeff Clarke' boomed from the Roker terraces as the team took a lap of honour before a capacity 47,000 crowd that had squeezed into a ground now beginning to be past its best, and one where thousands had been locked out.

In any successful season there has to be a number of valid candidates for the Player of the Year accolade and since Sunderland's individual honour was inaugurated this was the first season Sunderland had won anything so to become Player of the Year, Clarke had been absolutely outstanding.

Strangely the only ever-present in the side was not one of the candidates. Former England international right-back Steve Whitworth gave sterling service and was a model of consistency but since arriving late the previous season the fans had never taken to him. Twenty-goal top scorer Pop Robson had a good claim, as did reigning Player of the Year Shaun Elliott, Clarke's central defensive partner for much of the season, although pivot Rob Hindmarch also played a major role in defence, especially in the latter stages. Another with a terrific season under his belt was midfield maestro Kevin Arnott, a class act. Surprisingly for a promotion team who typically have a largely settled side, Clarke, Elliott, Whitworth, Arnott and Robson were the only players to not miss at least a dozen League games.

Despite the claims of Elliott, Arnott and Robson, Clarke was a most deserving winner. The only man to be Player of the Year at both Sunderland and Newcastle, Jeff had to overcome gigantic hurdles to win both. Controversially given a free transfer by Sunderland in 1982, he joined Newcastle and became the Magpies' Player of the Year in Kevin Keegan's first season at St James'.

'Kevin coming to Newcastle took the pressure off me,' says Jeff. 'As far as everyone was concerned, Newcastle consisted of Kevin Keegan and 10 others. Having come from Sunderland the less notice anyone took of me early on the better. I bedded in quickly and by the time I'd had a dozen good games I was accepted but of course had I started badly I'd have been a Sunderland reject and it would have been tough. In fact I enjoyed my time at both clubs and was fortunate enough to have good spells at both.' Indeed, in Alan Candlish's superb book *Ha'Way / Howay the Lads*, tracing the history of Wear–Tyne derbies, Clarke is justifiably named as the player of the 1980s.

If Jeff was in Kevin Keegan's shadow on Tyneside he had just as tall an order when he first came to Sunderland. Clarke came to the North East in 1975 as a raw and inexperienced centre-half as a makeweight in the deal that saw FA Cup-winning England international Dave Watson move to Manchester City. Watson's boots were big ones to fill but Jeff helped Sunderland to win Division Two in his first season. That year he played the first 31 games, the last of those seeing him break a bone in his foot in the first half of an away win at Orient, and still play on until the final whistle. When fit he had been a regular and popular choice ever since, although he did endure his share of injuries so missing the glamour and the glory of promotion were typical of his fortune.

Clarke's Player of the Year season at Sunderland began with a pre-season tour of Switzerland followed by a dismal showing in three Anglo-Scottish Cup ties before the League campaign kicked-off. Having gone agonisingly close the year before when suffering the fate Chelsea would this time round – by being overtaken in the promotion frame after completing their fixtures, in Sunderland's case in 1979 by Crystal Palace – Sunderland had changed manager. Coach Ken Knighton had succeeded long-term caretaker Billy Elliott. 'Ken Knighton walked in and I said something like, "Aye okay Ken," and he said, "It's boss now." He was a right Champagne Charlie,' recalls left-back Joe Bolton.

The fact that every game counts throughout a long season is illustrated by the opening two games of 1979–80. A point from an opening day goalless draw at Chelsea was precious in the final analysis while Birmingham, who would go up with Sunderland, were comfortably beaten in the first home game at Roker and when Fulham were despatched three days later it was without doubt a good start.

Sunderland may have had their eyes elsewhere when Oldham added to their Anglo-Scottish Cup win over the Red and Whites by inflicting a first League defeat of the season. This was sandwiched between a two legged League Cup tie with Newcastle. A two-legged tie which resulted in a pair of 2–2 scorelines and a penalty shoot-out on Tyneside.

'Ken Knighton had selected the five penalty takers before we even went out to play the second leg,' reveals Jeff. 'I was captain, I think, and was down to be one of the five, but when it came to it I couldn't take one. It went to sudden death and I still didn't take one. I absolutely bottled it! I remember while the shoot-out was taking place I was sat in the centre circle not even looking. Not taking a penalty was pretty pathetic but while I enjoyed the game I didn't fancy taking a spot kick. It was [Newcastle's] Jim Pearson who missed the decisive kick and he got loads of stick for it. I can remember thinking that could have been me.'

By mid-November, after a 3–1 defeat at Swansea, Sunderland had slipped into the bottom half of the table. It was hardly surprising the team were struggling as so much was being asked of them. The trip to the Vetch Field in south Wales was the Lads' fourth game in eight days. The previous Saturday Chelsea had been beaten at home but on the Monday Sunderland had played in London where they lost a League Cup replay to West Ham. Wednesday night had seen Sunderland play England! In celebration of Sunderland's centenary, an England XI won 2–0 on Wearside where Bob Latchford scored twice. By the time the Lads got to Swansea they must have been out on their feet compared to their opponents.

Sunderland's centenary had actually been in the middle of October but on that occasion the Black Cats had another extra fixture, beating Paraguayan outfit and reigning South American champions Olimpia Asuncion 5–2 in a friendly at Roker Park while top-flight Manchester City had also been beaten in a League Cup replay in the centenary month on top of a demanding run of League fixtures.

Freed from distractions, Knighton's team started to run into form as winter approached, although there was a November excursion to Wembley where the televised *Daily Express* five-a-side tournament was won splendidly with Newcastle hammered 4–0 in the semi-final. Solid home form was largely responsible for a rise to fifth from top by the turn of the year. The scorer of the winner in an away victory at Fulham that closed the decade was Argentinian Claudio Marangoni. Brought in for a club record fee earlier that month at a time when it was the vogue to sign players from the nation who had become world champions for the first time the previous year, Marangoni would be a star when he later returned to South America but he was a flop at Sunderland.

While Marangoni's move did not work out and he would leave before 1980 was over, another big money mid-season signing was Stan Cummins. Cummins was a great success along with the man who unwittingly wiped Clarke out at Cardiff, left-back Joe Hinnigan, who was never on a losing side as he played the last 14 games of the season. In March an England B game was held at Sunderland, Shaun Elliott playing in the match. Elliott was undoubtedly excellent but Clarke in the form he was in would have been just as good a choice.

Marangoni certainly was not cut out for the breakneck pace of a New Year's Day derby, which was lost 3–1 at Newcastle, or for an FA Cup tie with bottom of the First Division Bolton, who came to Roker and inflicted the only home defeat of the season in the scrappiest of games.

It was Wanderers' first victory in any competition since August. The silver lining to the Cup cloud though was that in leaving Sunderland to the cliché of concentrating on the League they did just that. After the first week of January only one more game would be lost as promotion was won. After that the squad jetted off to Florida and beat Fort Lauderdale in a friendly barely 48 hours after the hospitalised Jeff Clarke had his late-night champagne-bearing visitors.

Injury at Cardiff had curtailed Clarke's participation in the celebrations but promotion is won over a whole season and in the eyes of the supporters who follow the team week in, week out, Jeff Clarke was the man who had done most to lift the Lads back to the top level. Injury prevented him playing at all in the following season – Sam Allardyce came in as a replacement. Clarke's comeback arrived on the opening day of the 1981–82 season in which he would play 32 times before being released as manager Alan Durban looked to bring in Ian Atkins. Atkins would win the Player of the Year award in his first season but the fact that Clarke was simultaneously collecting the Newcastle Player of the Year accolade suggests that Sunderland should have kept a player the fans always admired.

Jeff Clarke at Sunderland
Debut: 2 August 1975: Middlesbrough 3–2 Sunderland
Last game: 8 May 1982: Southampton 1–0 Sunderland
Total appearances (all competitions): 215+3 as sub / 6 goals

Season by season
1975–76	40 games / 0 goals
1976–77	34 games / 0 goals
1977–78	24+1 games / 3 goals
1978–79	39+1 games / 2 goals
1979–80	48 games / 1 goal
1980–81	0 games
1981–82	31+1 games / 0 goals

Other clubs
Manchester City 1971–75
Newcastle United 1982–87
Brighton & Hove Albion (loan) 1984
Ankaragucu (Turkey, loan) 1987
Darlington 1987
Whitley Bay 1988

Non-playing
Newcastle United (community officer 1988 / coach 1993)
Nissan FC (physiotherapist 1997)
Sunderland (physiotherapist 1998–2001)
Leeds United (physiotherapist 2001–03)
Dundee United (physiotherapist 2003–)

1980–81   Stan Cummins

Division One: 17th out of 22
FA Cup: Third round, lost to Birmingham City in a replay
League Cup: Second round, lost to Stockport County
Top scorer: Gary Rowell, 11 goals, 10 League, 1 FA Cup
Ever present: Stan Cummins, 46 out of 46 League and Cup games, 10 goals
Official Player of the Year: Stan Cummins
SAFCSA Player of the Year: Stan Cummins

The 1980–81 season was to be an important one in the history of Sunderland. Until 1958 the club had boasted that it was the only club in the country to have only ever played at the highest level. A first relegation had taken six years to remedy but demotion again half a dozen years down the line had heralded a decade which, although it had witnessed sensational Cup success, had seen only one season played at the top level. Instant relegation had followed Bob Stokoe's 1976 promotion so now having marked the centenary season with promotion it was imperative that the Lads did not go straight back down again. They did not – but only just, and a man who had an awful lot to do with Sunderland stepping over the beckoning crevice that fell into the Second Division was a man who won the Player of the Year accolade in his first full season on Wearside – Stan Cummins.

This was the first season of the official Player of the Year award in addition to the Sunderland Supporters' Association version which was by now in its fifth year. The match programme, then called *The Roker Review*, printed coupons to fill in and send to the club's own Pools Office.

Cummins cost Sunderland's first £300,000 fee when he arrived from Middlesbrough in November 1979. A diminutive bag of tricks on the wing, Cummins instantly began repaying the investment. A dozen goals in 26 games made him second-top scorer as he helped fire Ken Knighton's side to promotion. Goals in his first two games – both at home – quickly endeared the ex Boro boy to his new fans. He soon became the first man in 17 years (since Nick Sharkey bagged five against Norwich in 1963) to score four goals in a match for the club, netted home and away in derby matches and, with a fine sense of theatre, scored a scintillating late goal to seal promotion before a capacity crowd – not a bad way to introduce yourself!

'Scoring four times against Burnley in a 5–0 win was a personal highlight for me. I've still got the ball from that match,' remembers Stan, whose goal at Roker against Newcastle proved to be the last home winner over SAFC's rivals for 28 years, though as Stan points out: 'I got another against them at Newcastle. That came from a long ball from Chris Turner. It bounced over the heads of the defenders and as it came to me I hit it on the volley to put us 1–0 up. We lost that game but it's nice to think I scored against Newcastle both home and away but the goal against West Ham is my favourite memory. It got us promotion! There's a few others that stand out but for me that one was special.'

Special it certainly was and the reward was a return to the big League and after an encouraging pre-season that included a Scandinavian tour, the curtain came up on the return to Division One. Stan was quick off the mark with goals in the opening two games as Everton and Manchester City were well beaten to put Sunderland top of the embryonic two-game table! A bumper crowd turned up for the next game only for Sunderland to go down by the odd goal in three to a Kevin Keegan-inspired Southampton, managed by a man whose name would be mud at Roker by the end of the decade – future Sunderland manager Lawrie McMenemy.

A sound point away to Manchester United sandwiched a lame two-legged League Cup exit at the hands of Stockport, despite Stan's third goal of the season, but a good away win at Leicester meant that a solid start had been made following promotion.

Cummins' old club Boro inflicted a disappointing third successive home defeat in the League and Cup but a good point at Spurs left the Lads unbeaten in five away games, with the only League goal conceded on the road coming at Old Trafford.

While Stan Cummins had become the darling of the crowd – his trademark shimmy leaving many a defender facing the crowd after being turned inside out – the ever popular Gary Rowell had endured a difficult 18 months. When Rowell scored in a thumping 4–1 win over Leeds it was the Seaham midfielder's first goal in a year and a half, largely ruined by injury. Top scorer for the two seasons prior to his injury, Rowell had not scored at all in the promotion campaign but would go on to be leading marksman for the three years after promotion, though Cummins would be just a single goal behind him this time round. The pair were on the score sheet together for the first time in a draw at Arsenal that kept the Lads a comfortable eighth in the 22-team division a dozen games into the season.

Prior to Cummins' move from Tees to Wear, the nature of Sunderland's relegation three years earlier left a bitter taste in supporters' mouths, so the trip to Coventry City was much anticipated given the Sky Blues' behaviour in the infamous Bristol City game. Strangely, Coventry had been invited to Roker Park for a pre-season friendly and though Sunderland won that game the tables were turned at Highfield Road where, despite Stan scoring, Sunderland slipped to only their second away defeat so far, the earlier one having been a trouncing at eventual champions Aston Villa. Coventry would get their comeuppance in the North East later in the season though with Cummins scoring his only penalty of the campaign.

Defeat at Coventry represented the beginning of a bad run. Just one win in nine games saw a slump from eighth to 19th. The last game of that run was a 2–1 reverse at Brighton, a defeat that would assume greater significance later. Things picked up with a 2–0 home win over Arsenal that featured a 40-yard rocket from centre-forward John Hawley but it was to be the last victory of a year that ended with defeat at Birmingham City in what was the first of three successive games against the same side.

Returning to St Andrew's in the FA Cup a week after the League defeat, Sunderland ground out a creditable draw but conspired to lose the replay in extra-time following a last-minute equaliser. Returning to form with the first back-to-back wins since the opening two games of the season, Stan scored against Norwich before Manchester United succumbed at Roker to lift the Lads back towards mid-table. The improvement was not sustained though and a Cummins goal against strugglers Leicester, who had been promoted with Sunderland, provided the only victory of the next six games. That bad run began with defeat at Southampton on a day when football was put into perspective by the death of Mel Holden at the age of just 26. Three years earlier, almost to the day, Holden had played his last game for the club. He died of motor neurone disease.

Having dropped to 17th, Sunderland's resurgence came courtesy of full-back Joe Hinnigan, who struck gold with a spell of four goals in three games including a brace in a convincing 3–0 victory over Coventry, where Stan also scored.

However, three weeks and three defeats later with the team again looking over their shoulders at what would have been another soul-destroying relegation, the board gave manager Knighton the bullet. Former player Mick Docherty – son of Tommy Docherty, who had been Chelsea's manager when they thwarted Sunderland's promotion hopes at Roker in 1963 – took over as caretaker manager.

Stan Cummins on the pitch at Wembley before the 1985 League (Milk) Cup Final.

Knighton's last throw of the dice had been to spend £180,000 on Bristol City centre-forward Tom Ritchie. He proved to be another of those players such as Brett Angell and Keith Bertschin who made a habit of scoring against Sunderland but who did not do as well after the Lads bought them. Ritchie had failed to score in any of the 11 games he played for Knighton so the ex-manager must have choked on his tea when news came though that Ritchie had grabbed a hat-trick as Docherty's first game was won 3–0. Ritchie scored again two days later in an Easter defeat at West Brom, but so long as Sunderland won their final home game against fellow strugglers Brighton they could expect to survive.

Roker Park was renowned for its roar but the quietest I ever heard it in the 30 years I watched football there was in the final minute of the Brighton match. An eerie hush slammed down like a guillotine as visiting full-back Gary Williams scored a last-minute winner at the Fulwell End. It seemed to spell a relegation which would mean Sunderland had gone down in each of the last three seasons they had played at the level fans expected Sunderland to be at. There was still one chance for Sunderland to save themselves. The problem was it was away to reigning champions Liverpool, who were about to win their third European Cup in five years.

If the Roker Roar was silenced against Brighton it was out in force at Anfield, where Sunderland's visit attracted 9,000 more than their previous home game against Manchester United. It was a day where wee Stanley Cummins walked tallest of all. Legend has it that Liverpool's Hetton-born manager Bob Paisley was happy for his side to take it easy and save themselves for their forthcoming European Final. Certainly Sunderland were fortunate to be playing Liverpool when they did not need to win. The Wearsiders duly won 1–0 with a first-half goal from Cummins. Joe Bolton, who made his 325th and last appearance for Sunderland that day, remembered it: 'The goal Stan Cummins scored was right in the corner. There's no way their 'keeper would have stopped that, no 'keeper would – not even Monty would have stopped it.'

Having scored on the day Sunderland were promoted, Cummins had now kept the Lads up too. The game is such a part of red and white folklore that it is strange to relate that Sunderland would have stayed up even if they had lost at Liverpool but nonetheless Stan had saved one of his finest goals for a famous day.

Stan Cummins at Sunderland
Debut: 17 November 1979: Sunderland 3–1 Notts County (scored)
Last game: 4 May 1985: Sunderland 0–4 Aston Villa
Total appearances (all competitions): 159+6 as sub / 32 goals

Season by season
1979–80	27 games / 12 goals
1980–81	46 games / 10 goals
1981–82	41 games / 5 goals
1982–83	32+1 games / 5 goals
1983–84	playing for Crystal Palace
1984–85	13+5 games / 0 goals

Other clubs
Middlesbrough 1976–79
Minnesota Kicks (loan) 1977
Seattle Sounders (loan) 1981
Crystal Palace 1983–84
Minnesota Strikers 1985

Nick Pickering

Division One: 19th out of 22
FA Cup: Fourth round, lost at home to Liverpool
League Cup: Third round, lost at home to Crystal Palace
Top scorer: Gary Rowell, 11 goals, 9 League, 1 FA Cup, 1 League Cup
Ever present: No one
Official Player of the Year: Nick Pickering
SAFCSA Player of the Year: Nick Pickering

The youngest player to win Sunderland's Player of the Year award, Nick Pickering, made his debut on the opening day of the season, having signed as a professional earlier that month on his 18th birthday. 'I don't mean this to sound big headed but I was just a young lad and no one else was as fit as me. It was my fitness that enabled me to do so well,' is how Nick looks back on the way in which he burst on to the scene. But he is being modest; there was a lot of natural ability to go with the super-fitness.

The 1981–82 season was a new dawn for more than just the South Shields teenager. Sunderland had a new manager in Alan Durban, a new strip in the much loathed Le Coq Sportif number that did away with the traditional red and white stripes in favour of a white shirt with pairs of thin red stripes and there was a new points system in operation. Three points for a win replaced the two points that had been in operation since the Football League kicked-off in 1888.

Durban had signed Scottish hard-man left-back Iain Munro, Sunderland's first Player of the Year Joe Bolton having refused Durban's offer of a 12 game 'trial' before a new contract was proffered. However, all the talk was about the new teenager in the team – not Pickering, but £355,000 record signing Ally McCoist. Like Pickering, McCoist was 18, albeit 10 months older than Nick. His 23 goals the previous season for St Johnstone had earned McCoist rave reviews in a team which had narrowly missed out on promotion.

McCoist had to settle for a place on the bench on the opening day of the season but there was a first start for Pickering. Fixture compilers did not like to make it easy for Sunderland in those days. A year later they would kick-off away to newly-crowned European Cup winners Aston Villa while on this occasion the first match was away to new UEFA Cup holders Ipswich Town. Many felt that Bobby Robson's team had lost out on the previous year's League title to Villa due simply to the demands of their Cup commitments.

'I'd played every game in pre-season and a few days before the first match at Ipswich Alan Durban told me I'd be playing,' recalls Pickering. They had a lot of big names including the two Dutchmen [Arnold Muhren and Frans Thijssen] as well as John Wark, Mick Mills, Terry Butcher and Eric Gates, who scored twice.'

Nonetheless Sunderland, who had finished the previous campaign by guaranteeing a second successive season of top-flight football for the first time in over a decade by winning away to a Liverpool side less than a month before they won the European Cup, produced a sterling display to emerge with a well-earned point from a thrilling 3–3 draw. McCoist had left the bench to create a goal for midfielder Mick Buckley with an audacious back-heel that whetted the appetite for the newcomer with Pickering's energetic and effective debut largely overlooked. It would be the start of a fabulous first season for Pickering while McCoist would score just twice and start less than half the games. 'Coisty' remained deservedly ever popular at Sunderland despite never fulfilling his potential until he returned to Scotland with Rangers but having started in

Nick Pickering in action in the 1985 League Cup Final. He would be on the winning side two years later with Coventry in the FA Cup Final.

the side on the opening day of the season Pickering would remain a regular until sold by Lawrie McMenemy four and a half years later.

Perhaps McCoist's high profile took the spotlight off Pickering, who, relatively untroubled by hype, could simply enjoy his football. 'That's a great point,' he agrees. 'Ally had come for a lot of money and had great potential. He would score some brilliant goals in training and went on to have a truly fantastic career but the attention on him did take the pressure off me and I could just play my game.'

Reigning champions Villa were the visitors for Pickering's home debut but left empty-handed as Nick played his part in an exciting 2–1 win, and the youngster kept his place despite a downturn in results and the return of Stan Cummins and Shaun Elliott. This pair – winners of two of the last three Player of the Year awards – had been allowed to miss the start of the season along with goalkeeper Barry Siddall after spending the summer playing on the other side of the Atlantic, Cummins and Elliott with Seattle Sounders, Siddall with Vancouver Whitecaps.

With memories still fresh in supporters' minds of the dreadful record run of 10 League games without a goal in the last relegation season five years earlier, Sunderland endured a similar run in the early autumn, going eight League games without finding the back of the net as they plummeted to the bottom of the table as new boss Durban struggled. Dropped to the bench in the middle of that run, Pickering was immediately restored as his strong running and ability on the ball were missed. 'I was ahead of my time because I was like a modern player is now,' says Nick. 'Because I was so fit I found it easy and I'd even get comments off opponents who would say, "Will you stop running!" ... or worse!'

The ending of the goal drought failed to brighten the gloom enveloping Roker Park as Cummins' goal at home to Manchester United barely merited the word consolation as the visitors inflicted Sunderland's heaviest home defeat since 1967, and one that to the end of the 2010–11 season had not been matched. In fact, Sunderland played well for a substantial part of that game only for Ron Atkinson's United side to run away with the match late on as they inflicted a 1–5 defeat.

Four days later, Crystal Palace – who had lost their last three Second Division games – came to Roker and won 1–0 in the League Cup, where at least Sunderland had found the net in the previous round against Rotherham. 'It was a bad time,' remembers Pickering. 'That's when a manager and his coaching staff really have to pick a team up. That season was a mixture of good performances and bad ones, typical of the ups and downs of a footballer's life, I suppose, but of course when you are a player you are being judged by everyone all the time.'

With the team struggling badly Durban, having noted how well Pickering was doing, turned to youth. Future England international Barry Venison and centre-forward Colin West were given debuts. When a goalless draw at fellow strugglers Middlesbrough – themselves in the middle of a run of 19 games without a win – was followed by Sunderland's own first victory in 13 League games with a shock win at Everton, hopes were high that a corner had been turned. It had not.

Home defeats by Brian Clough's Forest – a pulsating thriller Sunderland lost by the odd goal in five – and West Brom after the Lads led at half-time, combined with defeat at Brighton, left the Wearsiders bottom of the pile, lower even than Boro still on that winless run. Christmas 1981 did not look like being a good one but after being 2–1 down with 10 minutes to go away to Manchester City in the last game before Santa was due, the presents came early with sub Venison setting up an equaliser for Gary Rowell before lashing home a spectacular late winner.

Three Cup games would be played before League points were again contested, Liverpool winning a fourth-round tie at Roker after a replay was required to dispose of Rotherham once again. However, League survival was top of Sunderland's agenda ahead of Cup glory, so when a John Cooke strike at Wolves provided the first back-to-back League victories of the season it was a cause of delight notwithstanding the fact that the wins were separated by more than 40 days. It was to be Sunderland's last goal for half a dozen games as once again a goal drought set in with just one point taken in another dismal run in which Nick missed four of the five matches after being stretchered off at Villa Park. They were the only games he missed all year bar the one early season match where he was on the bench.

Alan Brown's solitary strike of the season ended the barren patch and earned a valuable point on Pickering's return before Nick scored the first goal of his career in a 2–0 Roker victory over Southampton, whose manager Lawrie McMenemy would later be the man who sold him. 'I was getting a bit worried because I hadn't scored and it was March. Mick Buckley found me at the back stick with a great cross and I stuck it away. I remember Ally McCoist got the other with a great goal when he cut in from the wing and bent it in.'

Goalscoring was Sunderland's Achilles heel. In the final analysis only the bottom two would score fewer with the Wearsiders averaging less than a goal a game. So after another run of four games without scoring, Sunderland had failed to net in 19 of their last 29 League fixtures. The man who made the difference was Colin West. Having only mustered two starts in his career and not even having been on the bench for over a month, he told Alan Durban he was the man to get the goals he needed. West was as good as his word. Restored to the side after a 2–0 home defeat to a Middlesbrough side without an away win all season, blond-target-man West weighed in with half a dozen goals in the last 11 games to rescue Durban's men, who suffered only two more defeats in the run-in. A best-of-season run of four wins and a draw in five games with Pickering scoring in a draw at Spurs and a win at West Brom even lifted the Lads to their best placing since mid-September. 'The one at West Brom was the goal from that year that sticks in my mind the most,' says Nick. 'It was a left-footer that flew into the bottom corner and I was well pleased with it.'

Having risen to the dizzy heights of seventh off bottom after having slumped to the foot of the table after the Boro defeat, Sunderland were brought down to earth as the wheels came off with a 6–1 hammering at, of all places, Coventry. With four games to go there was still work to be done. A year on from their dramatic last-minute Roker victory that left Sunderland needing to win at Anfield, Brighton came north again but this time were convincingly despatched 3–0. However, with only a solitary point gleaned from two away trips Sunderland were still in jeopardy as the final fixture approached.

Mid-table Manchester City had the potential to put Sunderland down as the Red and White Army faced yet another final day nail-biter. On the morning of Sunderland's last match Wolves were already doomed, Boro needed a miracle, although they were one of three of the seven threatened teams to have an additional game to play once the final whistle had gone on Sunderland's season. The Lads were one of four teams on 41 points ahead of Wolves and Boro and a point behind old foes Leeds, but it was Leeds who fell through the trapdoor, succumbing at relegation rivals West Brom and going down with Boro.

Midfielder Mick Buckley proved to be Sunderland's saviour with the only goal of the game against Manchester City. It had been Buckley who had scored from McCoist's back heel at Portman Road on the opening day. Buckley had netted twice that day and just once – a vital winner against relegation rivals Stoke – in between. As an Everton player Buckley's face had stared out from the match programme on the night of Sunderland's most recent relegation in 1977 at Goodison Park but he had played his part in keeping Sunderland up this time. So had Nick Pickering who, along with Buckley, had played the most League games, with teenager Pickering the highest appearance maker overall. 'Pickering's form, for one so young and playing First Division football for the first time, was remarkably consistent. He and Mick Buckley kept us going many a time when we were very flat,' noted manager Alan Durban in reflecting on 1981–82.

Colin West had made a real impact in the run-in but had started just twice before, centre-half Rob Hindmarch had been a tower of strength for most of the season while Shaun Elliott had been as consistent as ever. Little Stan Cummins had beavered away but the previous Player of the Year had only found the net four times while Gary Rowell was just one goal short of averaging exactly a goal every three games which took some doing in a goal-shy attack in which he often operated in midfield.

The silver lining to a clouded first season under Alan Durban though had undoubtedly been new boy Nick, whose head never went down and whose enthusiasm never waned. The leggy youngster covered mile upon midfield mile as he helped Sunderland successfully battle the drop. 'It would have been a crying shame if we had been relegated. I didn't feel nervous at all that season; I was just living the dream. To play for Sunderland at Roker Park and to score there was all I'd ever wanted to do.'

Four years later Pickering would play in the League (Milk) Cup Final for Sunderland in a year when relegation did come. By then he would be an England international after adding a full cap on a 1983 tour of Australia to add to his 15 Under-21 caps. In 1987, as a Coventry player, he would add an FA Cup winners' medal to his trophy cabinet. Interviewed on TV on the Wembley turf ahead of that game, when his mind should have been 100 per cent focused on

**Nick Pickering in training
at Roker Park.**

the FA Cup Final he was about to play, Pickering had a message for the watching nation, wanting to offer Sunderland good luck for their Play-off game against Gillingham the following afternoon. It was a poignant moment. 'Before the Cup Final with Coventry I got a telegram from Bob Stokoe wishing me all the best. It was a lovely moment. Winning the FA Cup was fantastic of course, and I was all emotional, but then the next day Sunderland went and got beat in the Play-offs and went down to the Third Division.' Nick Pickering was red and white through and through.

In later years Nick came back to work for the club as a community coach and for a while summarised Sunderland matches for the BBC on local radio. By then he had a long career behind him but in becoming Sunderland's Player of the Year for 1981–82 the 18-year-old illustrated that if you're good enough, you're old enough. It was a fact recognised by one of the finest and most admired sportsmen to come from the North East, probably Newcastle's greatest ever hero, Jackie Milburn. 'I won a North East Player of the Year award in my first year,' beams Pickering, 'which was presented by Malcolm Macdonald but had been voted for by a committee including Jackie Milburn. It was sponsored by Hennessy Cognac and the prize was a weekend in Paris that my wife Olwyn and I went on. It was great and I've still got the silver salver and the trophy I won for being Player of the Year at Sunderland.'

Nick Pickering at Sunderland
Debut: 29 August 1981: Ipswich Town 3–3 Sunderland
Last game: 25 January 1986: Sunderland 0–0 Manchester United
Total appearances (all competitions): 207+2 as sub / 18 goals

Season by season
1981–82	43 games / 3 goals
1982–83	44 games / 7 goals
1983–84	48 games / 1 goal
1984–85	45 games / 2 goals
1985–86	27+2 games / 5 goals

Other clubs
Coventry City 1986–88
Derby County 1988–91
Darlington 1991–93
Burnley 1993–94

1982–83   Ian Atkins

Division One 16th out of 22
FA Cup: Third round, lost to Manchester City in a replay
League Cup: Third round, lost over two legs to Norwich City
Top scorer: Gary Rowell, 18 goals, 16 League, 2 League Cup
Ever present: No one
Player of the Year: Ian Atkins
SAFCSA Player of the Year: Ian Atkins

Season 1982–83 peaked early, on the opening day in fact. Winning 3–1 away to newly-crowned European champions Aston Villa was a fine way for Birmingham-born Villa fan Ian Atkins to make his debut. 'My parents, who are deceased now, were born in Aston. They got married in the church a hundred yards from Villa Park and I made my debut for Sunderland at Villa Park. They had just won the European Cup, we were 1–0 down at half-time and we won 3–1. You couldn't write that script!'

An outstanding season for his first club Shrewsbury Town in 1981–82 had made Atkins' name, but Sunderland had a big advantage when it came to persuading the Midlander to move to the North East. Sunderland manager Alan Durban had given Atkins his League debut when Shrewsbury boss seven years earlier and paid £30,000 for him, with striker Alan Brown also going to Shrewsbury in part exchange. 'It's a dream move for me. I rate the manager as highly as I rate the club,' the 25-year-old Atkins told the Sunderland programme on his home debut. 'Stoke City were very interested but once Mr Durban stepped in I was always coming to Roker Park.'

Durban was just as pleased to have renewed acquaintances: 'Getting Ian Atkins from Shrewsbury is a good step in the right direction,' he said at the time. 'He's a good competitor wherever he plays and I'm as pleased to have him as he is at being here.'

A bright start to the season saw seven points accrued from the first three games but reality bit with a four-match losing run in the League that, having been ended with a four-goal showing over Norwich, was followed by a run of just a solitary League win in 14 League games, thanks to a Gary Rowell hat-trick against Arsenal. Nonetheless Atkins was loving life in the top flight. Speaking at Christmas 1982 just before the team started to climb away from the foot of the table, he explained:

'When you have spent the early years of your career playing in the Second, Third and Fourth Divisions, getting the chance to play in the First Division is absolutely terrific. When you've played in front of a few hundred fans at places like Halifax and Crewe you can really appreciate what it's like running out at Villa Park, Maine Road and Old Trafford. In simple terms I am very grateful to Sunderland Football Club and Alan Durban for believing that I could make a worthwhile contribution in the top flight. Despite our problems in the first half of the season I am enjoying my time with a good club.'

It had been a tough introduction to top-flight football for Atkins. Although Sunderland supporters largely did not realise it, the Brummie was making a similar transition to that made by Cup-winning hero Dave Watson a decade earlier. Watson was known as a centre-forward to Wearside fans before reverting to the centre-back role he had operated in at the start of his career midway through the triumphant FA Cup-winning season of 1972–73. In contrast Sunderland supporters saw Atkins as a centre-back on his debut at Aston Villa where the

Ian Atkins against Liverpool, December 1982.

opportunity presented itself due to regular centre-back Rob Hindmarch being suspended. From then on Durban utilised Atkins either in defence or midfield, whereas in his final season at Shrewsbury he had played the entire season at centre-forward.

Looking back, Atkins – who in 2011 is again on SAFC's books, working as a European scout – has no doubt that he was being seen in his best role in red and white: 'I'd got 19 goals the year before Alan Durban brought me in but I made my debut for Sunderland at centre-half, which is where Alan Durban thought my best position was and I agreed with him. Other people would have thought my best position was up front because of the number of goals I'd scored the year before but Alan knew me better than that. Centre-half was always my favourite position.'

The Gay Meadow club were in what is now the Championship and had escaped relegation by two points while reaching the quarter-finals of the FA Cup. Atkins' goal haul included two against top-flight West Brom in the League Cup but Sunderland had a promising young centre-forward in Colin West and midway through the season signed the veteran England front-man Frank Worthington. Ian was evidently just pleased to be playing First Division football, saying at the time: 'I'm just grateful to see my name on the first-team sheet. I got 17 [league] goals for Shrewsbury last season and I do like to get into the opposition penalty area but if Alan Durban wants me to play in the back four that's fine by me.'

Atkins had enjoyed good times with the Shrews. He had won a Third Division Championship (now League One) medal in 1979 in a season during which he scored against Wolves with a penalty in an FA Cup quarter-final in a Cup run that included a sensational victory over Manchester City. He was to score one of his four goals in his first season at Sunderland (all of which came at home) in a thrilling 3–2 win against City in February. This was in a spell of six wins in eight League games just after the turn of the year. It was a run that lifted the Lads away from the danger zone and bore out Atkins' Christmas message.

'Go down? You've got to be joking. There is no way we will be relegated. We will get better as the season goes on, I'm quite certain of that. I honestly believe our worst days are behind us…Even when we were at our lowest ebb nobody in our dressing room was even thinking about going down. I'm certain we can climb the table and finish a long way clear of the bottom three.'

He was right that Sunderland would improve. Bottom of the table at the turn of the year, Atkins' determined and classy performances, combined with the introduction of the experienced Leighton James to add to the know-how of Frank Worthington helped steer Sunderland away from troubled waters. In the end the Lads finished seventh from bottom but with just three points between them and relegated Manchester City it was a bit too close for comfort.

With just three games left, a run of two draws and five defeats from the start of April had dragged Sunderland back into the thick of the relegation battle they had begun to leave behind. Ian led by example, scoring in a home draw with eventual runners'-up Watford, who had inflicted a joint club record 8–0 defeat earlier in the season. Thankfully the defence tightened up. After Christmas, only in a 4–1 reverse at Ipswich did anyone score more than two against the Lads, who battled hard for a clean sheet to provide the base for a 1–0 win at Arsenal in the penultimate match of the season to mathematically guarantee Atkins' aim of continued top-level membership. A final day draw at home to West Brom was immaterial as with Manchester City and Luton facing each other in a relegation showdown to see which of them would make the drop with Brighton and Swansea, the Lads had the luxury of being safe with a game to spare. Manchester City got the axe with Luton boss David Pleat's memorable victory jig at Maine Road signalling City's demise.

Looking back at his Player of the Year debut season at Sunderland, Atkins recalls: 'We were near the bottom of the League and everybody was tipping us to go down but we beat Arsenal 3–0 with Gaz [Rowell] getting a hat-trick and then we drew with Man United and Liverpool. We had six clean sheets in a row which was fantastic and to captain the side was brilliant.'

The 'Ian Atkins–Gordon Chisholm combination at the centre of the defence' was one of the season's high spots noted manager Durban once safety was assured. As always in a close season

Ian Atkins celebrating against Manchester City, February 1983.

changes were afoot. Worthington's spell over, he was moved on. As was talented and popular young Scottish striker Ally McCoist, who became a legend at Rangers rather than at Roker: who knows what may have happened had Ally been persevered with. Local lads Mark Prudhoe and Mick Whitfield were deemed surplus to requirements after just 10 games between them, while midfielder Mick Buckley's time was also up.

Durban once again went back to an old club for a player he knew well as a key summer signing, bringing Paul Bracewell from Stoke City. Having had Mark Proctor on loan from Forest for a month in the spring, the ex-Middlesbrough man was bought to partner Bracewell as Sunderland's midfield axis, thereby cementing Atkins' position at the heart of defence from where he could direct operations.

Atkins would miss just three of 48 League and Cup games in his second and last campaign when his partnership with Chisholm was one constant in a season of change. Durban was sacked at the end of February with Sunderland without a League win since the turn of the year and out of the Cup. Len Ashurst took over following a single game with caretaker Pop Robson in charge.

Atkins played his part in helping Sunderland stay up. Four wins and a draw from the final seven games included a last-day victory at Leicester. After two seasons Ian Atkins had shown he was at ease in the top flight and he wanted to be at the top end so Everton was his next move. However, the transfer did not materialise until November and while Atkins played in pre-season matches for Sunderland at the beginning of 1984–85, a couple of reserve-team outings were his only appearances prior to his transfer.

'What happened was I went through pre-season with a hairline fracture in my foot,' explains Ian. 'It had got caught in pre-season on the beach at Aberystwyth but it was being treated as if it was a ligament problem. I still tried to get through it but that created an imbalance on my knee that became a cyst on my knee which put me out until October. Len Ashurst was in charge by now and wanted his own people at the club and that's why I left. There was never a problem, the manager simply didn't want me and that was fair enough, I've got no gripes with Lennie, he just wanted to build his own team.'

When Atkins moved, Everton had just won the FA Cup as well as reaching the League Cup Final and finishing seventh in the top flight for the second year running. The Toffees had a brilliant season as Atkins arrived, winning the League and the European Cup-Winners' Cup as well as reaching the FA Cup Final. But Atkins was unable to establish himself in a successful side, managing just half a dozen League games and a solitary substitute appearance in Europe. By September 1985, after just one second-season game in Everton blue, Atkins was on his way again.

'There were about six clubs I could have gone to from Sunderland including Norwich and Coventry and I spoke to a couple of them but Everton were top of the League at the time. Unfortunately when I joined Everton I was never fit and more or less had to do a pre-season in the middle of the season and Everton went on an unbelievable unbeaten run. I made my debut for Everton back at Roker Park when we beat Sunderland 2–1 at Christmas. It was incredible because I ended up winning a Championship medal and a European Cup-Winners' Cup medal but to dislodge Kevin Ratcliffe or Derek Mountfield was a tall order. I came into the side when someone was injured. I played centre-half, in midfield and even up front for Everton. Howard Kendall [the Everton manager] was fantastic, he knew it was nothing to do with money and I just wanted to play after captaining Sunderland. I was only about 14 months into a four-year contract but I wanted to be playing. Nowadays players tend to just sit on a contract in those situations but for me it was about playing football first. It was too good an opportunity to turn down when I joined Everton but eventually I left because I wanted to play football. I had the chance to join Sunderland again when I left Everton before I went to Ipswich. Lawrie McMenemy was the manager at Sunderland, who had been relegated by now.

'I still had my house in Sunderland and all I wanted to do was play football. Lawrie McMenemy spoke to me and wanted me to come to Sunderland on trial and play in a reserve game at Scunthorpe. I didn't think I needed to do that after being captain in the team's highest position since 1956 just over a year earlier and at the same time Ipswich offered me a deal so I went there. I'd have liked to come back to Sunderland even on an initial loan but Lawrie McMenemy wanted me on trial first and I don't think Everton would have allowed that. I'd have come back no problem, especially with still having a house in Sunderland and loving the area. I took it as an insult that he wanted me on trial. My family loved it at Sunderland and it broke their hearts to leave in the first place so it would have been great to come back. It's a special area that I love because nothing has ever really changed in terms of the mentality and the humour of the people. People like Kevin Ball for instance, comes from down south and loves the place. I'm delighted to be back at Sunderland now and have spent the last four years working as a scout. People know Sunderland is a big club but they don't know how big. Part of my job now is selling the club to potential players in Europe.'

In the eight years between leaving Everton and returning to Sunderland for the first time Ian had two and a half years at Ipswich and three and a half at Birmingham before moving into management with Colchester, who had just lost League status. Taking the U's to runners'-up spot was not enough for promotion so he accepted the role of assistant manager to ex-Leeds man Terry Cooper back at Birmingham. Still registered as a player, Ian made a handful of appearances which took the Villa fan to over 100 in Blues colours before deciding he wanted to be number one again and accepting a position as player-manager at Cambridge United in December 1992. With his new club already in trouble, Atkins fought an unsuccessful battle to prevent relegation from the 'new' First Division and resigned at the end of the season after making just two League appearances as he concentrated on managing.

Returning to Roker a month later as assistant manager to his old Ipswich teammate Terry Butcher, Atkins' second spell at Sunderland would be an unsuccessful one. Having been given more money to spend in the summer than any Sunderland manager in history, Butcher saw his side hammered 5–0 at Derby on the opening day, having lost several of his new faces in a pre-season car crash. It was emblematic of the season with Butcher given the chop after a home defeat by Southend left the club 20th in Division One after their fifth defeat in a row.

'Once a Sunderland man, you are always a Sunderland man. I came back as assistant manager to Terry Butcher but unfortunately things didn't work out for Terry and that affected me because I wasn't in control of my own destiny. When I came back I thought I was here for life…it broke my heart to leave,' reflects Ian, who is immensely proud that he was made Player of the Year in his very first season on Wearside. 'I won every single branch award that year. I was fortunate in that I won every single one and I've still got them or the majority of them at least,' says Ian proudly. 'It means a lot to win a Player of the Year award from supporters, especially for someone like me who had come from Shrewsbury and no one had really heard of. I was runner-up to Kevin Keegan in the Hennessy Cognac North East Player of the Year award too. I won Player of the Year awards at Shrewsbury, Ipswich and Birmingham, in fact everywhere except Everton.

'Sunderland is special. Once you put those stripes on it is like the blood in your body, you get a tingle in your arms because it is a great football area and the club matters so much to people. That's why to be voted Player of the Year at Sunderland is something to be really proud of and believe me I am.'

Ian Atkins at Sunderland
Debut: 28 August 1982: Aston Villa 1–3 Sunderland
Last game: 12 May 1984: Leicester City 0–2 Sunderland
Total appearances (all competitions): 86+1 as sub / 6 goals

Season by season
1982–83   41+1 games / 4 goals
1983–84   45 games / 2 goals
Sunderland 1993 (assistant manager June to December)
Sunderland 2008 (European scout)

Other clubs
Shrewsbury Town 1973–82
Everton 1984–85
Ipswich Town 1985–88
Birmingham City 1988–90
Colchester United 1990–91 (player-manager)
Birmingham City 1991–92 (player-assistant manager)
Cambridge United 1992–93 (player-manager)
Doncaster Rovers 1994
Northampton Town 1995–99 (manager)
Chester City 2000 (manager)
Carlisle United 2000–01 (manager)
Oxford United 2001–04 (manager)
Bristol Rovers 2004–05 (manager)
Torquay United 2006 (manager)

Division One: 13th out of 22
FA Cup: Third round, lost at home to Birmingham City
League Cup: Third round, lost at home in a replay to Norwich City
Top scorers: Colin West, 13 goals, 9 League, 2 FA Cup, 2 League Cup
Gary Rowell, 13 goals, 8 League, 1 FA Cup, 4 League Cup
Ever presents: Chris Turner, 48 out of 48 League and Cup games
Nick Pickering, 48 out of 48 League and Cup games
Player of the Year: Paul Bracewell
SAFCSA Player of the Year: Paul Bracewell

Having had last-gasp escapes in each of the three years since promotion, supporters' nerves were frayed to say the least. Manager Alan Durban had overseen the last two of those seasons but felt he was building an improving team. To that end his main summer transfer business had been to sign a pair of talented midfielders. He already knew what each player was capable of. Mark Proctor, signed from Durban's old Derby manager Brian Clough at Forest, had done well on loan at Roker towards the end of the previous season, while £225,000 had prised Paul Bracewell away from Stoke, where Durban had given him his debut four seasons earlier.

'The connection between us was that when I left school at 15 to sign as an apprentice at Stoke Alan Durban was the manager,' explains Paul. 'He left around 1981 when I was about to be out of contract and I signed for him at Sunderland. In fact though, Howard Kendall, who was player/coach at Stoke, was more of an influence on me because Alan Durban was a different kind of midfielder to me and got forward a lot more, but he gave me my chance. I remember being in his office with my parents when I signed as a kid. He said if I worked hard he'd give me my chance and he did that.'

Pre-season went swimmingly, Sunderland winning the Isle of Man tournament by beating St Mirren in the Final and also enjoying a 4–0 win over Middlesbrough at Roker Park. Once the real stuff started, though, Sunderland found games as much of a struggle as they had since promotion, taking just one point from the opening three games with centre-forward Colin West the only man to score. For Bracewell it was something of a false start as after helping Sunderland to a draw on his debut he limped out of the second game at Villa and was forced to sit out the next two matches.

Young winger Paul Atkinson debuted on the same day as 'Brace' and hit the winner as Wolves became the first side vanquished by the Red and Whites, a trademark Gary Rowell spot kick and an own-goal by future Sunderland man Peter Daniel seeing the Lads through to a 3–2 scoreline. Durban knew what an asset he had in Bracewell and was prepared to change a winning team to accommodate his new signing, dropping Wales international Leighton James to the bench to bring Paul back.

Already Bracewell had made an instant impact on the Roker faithful as he was evidently a player with a touch of class. Always on the move and a superb reader of the game, Bracewell knitted play together impressively, playing beautifully-weighted balls into the paths of his teammates. His touch and sharp incisive passing was reminiscent of Pop Robson and Tony Towers. Clearly Durban had signed a good 'un.

Sunderland hovered between 16th and 19th positions (out of 22) in the first three months of the season, managing excellent away wins at eventual champions Liverpool and also at

Arsenal. By the time Bracewell scored his first goal for the club with the only goal of the game away to Birmingham City, the Lads had unusually taken 10 points out of the last 12 away from home. But that was a flash in the pan as although Paul found the back of the net in the next game on the road the Lads were hammered 6–1 at Notts County.

Goalscoring was never Bracewell's forte. In total he scored just six goals in 270 appearances over three spells for Sunderland but with two of them coming in Sunderland's next win he found himself with four goals in six games at that stage, Brace's brace coming in a comfortable home win over West Brom between Christmas and New Year. 'They must have put something in the tea,' Paul jokes. 'I was never much of a scorer and only got something like 20 in my whole career but when I did find the back of the net they were often spectacular ones.' In fact Paul scored 21 in 747 League games but the astonishing thing here is that he played so many games given an appalling injury he suffered with Everton between his first two spells with Sunderland.

Chairman Tom Cowie's Christmas box to Alan Durban was to allow him to spend 200 grand on another of his Stoke old boys, Lee Chapman. He came from Arsenal and debuted as Sunderland ended 1983 by completing their third back-to-back victories of the season to lift them to a healthy 12th place. This was their highest position for three years outside of the opening month of the season as the table takes shape. It was to be the high point of the year and although the final position would be just one place lower, the second half of the season would be one of struggle with just one win in the next 14 League games.

Chapman had struggled at Arsenal after making his name at Stoke. He needed a fresh start and an excellent performance that included a goal on his third appearance in a solid 3–0 FA Cup win at Third Division Bolton augured well. Unfortunately, despite goals away to eventual runners-up Southampton and Manchester United, Chapman did not provide the spearhead Sunderland were looking for and come the end of the season he moved on without ever having scored in front of the home fans.

Chapman actually scored the final goal of Durban's two and three-quarter year reign. Evidently not impressed at how his last big buy had performed, Cowie gave Durban the sack at the beginning of March.

'When you look back we had a good young team with players like Barry Venison, Nick Pickering, Chris Turner, Mark Proctor, myself and others,' insists Bracewell. 'We were assembling some of the best kids around and I was bitterly disappointed when Alan Durban left as we weren't struggling badly. We didn't have much in the way of experience and were building for the future. Whenever you have a young team you get some up and down results just as Sunderland experienced in 2010–11 with a young team.'

Paul is correct in arguing that Sunderland were showing signs of building a decent team. Four of Durban's last five games were against the clubs who finished the season in the top four and only a 2–1 defeat away to Manchester United brought defeat against those four in that sequence along with a loss at top-half Tottenham.

After 30 consecutive appearances Bracewell was missing with a groin injury as striker Pop Robson took charge as caretaker for a well-earned draw with Arsenal and he was missing too for the next game as new manager Len Ashurst got off to a winning start against high-flying QPR. No outfield player has ever played as many games for Sunderland as Ashurst did between 1958 and 1970 and now, after a managerial career that included taking Newport County to a European quarter-final, 'Lennie the Lion' was given the challenge of managing his old club just a few days before his 45th birthday.

Two draws sandwiched three defeats following Ashurst's first match win. It was a tough start with six of his first eight games against top-half teams but Ashurst galvanised the side to a productive April that brought three wins and just one defeat from five fixtures.

Len recognised the value of Pop Robson who, having taken charge of the side before his own appointment, was persuaded to put his boots back on. 'Pop' had been concentrating on coaching since returning to the club in the summer. A class act throughout his career, Robson still knew how to find the back of the net and had scored on his only start of the season prior to Ashurst's arrival. Initially eased back as a sub, Robson scored on his second start under Ashurst as Everton were beaten and would become Sunderland's all-time oldest goalscorer with an important goal on his final appearance on the last day of the season.

That final game was at Filbert Street, where Leicester City were managed by Gordon Milne, who had been Coventry's manager on the night of Sunderland's controversial relegation in

1977. Also on Leicester's staff was Gerry Summers, who had succeeded Ashurst as manager at Gillingham and as there was no love lost between that pair there was zero chance of any 'Anfield 1981' style scenario. Sunderland had never been in a relegation position all season but – as usual – were in danger of going down on the final day. Wolves and Notts County were already doomed but there were eight teams who could join them.

With only one home defeat since September, at which point the Foxes had lost their opening six games, Leicester were no pushover and there was a feeling that – after the bad blood between Sunderland and Coventry when Milne was in charge combined with the little-known antithesis between Ashurst and Summers – Leicester would take pleasure in sending Sunderland down. No side outside the top six had scored more at home than Leicester, who had an exciting young striker by the name of Gary Lineker who had 14 goals in his previous 18 games. Stoke, old foes Coventry, Birmingham and WBA were all below Sunderland but all could overtake the Lads for whom a point would almost certainly be enough on goal difference but for whom a win would make survival certain.

Ashurst had won many scraps as a Sunderland player in the great team of the early sixties particularly and steeped in red and white he knew how much it mattered that Sunderland stayed up. In his unmissable and candid autobiography *Left Back In Time* Ashurst lifts the lid on how he engineered what proved to be a comfortable win with first-half goals from Chapman and Robson.

'With the situation as it was you would have thought that everyone at the club would be pulling together to ensure survival and First Division status. Far from it. I'd become aware that Everton, who at the time were a top First Division club and won the FA Cup that season, had set their sights on some of my better players. The situation had been simmering for a couple of weeks and came to a head on the Friday morning before that vital last game of the season when Paul Bracewell and Lee Chapman came to see me. They both wanted a transfer and intimated they were not fussed about playing at Leicester the following day, despite the fact that I had named them in my starting line up. Both intimated that they did not want to be at the club the following season. With the team bus leaving within the hour I had to respond quickly.

'What was paramount was Sunderland's First Division survival; next season could look after itself. Thinking on my feet, I gave them an ultimatum: "Win at Leicester tomorrow and you will be at another club for the start of next season." Both were magnificent the next day with Bracewell Man of the Match, along with captain Ian Atkins, another player who wanted to depart.'

With other results falling Sunderland's way the points – from a 2–0 victory in which Chapman scored – lifted the Lads from 16th to 13th, safe by four points and astonishingly in the club's highest place since 1956. Paul's own recollection of his first departure from Sunderland differs from Len Ashurst's. 'Lennie came in and probably thought I was someone he could get money for to help him build a side. That's the way things go because that's football and there's no hard feelings.'

Bracewell joined a club pushing for honours and within a year had three medals to his name. Brace played a total of 57 games in his first season at Goodison as Everton won the League and the European Cup-Winners' Cup as well as reaching the first of what would be four FA Cup Final appearances of Brace's career, all of which were lost.

The touch of class Sunderland supporters had noted from Bracewell's first appearances brought Paul an England debut in the summer after his first season at Goodison. There was to be one more fabulous season for him at Everton before serious injury wiped two seasons from his career. Returning in 1988–89, Bracewell played in half of Everton's games before returning to Sunderland. Strangely that would follow an appearance in the FA Cup Final but when another FA Cup Final proved to be the last game of his second spell at Sunderland it proved to be a controversial departure.

The midfielder had evidently lost half a yard of pace following his injuries but the touch of class was still there and under his old Stoke teammate Denis Smith, Bracewell steered Sunderland to promotion. That elevation followed the first of his two Wembley appearances for the Lads, Sunderland actually losing to Swindon but famously going up anyway after Swindon were punished for financial wrongdoing.

Putting his injury problems behind him, Bracewell played over 40 games in each of the three seasons of his second stint on Wearside. Relegation in the middle of those was followed by a season of struggle in Division Two only for a glorious Cup run under Malcolm Crosby to lead to Wembley. Captaining Sunderland in the 1992 FA Cup Final which was lost 2–0 to Liverpool (whom he had twice lost to in Cup Finals before), Bracewell proceeded to stun Wearside by walking out…and signing for Newcastle.

On Tyneside, where he had been offered a longer contract than on Wearside, Paul won promotion under Kevin Keegan and enjoyed a couple of good seasons in the top flight before being drawn to Sunderland for a third spell.

His old Everton midfield partner and room-mate Peter Reid having taken over at Roker Park, Bracewell was the obvious choice to come in and assist Reidy and so Paul returned in the dual role of player and assistant manager. As in 1990, Paul helped Sunderland back to the top flight, this time as champions. He was the only ever present in the final season at Roker Park as the team went down again and would play just three more times in the first year at the Stadium of Light before moving on to become player-coach at Fulham under his old Newcastle boss Keegan.

'Brace' in action against Southampton's former Liverpool man Jimmy Case.

As he had done at all of his clubs, Paul impressed, so much so that he succeeded Keegan when he became England supremo in 1999. Following a year in charge Bracewell was replaced by Jean Tigana with his own next port of call being Halifax Town, where he spent a year in charge before resigning four games into the 2001–02 season.

With a total of 270 appearances in his three spells on Wearside, Paul Bracewell played more times for Sunderland than any other club. He was always a hugely influential figure as a skilful passer of the ball and intuitive reader of the game. Winning the Player of the Year award in his first season at Roker when he was at his best is something Paul his rightly proud of: 'To be voted Player of the Year by the supporters is a fantastic honour. I was still relatively young and had come to the club for £250,000 which is a lot of money so there was pressure there.'

These days Bracewell channels his energy into 'Complete Football', a venture that provides excellent football facilities, offers youth coaching and runs five, six and nine-a-side Leagues. 'It's going really well and I enjoy it. Grass roots football is so important to the future of the game and there's a massive demand for what we offer. We're opening a new site in Liverpool and looking to roll it out across the country.'

Bracewell's Player of the Year season at Sunderland came in his first single year at the club but he has had two further spells on Wearside and you never know, there could be a fourth in some capacity in the future.

'I enjoyed my time at Sunderland although I was disappointed when the manager left part of the way through my first year. It didn't put me off though because it's a great club and I kept coming back.'

Paul Bracewell at Sunderland
Debut: 27 August 1983: Sunderland 1–1 Norwich City
Last game: 23 September 1997: Bury 1–2 Sunderland
Total appearances (all competitions): 268+2 as sub / 6 goals

Season by season
1983–84	44 games / 4 goals
1989–90	45+1 games / 2 goals
1990–91	43 games / 0 goals
1991–92	49 games / 0 goals
1995–96	44 games / 0 goals
1996–97	41 games / 0 goals
1997–98	2+1 games / 0 goals

Other clubs
Stoke City 1978–83
Everton 1984–89
Newcastle United 1992–95
Fulham 1997–2000 (player-coach then manager)
Halifax Town 2000–01 (manager)

Chris Turner

Division One: 21st out of 22 – relegated
FA Cup: Third round, lost to Southampton
League Cup: Finalists, lost to Norwich City at Wembley
Top scorer: Bob Lee, 13 goals, all League
Ever present: Chris Turner, 53 out of 53 League and Cup games, 15 clean sheets
Player of the Year: Chris Turner
SAFCSA Player of the Year: Chris Turner

Chris Turner's Player of the Year season was his last at Sunderland. The first goalkeeper to be awarded the club's individual honour, Turner was made captain for the day on his farewell performance and performed as heroically as he had all season in an already relegated team. 'It was a disappointing year for the club but a tremendous season for me personally and being asked to captain the club as a goalkeeper on the last day was a massive honour for me,' says Chris.

It had been a tumultuous season. Turner had been the single most influential figure in a 10-game run to a Wembley Cup Final but had been powerless to stop a slide in the second half of the season from mid-table at Christmas to relegated with a dozen points still to play for.

It was Chris' sixth season at Sunderland. For the first three he had competed for the first-team shirt with Barry Siddall, coming out on top in terms of appearances in his first two seasons and being second choice for most of the third. For the second half of his time at Sunderland though Turner was the undisputed number one. Having recovered from a fractured skull which curtailed his season in 1982–83, Turner never missed a game in his last two seasons at Roker

Chris Turner boards the bus at Roker Park en route to Wembley in 1985.

Park, his final match being his 101st consecutive appearance prior to a club record equalling transfer to Manchester United.

1984–85 was Sunderland record outfield appearance maker Len Ashurst's first full season as manager of the club. Turner was already at Roker when Ashurst was installed but Len had given Chris his League debut at Sheffield Wednesday in 1976 and knew what a good 'keeper he was, not least as Chris had won the Young Player of the Year award at Hillsborough.

The opening day of the season saw England 'keeper Peter Shilton beaten within two minutes by new Ashurst purchase Gary Bennett as Southampton were defeated 3–1. By two days before Bonfire Night, following back-to-back 3–0 home wins, Sunderland were seventh. Beyond the embryonic stages of the August and September League tables it was higher than Sunderland had been since way back in 1956. Three nights later another Turner clean sheet helped Sunderland to an extra-time victory over Nottingham Forest, managed by the man who held a grudge against his former SAFC teammate Ashurst over the injury that led to the premature end to his own playing days: Brian Clough.

Having already knocked out Crystal Palace in the Milk Cup (as the League Cup was called then), Sunderland would progress to the Final largely thanks to a series of inspirational performances by Turner. Only six goals were conceded in the 10 games of the competition but having done so much to get the Lads to the Final Chris Turner had no chance with the goal that beat him at Wembley.

'I'd say my best performance was in the home Cup game with Spurs that finished 0–0,' says Turner. 'Everybody goes on about the penalty save in the replay but in the first game at Roker it really was one-way traffic and Tottenham should have buried us. I had one of those games where I just saved everything. Regarding the penalty save, normally if you save a spot kick it's because it's not been struck properly but Graham Roberts got a good connection and I managed to get a strong hand on it. Anything to my right I always fancied saving and it couldn't have come

Chris Turner (3rd from left), along with (from left): Steve Berry, 1981–82 Player of the Year Nick Pickering and David Corner.

at a more important time, being near the end. When it came to the Final it was a disappointing goal to concede. Young David Corner made an unfortunate decision to try and let the ball go out of play for a goal-kick but lost possession. The ball was played back to Asa Hartford. I had his shot covered and had started moving to my left to gather it when it clipped off Gordon Chisholm and deflected in the opposite direction leaving me powerless to stop it. We didn't deserve to win that Final but we didn't deserve to lose it either. It was a poor game where the breaks went against us and we knew it wasn't going to be our day when Clive Walker hit the post with a penalty.'

Playing in front of Chris in central defence, Gary Bennett acknowledges Turner's vital role in that Cup run: 'Chris was a great 'keeper especially in the 84–85 season in the League Cup run when we got to the Final. Without him making the saves he did I don't think we would have got there. He was a great shot stopper.'

For any player a showpiece occasion is something to look forward to. In his autobiography *Left Back In Time*, manager Len Ashurst uncovers the financial squabbles going on behind the scenes but Chris says, 'We didn't focus on finance too much but little things like that come with getting into a Cup Final and it happens at every club. What hit us when we got to the ground was that our wives and girlfriends were stuck at the back miles from where they should have been. They were all in new outfits and had been looking forward to the big occasion as much as we had but they hadn't been looked after and that was a grind to us.'

After the Wembley defeat, vanquished semi-final foes Chelsea extracted some revenge with a 2–0 win at Roker in the first match after the trip to the Twin Towers. This was followed by defeats to both the red and blue halves of Merseyside to leave the Lads in free fall and heading for the relegation trapdoor. With Turner doing his best to stem the flow, three successive clean sheets offered some hope but with the side able to score just one goal in those games the League position remained unaltered as it would to the end of the campaign. Only doomed Stoke and their record low points tally (a record that remained until 2006 when Sunderland got even fewer than the Potters' measly 17) kept the Lads off the bottom.

The last six games brought just one point. The fact that came from a thrilling 2–2 draw away to high-riding Manchester United illustrated that there was more talent in the team than the League position indicated. But with Sunderland managing just one goal in total from the five other games in the run-in, Turner was always fighting a losing battle in more ways than one.

The Ipswich side which came to Roker on the final day of the season were far from the free-flowing stylists the Suffolk side had boasted during Bobby Robson's time in charge. They would have been Sunderland's Wembley opponents had they not lost to a goal from future Sunderland manager Steve Bruce in their semi-final with local rivals Norwich. At this time Ipswich were managed by Bobby Ferguson, who would later become first-team coach at Roker Park under Terry Butcher, who was one of a trio of future Sunderland players in the Ipswich line up along with Eric Gates and George Burley. The visitors overran a demoralised Sunderland with striker Kevin Wilson putting the seal on Sunderland's unhappy season with his second goal, and the match winner, a minute from time. However, had it not been for Turner, Sunderland would have been well beaten.

Chris would go on to make 64 League appearances for Manchester United before returning to his first club, Sheffield Wednesday, with whom he would win the League Cup – beating Manchester United in the 1991 Final. In a distinguished career, Turner played more for Sunderland than any other club and reveals that he could possibly have played even more.

'I played every game in my final two years at the club and could have stayed. When I got the chance to sign for Manchester United just as we'd been relegated the pull was so strong that I knew I'd regret it for the rest of my life if I didn't take the opportunity. The most disappointing thing for me was that later, when I wasn't getting a game at Man Utd, Sunderland tried to get me back but it didn't come off because they couldn't get the finance together. I'd have loved to have come back and I still love watching Sunderland now whenever I visit the Stadium of Light. It's a great club with fantastic supporters. I loved my time at Roker Park. It wasn't as glamorous as Old Trafford or Highbury but to me it was magical. One of my first matches was a night match in the League Cup against Manchester City who were managed by Big Malcolm Allison and had a million-pound striker in Michael Robinson but we won 1–0. It was pouring and the conditions were bad for a goalkeeper but I played well and felt confident and it set a seal for me with the supporters.'

Chris Turner at Sunderland
Debut: 11 August 1979: Sunderland 1–2 Oldham Athletic, Anglo-Scottish Cup, appeared as sub
Full debut: 29 September 1979: Sunderland 1–1 Preston North End
Last game: 11 May 1985: Sunderland 1–2 Ipswich Town
Total appearances (all competitions): 223+1 as sub

Season by season
1979–80	31+1 games
1980–81	31 games
1981–82	19 games
1982–83	41 games
1983–84	48 games
1984–85	53 games

Other clubs
Sheffield Wednesday 1975–79
Lincoln City (loan) 1978
Manchester United 1985–88
Sheffield Wednesday 1988–91
Leeds United (loan) 1989
Leyton Orient 1991, 1993 (assistant manager), 1994 (joint manager)
Leicester City 1995 (coach)
Wolverhampton Wanderers (youth team coach)
Hartlepool United 1999–2002 (manager)
Sheffield Wednesday 2002–04 (manager)
Stockport County 2004–05 (manager)
Hartlepool United 2006–10 (director of sport, manager 2008–10)

1985–86   Mark Proctor

Division Two: 18th out of 22
FA Cup: Fourth round, lost in a replay away to Manchester United
League Cup: Second round, lost 5–4 on aggregate to Swindon Town
Full Members' Cup: Eliminated at group stage
Top scorer: Eric Gates, 11 goals, 9 League, 1 League Cup, 1 Full Members' Cup
Ever present: No one
Official Player of the Year: Mark Proctor
SAFCSA Player of the Year: Shaun Elliott

As in 2002–03, a terrible season would see the Player of the Year award go to a player who missed the first half of the season: 17 years hence, youngster Sean Thornton would win the award in the 19-point relegation season despite not debuting until January. In 1985–86 midfielder Mark Proctor became Player of the Year after his seven goals in 19 League games left him just two League goals behind top scorer Eric Gates as he played an influential role in preventing the season from ending in total disaster and humiliation. Mark's goals in the last two games of the season ensured escape from relegation to the Third Division for the first time in the club's history. As it was, Sunderland finished in their lowest ever position.

This was the first season when the two major Player of the Year awards had different winners. Since the introduction of the club's official Player of the Year award in 1980–81, each season had seen the same player win both the official and longer-standing SAFCSA trophy. However, while captain Shaun Elliott repeated his 1978–79 success by lifting the Supporters' Association award, it was Mark Proctor who took the official title. Carried out in conjunction with the *Sunderland Echo* and sponsored by the Sunderland & Shields Building Society, this official award existed for many years alongside a Player of the Month award regularly featured in the club's match programme.

In those pre-internet days, voting was done via forms available in the club's promotion office as well as the offices of the *Echo* and the Building Society. Supporters were encouraged to vote by the incentive of the chance to have lunch with the winning player, with junior voters offered a tour of the ground along with a strip and match tickets.

'I came third in the North East Player of the Year award that season as well which came as quite a shock to me,' says Proctor in 2011, back at his home-town club Middlesbrough where he had begun as an associate schoolboy in 1975. 'Proccy was a joker,' says his former teammate Gary Bennett. 'He and David Hodgson were the best of friends. He was a lovely lad and now [in 2011] is first-team coach at Middlesbrough and works with my son who is a young player there. Proccy's a great lad, a great passer of the ball and a tremendous midfield player.'

In what was a dreadful season for all associated with SAFC, it seems that Mark's winning of the Player of the Year award came as a reflection of the fact that he was unaffected by the disillusion and frustration surrounding the club because, as he explains, he was simply enjoying playing:

'It was an absolutely fantastic time for me because I'd reached the stage where I thought my career was possibly finished. I'd missed the Milk Cup Final which was a big blow as I thought I'd never get another chance to play at Wembley although as it worked out I did [in the Zenith Data Systems Cup for Boro versus Chelsea, five years almost to the day after the Cup Final he missed]. I won a couple of Player of the Year awards at Boro as a youngster and collected another

award when I was with Sheffield Wednesday but the Sunderland one was a surprise given that I'd only played the second half of the season.

'I came back in the December and was a humble, happy young man who was just so pleased to be playing again. When you think your career might be taken away from you and you find you can play again you do so with such joy.'

1985 had been a write-off for the midfielder. 'The injury happened at St James' Park on the day we finished with nine men when Howard Gayle and Benno [Gary Bennett – on New Year's Day 1985] were sent off. I pulled my groin in that match which later developed into a pelvic strain. I ended up attempting more comebacks than Frank Sinatra but just kept breaking down.'

He lasted just 17 minutes of a pre-season friendly at Aston Villa and then worked his way back. Astonishingly for a player who had struggled with injury for so long, when he came back at the end of November he played twice in less than 24 hours. Having played 90 minutes on a Tuesday night at Roker Park as the reserves beat Rotherham 4–3, Proctor then requested and received permission to play for the youth team in a charity match the following day. He managed almost another full game, scoring twice in a 7–1 win over Bedlington Juniors at Ashington's Portland Park in a game played as a fund-raiser for people in Senegal.

Two more reserve outings, the last of which saw him score from the spot in a big win at Port Vale, earned him a first-team recall three days later at Blackburn. Ending in a 2–0 defeat, the scoreline mirrored that of the season's opening-day fixture against the same opponents, managed by future Sunderland assistant boss Bobby Saxton.

Saxton would be at Sunderland under Peter Reid when Sunderland were flying in the early days at the Stadium of Light. In contrast, new manager Lawrie McMenemy, who had taken over from Len Ashurst, turned out to be an unmitigated disaster. The Rovers' return left Sunderland 15th in the Second Division.

McMenemy's name is loathed by Sunderland supporters as he oversaw an incredible decline in the club's fortunes yet when chairman Tom Cowie secured the Saltwell Park born 48-year-old, the acquisition was looked upon as a major coup. First choice for the fans was former Sunderland forward Brian Clough, the charismatic man who had taken both Derby and Nottingham Forest to the League title and won the European Cup twice with Forest. If Clough could not be secured then McMenemy was seen as the next best thing. A manager with a major media profile, he was a popular appointment and had a trophy on his CV having taken Second Division Southampton to FA Cup Final success against Manchester United three years after Sunderland had beaten Leeds.

In the 1960s, McMenemy had worked under ex-Sunderland manager Alan Brown as a coach at Sheffield Wednesday but while Brown was a devotee of youth, McMenemy went to the opposite end of the spectrum and cast aside Sunderland's promising youngsters in favour of ageing big-name imports which was a strategy that had served him well with the Saints.

Optimism abounded in the stands for the first game under a man fans felt would put Sunderland back on the map. The opening day saw debuts for former England and Ipswich forward Eric Gates, former European Cup winner and Scottish international Frank Gray, experienced former Crystal Palace target man Dave Swindlehurst and Republic of Ireland international goalkeeper Seamus McDonagh. Having lost former 'keeper Chris Turner to Manchester United for a joint club record fee, goalkeeping would prove to be a problem for the side for much of the season.

In the opposite dugout for the first game after relegation, McMenemy's counterpart Saxton had played for Brian Clough at Derby and liked to see football played effectively and attractively. With the August sunshine heralding the start of the McMenemy era, Sunderland's new-look side barely got the ball off a fluent Rovers outfit who won much more comfortably than the 2–0 scoreline in the record books suggests. It was a sign of things to come at Sunderland. It was the first of five defeats in a row without so much as scoring a goal.

Things were so bad that claiming a point from a home game with Grimsby Town was a cause for celebration as Sunderland had actually scored – a mere 494 minutes into the season. McMenemy kept changes early on to a minimum as he gave the team a chance to get to know each other's games, although his former Southampton player Reuben Agboola – who had been devastated at McMenemy's appointment – was discarded after just three games.

Finally a brace from home-grown England international Nick Pickering provided a belated victory away to Shrewsbury. It was the first of seven wins in 11 League games that lifted the

Lads up 10 places from bottom to 12th by mid-November. With the top three promoted and no Play-offs to aim for the season already looked over but there was drama to come at the wrong end of the table.

Proctor's first game at Roker Park of 1985 arrived three days before Christmas, when he helped earn a draw with Crystal Palace, but there was better news on Boxing Day as Sheffield United left empty-handed. Despite ending the year with a two-goal loss at his home-town team of Boro, Proctor's inspired return brought him the December Player of the Month award.

They were tough times with just two League wins in 17 games. Two weeks after beating the Blades, a Nick Pickering hat-trick in a 4–2 hammering of old rivals Leeds was more than welcome but led to McMenemy cashing in on Pickering by selling him after just one more match.

While Pickering joined Ashurst signings Peter Daniel and Clive Walker in being discarded by the new manager, McMenemy meanwhile was constantly investing in the transfer market and sticking to his policy of bringing in big names who, while past their best, he hoped would be good enough still to get Sunderland moving onwards and upwards.

Sunderland-born full-back Alan Kennedy had scored the winner in the 1981 European Cup Final for Liverpool and had scored in the penalty shoot-out of the 1984 Final as he collected another winners' medal. Joining Kennedy in the opposite full-back berth was ex-Ipswich stalwart and 1978 FA Cup winner George Burley.

'They were all bought on the back of Lawrie McMenemy's policy of buying senior players,' recalls Proctor. 'It was a strange season that all went a bit "Pete Tong" and I'm sure that if asked those senior players would say that their performance level wasn't great and that in turn didn't help the younger lads in the team. From my own point of view I was just so glad to be playing after all of my injury problems that my recollections are all positive despite the problems of the time.'

As well as introducing Kennedy and Burley at full-back with the previous numbers two and three – Venison and Gray – being utilised in midfield, McMenemy had ongoing problems in goal. Sunderland used three 'keepers in 1985–86 and they were all signed on loan. McDonagh endured a difficult time, at one point even questioning the size of the goals at Grimsby. He was followed by long-time Liverpool reserve Bob Bolder who initially did well, looking to command his penalty area.

Bolder's arrival coincided with an upturn in results and, thinking they had solved their problem, Sunderland paid £30,000 to convert the loan into a signing, but before long Bolder's confidence began to sag as results fell away and by early February he had played his final game and ended the season on loan to Luton where he was content to be back-up to first-choice goalie Les Sealey.

Joining on loan from Luton in exchange for the loan of Bolder, Sunderland acquired Andy Dibble, a man who played in the League for nine clubs in his career. Inevitably for a jobbing goalkeeper often playing for clubs on a short-term basis, sometimes they proved a success and sometimes they did not work out for him. However, Dibble became something of a cult hero at Sunderland as he played a major role in his dozen appearances in ensuring a bad season did not become a disastrous one.

Sunderland were gradually being sucked towards the bottom of the table. Proctor chipped in with a couple of goals but eventually injury caught up, forcing him out of three games in late March.

Andy Dibble.

Mark Proctor leads out the squad at Wembley but he was unavailable for the showpiece due to long term injury.

Sunderland had dropped to one spot off the relegation places as they went into a 10th game without a win in Dibble's sixth match. A 4–2 victory over bottom-of-the-table Fulham saw Proctor return and score twice to begin a run of five goals in the final seven games as he guided the Lads to safety. The win over Fulham was the first of four from the final seven fixtures that enabled Sunderland to escape the drop into Division Three.

Following the Fulham result though, a draw, a win and two defeats meant that nothing less than maximum points from the remaining two home games would guarantee survival. On the morning of Sunderland's penultimate game at home to fellow strugglers Shrewsbury Town, Fulham were already down and debt-ridden Middlesbrough were almost certain to join them but could still finish above Sunderland with Blackburn, Carlisle and Shrewsbury the other sides in danger.

Clean sheets had been rare commodities with just four in 40 League games but with Elliott commanding and Dibble excelling somehow Sunderland put together their only back-to-back shut-outs of the season with Proctor scoring in both games as 2–0 victories were carved out. 'I remember smashing one down the middle to score against Shrewsbury, I think it was in front of the Fulwell End, and then I managed to bury a penalty against Stoke when we won that match as well,' recalls Proctor, who had also scored in the previous game at Brighton.

In the final analysis Sunderland finished fifth from bottom, four points clear of Carlisle, who joined Boro in going down. A relieved McMenemy waved a white handkerchief at the 20,631 who had witnessed the final-day escape. A year earlier Sunderland had been playing in the top flight and a Wembley Cup Final but had almost tumbled to successive relegations. Hope springing eternal, McMenemy's message was 'next year, it will be different'. It was one of two seasons Lawrie McMenemy was in charge of Sunderland. Astonishingly it was not the worst!

The manager intended a clear-out and seven of those who played against Stoke would never play for the club again, including SAFCSA Player of the Year Elliott.

It was a dreadful season in which the club finished lower than ever before. In choosing Proctor as the Player of the Year, the fans went for someone who had made a real impact after returning from long-term injury, bringing class and composure to proceedings and perhaps significantly, supporters made a statement by voting for a player not brought in by the new manager. Similarly the SAFCSA choice, Shaun Elliott, was a local lad, not one of the manager's big-name flops.

Proctor at his peak was a terrific player. An England Under-21 international, he was an assured and astute passer of the ball, capable of playing the bulk of his career in the top flight. Paired with Paul Bracewell in 1983–84, the duo provided the engine for a side that had potential. Sadly, injury and upheaval at the club meant that Mark's time on Wearside did not allow the Teessider to witness Wearside at its best and yet he loved it.

'I had five fantastic years there. I was living in Middlesbrough at the time so it was near home and I loved Sunderland and Roker Park and have massive affection for the club and its supporters. Apart from the year I had out with injury it was a great time for me. I had loads of managers in my time there including quite a few temporary ones but I also had the opportunity to work with some really great experienced players such as Frank Worthington and Leighton James.'

One year on from his assistance in a great escape, Proctor missed a couple of pressure penalties as Sunderland succumbed to relegation to the Third Division, although he scored twice in the first leg of the infamous Play-off with Gillingham. Nonetheless Proctor was a good servant of SAFC, a fine footballer and one who always gave his all.

Mark Proctor at Sunderland
Debut: 19 March 1983: Sunderland 1–1 Swansea City
Last game: 31 August 1987: Sunderland 4–1 Mansfield Town
Total appearances (all competitions): 136+2 as sub / 23 goals

Season by season
1982–83 5 games / 0 goals
1983–84 46+1 games / 3 goals
1984–85 22 games / 2 goals
1985–86 22 games / 7 goals
1986–87 35+1 games / 11 goals
1987–88 6 games / 0 goals

Other clubs
Middlesbrough 1975–81
Nottingham Forest 1981–83
Sheffield Wednesday 1987–89
Middlesbrough 1989–93
Tranmere Rovers 1993–95
St Johnstone 1995
Whitley Bay 1995
South Shields 1996–97
Hartlepool United 1997–98

As coach/manager
Darlington 2004–06
Hibernian 2006–07
Livingston 2007–08
Middlesbrough 2008–

Division Two: 20th out of 22 (relegated via Play-offs)
FA Cup: Third round, lost to Wimbledon
League Cup: First round, lost to York City
Full Members' Cup: Second round, lost to Bradford City
Top scorer: Dave Buchanan, 11 goals, 8 League, 3 League Cup
Ever present: No one
Player of the Year: Gary Bennett
SAFCSA Player of the year: Gary Bennett

Like the 1979–80 Player of the Year Jeff Clarke, Gary Bennett had been a young centre-half at Manchester City. 'Benno' was brought to Sunderland by Len Ashurst, who had had him at Cardiff, and Gary wasted no time in endearing himself to his new fans by scoring against England 'keeper Peter Shilton within two minutes of his first game in 1984. That had been in the top flight. By the end of this season Sunderland and Gary would be in the Third Division despite his best efforts to save the club. By the time Benno moved on over a decade after his arrival, the Lads were in a much healthier state in the early stages of the Peter Reid era, Gary had become the first man to represent the club at Wembley three times, had collected another Player of the Year trophy and had risen to fifth on the list of all-time Sunderland appearance-makers. It is also worth pointing out that as the first popular black player to play for Sunderland Gary had done more to tackle racism than anyone else in modern times, something he has carried on to the present day through his selfless work with 'Show Racism the Red Card'.

Red cards were something Benno got used to. The first Sunderland player ever to be sent off five times – a dubious record now jointly shared with Kevin Ball – being sent off was not necessarily something to turn fans against you. Granted, if they are ridiculous reds fans rightly curse a player's stupidity but if they are for things like wrestling David Speedie in the Clock Stand paddock at Roker Park then they only add to your reputation. Bennett played with passion. He bought into the region in the way Niall Quinn looks for players to do so when they come to the club, something Benno illustrates by the fact that he still lives in Sunderland despite being a Mancunian.

A Wembley finalist in his first season as Sunderland lost the League Cup showpiece and ended up being relegated with their conquerors Norwich, Benno survived the cull of Len Ashurst's players when Lawrie McMenemy took over, but in this 1986–87 campaign suffered his second relegation in his first three years in the North East. McMenemy's first season had almost ended in disaster but there was no escape from demotion to the Third Division this time round.

'After getting through that first season under Lawrie McMenemy there was a feeling within the club that we were going to go places now and we thought that things couldn't get any worse than they'd been in his first season.' So says Gary Bennett of what became the worst season in the entire history of the club right from its humble beginnings in 1879. A decade and a half later Sunderland would twice set unwanted records for the lowest ever points totals in the top flight in years when the Sunderland Supporters' Association did not award their Player of the Year trophy, but despite the fact that in 1987 one of the proudest clubs in the land slumped into the Third Division for the only time in their long history, Gary Bennett was voted Player of the Year in recognition of his unstinting efforts to try and keep the club up. It was the first of two Player of the Year awards Benno would win in 11 years at Roker Park.

'I was made captain under Lawrie and going into the second season under him we were optimistic, especially looking at the players we had and we felt that we should win the League.' The big names McMenemy had recruited had had a year to acclimatise to the differing demands of the Second Division compared to the glamorous stages they had been used to. A disastrous start had derailed the ambitions of Sunderland's first campaign under their high-profile manager and – as Gary says – the opinion within the club was that Sunderland were now ready to take off and return to the top flight they had only left a couple of years ago.

The season actually began with an encouraging away win based on a solid clean sheet at Huddersfield. Efforts were made to draw a line under McMenemy's first year with forward-thinking commercial manager Alec King drawing 2,500 hard-core fans to the Sunderland Empire for a rallying pre-season Roker Revival meeting. Optimists got ahead of themselves with the idea that the gruelling first season under McMenemy was all a bad dream and from now on it would be plain sailing back to the top flight, left behind a year ago. Seventy-two hours later that bubble had burst as Third Division York City handed out a 4–2 hiding in a League Cup first leg at Roker Park where fewer than 10,000 bothered to turn up. Those that attended did see a youngster by the name of Marco Gabbiadini come on as a sub for the Minstermen, who were managed by the man who would a year hence start Sunderland on the road to recovery, Denis Smith.

For now though McMenemy was at the helm of a ship he was taking down. Bob Murray had taken over from Tom Cowie as chairman in the summer and the man who would become the longest-serving chairman in the club's history liked to point out that like the *Titanic*, Lawrie McMenemy should never have left Southampton. Seven players had left over the summer including crowd favourite Shaun Elliott and promising England Under-21 star Barry Venison while the only outfield debutant on the opening day – Dave Buchanan, who scored – had come from Blyth Spartans.

McMenemy's first home League game of his second season brought a draw with Brighton (who would finish bottom) before the second leg of the League Cup clash with York, which brought an improved 3–1 win that made the aggregate scores level at 5–5 with Sunderland duly eliminated after extra-time on the away goals rule. The 6,480 who witnessed that outcome at Bootham Crescent could have no idea that the away goals rule would return to haunt the Lads in eight months time but if any further evidence was needed that Sunderland were in trouble it came in the very next game when Blackburn hit the Lads for six. The writing was on the wall – McMenemy's honeymoon was over and divorce papers were in the process of being filed.

The autumn, however, saw cracks papered over as a run of just one defeat – away to eventual champions Derby – in nine games saw Sunderland rise to fifth by the end of October. It would be the highest position of the season but with the Play-offs being introduced this season there was renewed hope that Sunderland would be involved. However, just seven more victories in the remaining 30 games ensured that they were at the wrong end of the table.

Defeat despite a Benno goal away to Sheffield United at the start of November began a run of five and a half months during which just five games were won, the team plummeted and hope evaporated. When Sheffield United made the return trip to Sunderland just 8,544 paid to enter Roker Park. When the Blades inflicted another home defeat after a woefully disorganised display many of that meagre crowd assembled in the car park outside the main entrance to voice their displeasure in vehement style. Eighty-five years earlier Sunderland had been forced to play a home game at Newcastle after Roker Park was forcibly closed after a riot following a game against Sheffield Wednesday; if the crowd could have laid their hands on Lawrie McMenemy after the defeat by the red and white half of Sheffield it would have been carnage on a comparable scale to the turn of the century.

Gateshead-born McMenemy did not hang around to give the irate supporters the chance to run him out of town. That night the man dubbed 'Mackem-enemy' infamously did a midnight flit, leaving his all-expenses-paid club house in the dead of night without even informing the man who had appointed him, former chairman Tom Cowie, who later learned Lawrie had legged it from the local press.

'We found out through the press which is how come most people found out. There were rumours that he had a deal with the *Sun* where he did a weekly page,' remembers Gary, who at least did hear from Lawrie shortly afterwards. 'Later Lawrie wrote a letter to me as captain saying he was sorry to be leaving and wishing the lads and the club all the best and wishing that we'd be able to keep the club in the division and saying he was sorry that things hadn't worked out. He was great to play for as far as I was concerned. He didn't take much of the training but when you talked about high-profile managers he was at the top of the list. He was one of the first managers who came to a club and brought all his backroom staff with him. In bringing in his own staff he made big changes and we didn't actually see much of Lawrie to be fair because he was doing a lot in the public eye but when he was around he was a great fellow to talk to.'

Nine years later chairman Murray had success in avoiding relegation when appointing Peter Reid as manager with seven games to go – although that would also signal the end of Bennett's time at the club. On this occasion in 1987, having seen the manager vanish in his own first year as the head of the board, Murray knew SAFC needed a saviour. He turned to the man who had worked a miracle in his previous spell as Sunderland manager, Bob Stokoe.

'I was excited,' says Gary of the arrival of the 1973 FA Cup-winning boss. 'We'd heard a lot about Bob Stokoe and what he'd achieved. We were hoping that he could work his wonders in the games that we had left and keep us in the division. It was a pleasure to myself to think that I'd be at Sunderland and have Bob Stokoe as a manager because I thought I'd be able to learn from him but as we know it didn't work out in the end.'

Stokoe's first game in charge in a decade was away to Bradford. By now back at Valley Parade after the tragic fire disaster that put the ups and downs of football clubs into perspective, Bradford had beaten Sunderland on home turf earlier in the season at the gigantic Odsal Stadium in the Full Members' Cup – the last game SAFC ever played in that competition. Despite taking the lead in Stokoe's first game 'the Messiah' was unable to work another miracle as Bradford fought back to win, a mistake by goalkeeper Iain Hesford contributing to the defeat which left the Lads one off the bottom.

With football's unerring ability to conjure up quirks of the fixture list, Stokoe's first home game back in charge was against none other than 1973 FA Cup Final opponents Leeds. Again Sunderland led but Hesford conceded an equaliser from close on 40 yards after being caught off his line, leaving fans wishing Sunderland had brought back Monty as well!

A year earlier a win over fellow strugglers Shrewsbury had been crucial and Bennett produced the only goal of the game at the Shrews' Gay Meadow to give Stokoe his first win and renew hope of staying up. Despite Bradford inflicting their third 3–2 victory of the season, another single-goal win at home to Crystal Palace, backed up with a point at Millwall, left Sunderland two places clear of the drop with just one game to play.

Mid-table Barnsley had nothing to play for as they visited Roker with Sunderland's destiny in their own hands. However, the Wearsiders' ability to snatch defeat from the jaws of victory saw them conspire to miss a penalty and lose a game there for the taking in front of the biggest crowd of the League season.

Finishing third from bottom meant that Sunderland were involved in the newly-introduced Play-offs. Play-offs, or Test Matches as they were called then, had been in use between 1893 and 1898, Sunderland having successfully contested them in 1897. Brought back in 1987, they have rid football of the meaningless end-of-season run-ins of mid-table sides and brought about intense drama that Sunderland have suffered from more than most. The experience of 1987 would be as bad as any for the Red and White Army.

Paired with Gillingham, who had finished fifth in the Third Division, the first leg was lost 3–2 in Kent, where Tony Cascarino scored a hat-trick. The feeling was that surely Sunderland could not drop into the Third Division. It was as unthinkable as the club's first

Gary Bennett (left) takes on Howard Gayle in pre 1985 League Cup Final training.

ever relegation out of the top flight in 1958 but that had happened and so the worst nightmare would come true again. Within three minutes Gillingham scored to extend their aggregate lead to 4–2. Showing a fighting spirit so often missing under McMenemy, Sunderland hit back with two goals in five minutes from Eric Gates and then – having been denied two stonewall spot kicks including one when Bennett was fouled – Sunderland had the opportunity to lead from a penalty. However, as in the Barnsley game where the Lads could have saved their skins, it was missed by the normally reliable Mark Proctor – the previous season's Player of the Year.

Iain Hesford, the Sunderland 'keeper who had dropped more clangers than he cared to remember, then showed his quality by saving a penalty only for that man Cascarino to score anyway as Sunderland failed to clear. At 5–4 down on aggregate it was time for desperate measures: 'I swapped positions with Dave Swindlehurst,' recalls Bennett, who was still giving his all despite being nowhere near 100 per cent fit. 'Swinders went back to play centre-half and I went up front and managed to score a goal to send us into extra-time. A cross came in and I managed to get my head to it. Everything just fell into place, there was uproar when it hit the net.'

Benno had made it 5–5 on aggregate with an identical 3–2 home win in each leg. Ignore Gary's modest 'A cross came in and I managed to get my head on it' description. He had no right to get to the ball but being a lad who played with heart, passion and sheer desire, he launched himself at it and scored a goal that had extra-time not gone badly would still be thought of as one of the greatest goals in the club's history.

'The 90 minutes were up almost straight after my goal,' says Gary. 'The Play-offs were new to everybody, no one was familiar with them and we didn't know what was happening. I remember going into it [extra-time] thinking, "Do away goals count?"…there was extra-time to think about and would away goals count then? We thought, "Is it going to penalties or what?"'

As with the start of the game, Gillingham caught Sunderland cold, Cascarino netting his fifth goal of the tie. Although Keith Bertschin managed to make it 4–3 on the day and 6–6 on aggregate, Sunderland were duly relegated – the only team in history to be relegated on away goals. This, despite the fact that the scores had been identical in the two legs in the 90 minutes; relegation on away goals came down to the fact that extra-time had been played on Wearside.

Relegated to the status of associate members of the Football League, Sunderland, one of the oldest and proudest clubs in the land, the club of the 'Team of All the Talents', the 'Bank of England Club' and of 'Stokoe's Stars' had sunk to an unfathomable depth. It was not Stokoe's fault, and after his efforts to save the club he left, as did several of McMenemy's recruits. You know the value of people though when they stand up to be counted in the toughest of times. For Gary Bennett to be Player of the Year in this most dreadful of seasons tells you all you need to know about the man. Gary never went missing, led from the front…and just three years later would be back in the top flight with Sunderland.

Gary Bennett at Sunderland
Debut: 25 August 1984: Sunderland 3–1 Southampton (scored)
Last game: 15 April 1995: Sunderland 1–1 Luton Town
Total appearances (all competitions): 434+9 as sub / 25 goals

Season by season
1984–85	46 games / 3 goals
1985–86	33 games / 4 goals
1986–87	48 games / 5 goals
1987–88	43 games / 2 goals
1988–89	44+3 games / 3 goals
1989–90	47 games / 3 goals
1990–91	43 games / 2 goals
1991–92	44+2 games / 3 goals
1992–93	16+1 games / 0 goals
1993–94	46+2 games / 0 goals
1994–95	23+1 / 0 goals

Other clubs
Ashton United 1979
Manchester City 1979–81
Cardiff City 1981–84
Carlisle United 1995–96
Scarborough 1996–98 (player-coach)
Darlington 1998–2000
Darlington 2000–01 (manager)
Worksop Town 2001
Scarborough 2001

Eric Gates

Division Three: First of 24
FA Cup: Second round, lost to Scunthorpe United
League Cup: First round, lost to Middlesbrough over two legs
Sherpa Van Trophy: Quarter-final, lost to Hartlepool United
Top scorers: Marco Gabbiadini, 22 goals, 21 League, 1 Sherpa Van Trophy
Eric Gates, 21 goals, 19 League, 1 FA Cup, 1 League Cup
Ever present: John Kay and John MacPhail, each 46 out of 46 League. MacPhail also played
all eight Cup ties with Kay playing in six of the knockout games
Player of the Year: Eric Gates
SAFCSA Player of the Year: Eric Gates

Having endured two terrible years with Sunderland following his return to his native North East after a glorious career with his first club Ipswich, Eric Gates enjoyed an Indian summer on Wearside. He played a major role in the red and white renaissance once he was partnered with new signing Marco Gabbiadini. The pair earned the nickname the 'G-Force' and were tailor-made for each other in a similar manner to how Niall Quinn and Kevin Phillips teamed up a decade further down the line.

So much of football turns out to be luck rather than judgement. When new boss Denis Smith returned to his former club York City to poach teenage striker Marco Gabbiadini it was with the idea of partnering Marco with Keith Bertschin rather than Gates who was replaced by Gabbiadini for Marco's first two games. However, injury to Bertschin allowed Gates back into the side to partner Marco. 'I broke my jaw at Fulham in Marco Gabbiadini's second match,' remembers Bertschin. 'Eric Gates had been off form but got back into the team in my absence. He was such a great foil for Marco that even though I did well when I played I couldn't get a game a lot of the time.'

Gates and Gabbiadini came together for the first time in a home game against Aldershot, where the pair immediately clicked. 'Gabbers' scored twice on the G-Force's first outing and a week later both of them grabbed a brace as Sunderland went to the top of the League. It was 10 October and from then on the Lads would never drop out of an automatic promotion spot, eventually finishing nine points ahead of runners-up Brighton.

From the day the G-Force was formed, League defeat would be tasted just once in four and a half months – the response to that being a 7–0 victory in the next match with Gates becoming the first player since Stan Cummins seven years earlier to score four times in one match.

Gates had found the perfect partner in Gabbiadini. By now in his early thirties, Eric had lost a little of the sprightly zip over the first two or three yards that had helped make him such an attacking livewire in Bobby Robson's great Ipswich side of the early 1980s. What he still had though was the footballing brain to play people into space with perfectly weighted passes. Since coming to Sunderland under Lawrie McMenemy, Gates had been expected to largely play off the front-man. Mainly that had been veteran target man Dave Swindlehurst and latterly Keith Bertschin. While Eric was no slouch, he was no longer a whippet either. Once Gabbiadini came along, Gates' role changed. Instead of looking to latch on to balls knocked down from the centre-forward, his role switched to being seen more as the provider, and boy, did he know how to set them up for Gabbiadini.

The captain of the team in Eric's era was Gary Bennett and Benno recalls the improvement: 'Everybody knows what Eric went through in his first couple of seasons here because it took him a while to adapt but once Gabbiadini came along, all of a sudden they clicked. Eric was an excellent footballer.'

Manager Smith had been known as a rugged centre-half but the team he built at Sunderland was a stylish one who played their way from the Third Division to the top flight in three years powered by the G-Force.

The method was to build the team around the idea of getting the ball into Eric's feet. Marco was on the same wavelength and would make his run as Gates took possession. With a seemingly telepathic understanding, the former England international would play the ball into Gabbiadini's path and watch with satisfaction as his protégé would power on to blast the ball home.

As confidence blossomed supporters saw more of Gates 'the finisher' as Eric too began to find the back of the net on a regular basis, ending up with just one goal less than Gabbiadini in their first season: 21 to Marco's 22.

When Eric netted four against Southend on future Player of the Year Richard Ord's debut in November, it was the first time in 20 years that Sunderland had scored seven goals in a game. Later the same month they did it again and while Eric did not score on that occasion against Rotherham United - he was subbed to save him for more important games - he had turned on a master class of creation as Sunderland stormed to a 6–1 half-time lead. Goodness knows how high the score that night might have been if Gabbiadini was playing but Marco missed out as the game was in the Freight Rover Trophy, which Sunderland found themselves contesting as members of the Third Division. Less than a month after their annihilation in what the Millers must have renamed the Fright Rover rather than the Freight Rover Trophy, Rotherham returned to Roker in the League where, after destroying them with his passing, Eric this time demonstrated his finishing with a hat-trick.

There have been too many occasions when everything has gone wrong for Sunderland but 1987–88 was a season in which – Cups aside – pretty much everything went right. Over 46 games the team averaged exactly two goals a game and the tally of 93 points was a new club record.

Fittingly it was Eric who scored the goal that sealed promotion, a typically sharp finish for the only goal of the game at Port Vale. Gates added another as Northampton were beaten 3–1 in the final home game and the ex-England international pulled the strings as Sunderland said farewell to the Third Division, signing off with a 4–1 win at Millmoor, thus taking the goals tally against Rotherham to 14 for the season.

It was not all about attacking even though penalty-taking centre-back John MacPhail set a club record number of goals for a defender with 16. Running Eric Gates closest for the Player of the Year award was goalkeeper Iain Hesford. Probably the player to endure the toughest time in the relegation season, Hesford had been sidelined by Smith at the start of the season. To begin with Sunderland had employed loan 'keeper Steve Hardwick but he had declined to stay on citing the difficulties of playing before North East crowds, having previously been at Newcastle.

This resulted in Hesford having to be recalled for a game away to Gillingham, the very side who had caused Sunderland's relegation by beating them in the Play-off semi-final and, moreover, a team who had registered 8–0 and 10–0 wins in their last two home games. To his enormous credit, Hesford helped Sunderland to a goalless draw that night and missed just one of 40 games as he earned himself a medal to ensure that like Gates, despite being a member of the team who went down, he could leave Sunderland with his head held high.

It has been bad enough in recent decades to see Sunderland yo-yoing between the top two tiers but thankfully the year in the Third Division proved to be just the one season. The achievement of Denis Smith and his team in quickly closing the worst chapter in the Sunderland story should never be underestimated. Denis Smith had nothing to do with the Lads being there in the first place but having been part of the side which took Sunderland down, Eric Gates helped to redeem himself by being a major influence on the club bouncing back and putting smiles back on everyone's faces.

Gatesy would keep doing that for another couple of seasons and in later years through his extensive work covering Sunderland, firstly as a local radio summariser alongside future BBC World Cup Final commentator Guy Mowbray, and later as one of the 'Three Legends' alongside similar favourites from the Tyne and the Tees. More recently Eric combines the life of a farmer near Sunderland by being a regular compere at all kinds of talk-ins and supporters' get-togethers across the region.

Eric Gates at Sunderland
Debut: 17 August 1985: Sunderland 0–2 Blackburn Rovers
Last game: 28 May 1990: Swindon Town 1–0 Sunderland (Wembley)
Total appearances (all competitions): 199+21 as sub / 55 goals

Season by season
1985–86	44+1 games / 11 goals
1986–87	26+8 games / 9 goals
1987–88	49 games / 21 goals
1988–89	34+10 games / 4 goals
1989–90	46+2 games / 10 goals

Other clubs
Ipswich Town 1972–85
Carlisle United 1990–91

Marco Gabbiadini

Division Two: 11th out of 24
FA Cup: Third round, lost to Oxford in a replay
League Cup: Second round, lost to West Ham Utd over two legs
Simod Cup: Second round, lost to Blackburn Rovers
Top scorer: Marco Gabbiadini, 23 goals, 18 League, 3 League Cup, 2 Simod Cup
Ever present: No one
Player of the Year: Marco Gabbiadini
SAFCSA Player of the Year: Marco Gabbiadini

Having fired Sunderland to promotion in his first season when his brilliant partnership with Eric Gates helped veteran Gates to become Player of the Year, Marco Gabbiadini swept to the 1988–89 Player of the Year award and a year later became the first man to retain it.

The 1988–89 campaign was the first after promotion from the sojourn to the Third Division. Sunderland had struggled horribly in the two seasons they had spent at what is now 'Championship' level since dropping out of the top flight in 1985. Under Denis Smith the first aim was to consolidate following promotion and then push on to get the club back to what supporters feel is the club's rightful home at the top level. No club can claim to have a divine right to be in the top tier, but Sunderland, having gone two decades longer than any other club without playing in any division other than the top one, certainly feel as if it is their natural home.

Before they could contemplate being among the elite again however, the Wearsiders had to ensure they could cope with playing at their new level. It is almost unheard of now for a team to go into a new season without some new faces in the side on the opening day but having seen his men win their League in style Denis Smith kicked-off the new campaign with a team made up of those who had served him well thus far.

The Lads began with a home draw against a Bournemouth outfit that had avoided the relegation Play-offs by just three points the year before. It represented a point on the board but indicated a slow start, which was what was in store. By the end of September Sunderland were fourth from bottom and were without a win in the League, having drawn four and lost two with Colin Pascoe the only man to join opening-day marksman Gary Bennett on the Division Two scorers' list. Marco had missed a couple of games but had found the net against his former club York in the League Cup.

Whereas the 'G-Force' had ripped Third Division defences to shreds, the front two were not having the same joy early on so Smith acted, bringing in big, bustling Billy Whitehurst to partner Gabbiadini instead of Gates, who would not start a game in 10 weeks during which he was always sub but rarely left the bench.

Talk about chalk and cheese. The difference between Gates and Whitehurst as a front partner was like the difference between the *Daily Sport* and the *Guardian* or Jedward and Gustav Mahler. Whereas Gates was always about touch and finesse, Whitehurst was all about being big and brutal. The ball was not Billy's friend but the hope was that Gabbiadini would profit from playing alongside a six-foot ex-brickie whose former clubs included Retford Town, Bridlington Trinity, Mexborough Town and Newcastle United.

It seemed to do the trick. Marco got his first goal at this level on the first occasion he and Whitehurst started together, with Sunderland landing their first three points since promotion and netting three goals against Oldham into the bargain. Three days later the pair of them were

Marco in Typical pose, powering towards the Fulwell End.

on the score sheet together as Leeds were beaten. Although a couple of blanks were drawn on the road the new-look front two were clicking into gear in front of the home crowd. Whitehurst joined two-goal Gabbiadini among the scorers in a 4–0 win over Swindon, which was the biggest home League win outside the Third Division since just prior to promotion eight years earlier. In the next game versus Blackburn Marco made it five goals in four home games, all of which were won.

'When I played up front with Billy Whitehurst it was just about the only time in my entire career that I played alongside a big man,' says Marco. 'In the latter stages of my career I was sometimes used as something of a target man myself because while I wasn't the biggest I wasn't bad in the air and could hold the ball up. I enjoyed playing with Billy. He always looked after me and if anyone was giving me a hard time he'd make sure they had an even harder one! However, we always tried to play good football at Sunderland. We were an attacking team whose philosophy was we'll always aim to score more than the opposition. That worked well for us to begin with but it was probably epitomised by the relegation season [1990–91] where we lost a lot of games 3–2 but always tried to play positively.'

In a spell when fixtures were paired two at home and two away, the next couple of away trips brought a great point at eventual runners-up Manchester City and four goals in a big win at Oxford, with both Gabbiadini and Whitehurst registering once again. Now into November, the Lads were steadily climbing the table after their bad start and when Marco scored in a terrific draw away to eventual champions Chelsea it looked as if Smith was succeeding in consolidating after promotion.

The match at Stamford Bridge, though, would be the last time either Gabbiadini or Whitehurst found the back of the net in the League before Whitehurst was offloaded along with 'keeper Iain Hesford in part exchange for new club record signing Tony Norman from Hull. Former Hull forward Whitehurst was the bait to tempt the Tigers to part with their star 'keeper. Barnstorming front-man Billy feels that Gabbiadini's wish to play alongside Gates contributed to his departure: 'I think it was a stumbling block with me at Sunderland because I think Marco preferred to play with Eric and he was the kingpin at the time so I think that was something that prompted Denis Smith to get rid of me...and to be honest, I'd been in the George Washington Hotel for the whole time I was at the club so I was on the beer and that might have prompted Denis [Smith] to let go of me.'

The G-Force combination had been restored a week before Christmas with both scoring as a 4–1 win at Plymouth ended a barren run of seven games without a win. It was the start of five wins in six League games, the last a 1–0 win in the reverse fixture of the opening day against Bournemouth which propelled Sunderland to a season's highest placing of sixth.

A run of three defeats and just one goal turned Denis Smith's mind to having another big centre-forward to replace Whitehurst. His choice was a German called Thomas Hauser who, after debuting as a sub, was inevitably dubbed 'U-boat'. Hauser's first appearance coincided with a return to winning form on a day of reunions: Marco getting one of the goals in a 2–0 win over Hull with Whitehurst, and both 'keepers facing their former clubs.

Victory over the Tigers only punctuated a run of losses and despite both Gabbers and Gates scoring in a home defeat at the hands of Man City it was not long before Gates again found himself benched as new man Hauser was given his chance. More mobile than Whitehurst – in the way that a tug is quicker than a dredger but its still a tug – Hauser's touch was little better than Big Bad Billy's but nonetheless the new pairing got off to a good start, Marco scoring four times in their first two starts together, including a hat-trick against Ipswich. That was an astonishing day for Gabbiadini, who was sent off in the aftermath of completing his first treble with a penalty for lashing out at Ipswich's Blyth-born Tony Hume, leaving the hat-trick hero to depart before play could resume. It was Gabbiadini's second red card in two months, having also been dismissed in the January FA Cup defeat at Oxford.

There would be only one win and one goal from Gabbiadini in the next five games but the final five began with three successive victories – the third with a Marco winner at Oxford for his 23rd goal of the season in all competitions.

A final position of 11th was modest in the light of Sunderland's rich history but this was not a time for history. The reality was this was the highest position since relegation from the top flight in 1985 and a solid step back towards the top level. Moreover, Marco had shown that he could find the net regularly at this level and would be a vital part of the team Denis Smith would steer to a second promotion in three seasons the following year.

The 1988–89 campaign had seen attacking midfielder Colin Pascoe reach double figures as second-top scorer and stalwarts Gary Bennett and Gordon Armstrong had been solid regular members of the team. As had centre-half John MacPhail and midfielder Gary Owers, while new goalie Tony Norman had impressed since his Christmas arrival, but there was no doubt as to who the main man was at Sunderland. Marco turned 21 in the middle of this season and was living the dream. 'When I first came to Sunderland the previous season I was only 19. You don't know yourself at that age how far you can go in the game. Sunderland were at the same level I'd been playing at with York when I signed so I was comfortable with that but I hadn't played much with York as I was only young. This was before the time that football was on the TV seven days a week so while I knew Sunderland were bigger than York I had no idea about the vast history or how big the club was and how much press coverage and interest there was. I soon discovered that everyone was interested in the football club. I was always confident in myself but never quite sure how my career would progress but at Sunderland I felt I was in the right place.'

Teammate and fellow two-time Sunderland Player of the Year Gary Bennett smiles broadly at the mention of Marco and comments, 'Marco was an exciting footballer and any supporter of that era who was going to the game knew that it was an exciting time because Marco could make something out of nothing. He was a powerful lad because although he wasn't the biggest he had pace and if you gave him the ball he was capable of sticking it in the back of the net. He scored some tremendous goals for Sunderland.'

Those tremendous goals made Marco the darling of a crowd desperate for a hero. 'The fans were fantastic with me and still are,' he says. 'My mum and dad always supported me and came to games and my wife Debbie was always there too from my second season onwards and they were always part of it. When the whole place was singing, "Ole ole, ole, ole, Marco, Marco" it was brilliant. As a striker you get to do the nice bit of football because you finish things off and if you put the ball in the back of the net you get the credit. You need to have a bit of humility though and realise that the rest of your teammates have worked to create the chances for you as a striker. I'll never forget those years at Sunderland and still now I treasure them.'

Marco Gabbiadini at Sunderland
Debut: 26 September 1987: Sunderland 0–2 Chester City
Last game: 21 September 1991: Sunderland 1–2 Grimsby Town
Total appearances (all competitions): 183+2 as sub / 87 goals

Season by season
1987–88   39 games / 22 goals
1988–89   43+1 games / 23 goals
1989–90   57 games / 26 goals
1990–91   34+1 games / 11 goals
1991–92   9 games / 5 goals

Other clubs
York City 1984–87
Crystal Palace 1991–92
Derby County 1992–97
Birmingham City (loan) 1996
Oxford United (loan) 1997
Stoke City 1997–98
York City 1998
Darlington 1998–2000
Northampton Town 2000–03
Hartlepool United 2003–04

1989–90   Marco Gabbiadini

Division Two: Sixth out of 24, promoted via Play-offs
FA Cup: Third round, lost to Reading
League Cup: Fifth round, lost to Coventry City in a replay
Zenith Data Systems Cup: First round, lost to Port Vale
Top scorer: Marco Gabbiadini, 26 goals, 21 League, 1 Play-off, 4 League Cup
Ever present: Marco Gabbiadini and Eric Gates, each 46 out of 46 League. Each played 12
of the 13 knockout games
Player of the Year: Marco Gabbiadini
SAFCSA Player of the Year: Marco Gabbiadini

Marco Gabbiadini is the only player to retain the official SAFC Player of the Year award. In recent years both Julio Arca and Danny Collins have won the SAFC Supporters' Association's respected Player of the Year honour two years running but Gabbiadini is the only man who can claim to have held on to the official award, and into the bargain was the first man to win any of the versions of the Sunderland Player of the Year in successive seasons. Having missed the first few weeks of the 1987–88 campaign prior to his transfer as a teenager from York City, Marco in fact was named Player of the Year in each of his first two full seasons at the club.

The 1989–90 season would begin at Newcastle – a friendly at Newcastle Town in the Midlands – and be remembered mainly for Marco's magnificent goal at Newcastle United in the Play-off semi-finals prior to Sunderland being controversially promoted after losing the Play-off Final at Wembley.

Left-back Paul Hardyman was the solitary debutant in an opening-day away win at Swindon. Ironically Swindon would be Sunderland's Wembley opponents in the 59th and final game of the season which Hardyman would miss through suspension. Like Gabbiadini the previous season against Ipswich, Hardyman had been sent off following a Fulwell End penalty, in his case in the last minute of a Play-off semi-final against Newcastle after Marco had been felled for the spot kick.

That would come in the final home game of the season. In the first against Ipswich both Gabbiadini and Gates would score but on a torrid night for future Player of the Year Richard Ord, the visitors ran out 4–2 victors. Despite that setback, Denis Smith's side made an assault on placing themselves upon the early front runners. A home win in the Wear–Tees derby after coming from behind was followed up with a good away point at West Brom thanks to a Gabbiadini strike before Marco blasted a hat-trick in a big home win over Watford.

Already named as the 'North East Young Eagle of the Month' for August, Gabbers roasted former Newcastle defender Glenn Roeder in the Hornets defence to fire Sunderland into second place after five games. Marco would wait a month for another League goal but with the Lads unbeaten in that spell his strike in a narrow home win over Bournemouth had Sunderland still in an automatic promotion slot with 10 games gone. A week later at Leeds Marco shook the hand of his brother Ricardo as the latter replaced him as a sub. It would be the younger brother's only appearance for Sunderland though and a rare disappointment in that he never got the chance to partner his brother in the Sunderland attack.

Ten days before Ricardo's big moment, Marco grabbed a brace in the League Cup at Fulham – where he had scored his first Sunderland goals almost exactly two years earlier. Since then Marco had gone from unknown teenage hopeful to Sunderland's main man. Scoring 53 goals in 94 games since his transfer made him hot property and had given Sunderland supporters a real

Marco Gabbiadini with his brother Ricardo. Marco is on the right.

goalscoring hero after several years in the doldrums. 'Ole, ole, ole, ole, Marco, Marco' was the chant that constantly tumbled from the terraces. Within a decade terraces would be a thing of the past at Sunderland but this was before the Hillsborough disaster, the Taylor Report that followed it and the decision to uproot after nearly a century at Roker Park towards a new stadium fit for a new century. Marco in full flight, thighs pounding like the engines at Ryhope Pumping Station, was a sight that got people off their seats if they had them. A ball played by Gates in front of Gabbiadini for him to steam on to was something to set the pulse racing. Gabbers in possession and bearing down on goal was the most exciting sight supporters had seen since Billy Hughes and Dennis Tueart in their heyday in the early seventies. For a generation who grew up watching Marco fire Sunderland from the Third Division to the first in next to no time, the name Gabbiadini is virtually superfluous. Like Raich, Charlie and Julio, there can be only one Marco and that constant 'Ole, ole, ole, ole, Marco, Marco' chant would be the soundtrack to the goals the Nottingham-born son of an Italian father scored in a smidgen over four seasons at Sunderland.

Gates and Gabbiadini was the best strike partnership Sunderland enjoyed between the 1973 Cup triumvirate of Hughes, Halom and Tueart, and the Quinn–Phillips combination that came along a decade after the G-Force were first paired. Marco's pace and power dovetailed with the experienced Gates' brain to devastating effect. 'Eric was a top player,' says Marco. 'I remember as a kid I'd watched him on television being one of Ipswich's main men under Bobby Robson on big European nights. When he'd first come to Sunderland it had all gone wrong for him to start with but we hit it off and played to each other's strengths.'

Ever present in all 46 League games, an astonishing feat for a striker who came in for some rough treatment, Marco had learned to calm the temper that had brought him two red cards in the previous season. He missed only the first of the 13 Cup and Play-off games, which was the first leg of the League Cup tie with Fulham that he settled in the return leg.

Like almost all forwards, Marco got goals in batches. Throughout the autumn Sunderland's form was up and down, bad defeats at West Ham and Leeds followed by three wins in a row in a spell when Marco managed just a single strike in eight League outings.

Without a Cup run since reaching the Final of the Milk (League) Cup in the year they dropped out of the top flight (1985), the Lads found themselves progressing in the same competition. Gabbiadini goals in both legs of a tie with Bournemouth disguised his temporary lack of League goals.

The eighties ended with an unbeaten run of 11 games when, despite four draws in five games, Sunderland ended the decade in third place. Having been the Young Eagle of the Month again in November, Gabbiadini gave his adoring public a Christmas present with a Boxing Day winner against Oxford. He was also on the mark in the final game of the year, as Port Vale claimed a draw on Wearside where Thomas Hauser scored the final goal of the decade, just as he would net the first of the nineties.

The German did not have a bad goals record, finishing with six goals in as many starts in the League. 'U-boat', however, played another 18 games as sub in all competitions together with an additional Cup start when he stood in for Marco at Fulham, but remained on six goals. No one other than Gabbiadini reached double figures in the League. The ageing Gates could still create but with just six goals in 36 Division Two games he was finding it tougher to score in the higher division - having managed just four in 37 games in the first year following promotion. Midfielders Gordon Armstrong and Gary Owers contributed 17 between them in the League but it was clear that the onus was very much on Marco.

Marco scored 26 goals in total, including 21 in the League. None of these were penalties, full-back Hardyman having taken over spot-kick duties. With penalties Marco could have topped 30 for the campaign.

The nineties began badly. A New Year's Day defeat at Hull was followed by FA Cup elimination at Third Division Reading, who would draw Newcastle in the next round. Sunderland's knockout games with Newcastle would come soon enough but before then the losing run continued with a three-goal defeat at Boro, where the opening goal came from the man who would be the player who would replace Gates as Gabbiadini's partner by the summer – Peter Davenport.

Sunderland had reached the quarter-finals of the League Cup with a big pre-Christmas replay win over Exeter City after a controversial night at the 'other' St James' Park. The alleged off-the-pitch high jinks in the West Country would pale into insignificance next to the quarter-final tie with top-flight Coventry however. The 1977 shenanigans involving the Sky Blues that saw Sunderland relegated still rankled with the Red and White Army so City were not the most popular visitors on a cold January night.

The game itself was a relatively uneventful goalless draw but the sides each lost a man after Gary Bennett jumped into the Clock Stand Paddock to 'finish off', in his own words, the aggravating midfielder David Speedie. Bennett and Speedie had come to blows before in the semi-finals of the same competition five years earlier [when Speedie was with Chelsea] so they had history just as Sunderland and Coventry did. A week later Coventry wiped the floor with the Wearsiders, four goals from Steve Livingstone giving him the night of his life. It was only one goal less than his entire career League total as a Coventry player.

Between the two Coventry Cup games Marco grabbed a 22nd birthday goal in a draw with West Brom. With Sunderland's next match away to Newcastle, at a time when his team had gone seven games without a win, Denis Smith took his squad to Blackpool for a few days' derby preparation. Red and white duly outplayed black and white in a howling wind and were unlucky to only draw. In years to come Magpies defender Nikos Dabizas would infamously claim Sunderland's Quinn–Phillips partnership was predictable and then watch helplessly as Superkev twice stuck the ball past them. The Magpies had not learned in 1990 either, as in the February

Marco won an England 'B' cap against Czechoslovakia at Roker Park in 1990.

game at St James' the G-Force traded passes before Marco sped though to score, and although they knew it was coming, all the Mags could do in the Play-off come the end of the season was watch Gates and Gabbers destroy them again.

Two more matches would follow the League trip to Newcastle before Sunderland would win again, two goals from Thomas Hauser beating Brighton before Marco hit a purple patch. Six goals in seven games climaxed with four wins in a row as the Lads hit form at the right time.

Marco's goals record could not be ignored and he was called-up for an England B international against the Czechoslovakia at Roker Park three days after the penultimate home game of the season, England winning 2–0 with a brace from Arsenal's Alan Smith.

With the Yorkshire Uniteds of Leeds and Sheffield comfortably ahead in the automatic places Sunderland did enough to finish in the Play-off places, finishing sixth, level on points with Blackburn and Swindon in the places above them. In third place were Newcastle, who had finished six points ahead of Sunderland. The Wearsiders, though, had been the better side in both derbies and had they got the wins they deserved in both games would have seen the roles reversed and been level with the Magpies, so there was plenty of confidence that Sunderland would come out on top.

Not unusually, followers of the Tyneside club proclaimed success before it was achieved. Having managed a goalless draw in the first leg at Roker many thought all they had to do was turn up and beat the Mackems at home. That ignored the fact that apart from being outplayed twice already, Sunderland had also managed their second-highest number of away wins since the club's best ever season of 1912–13 when the League had been won and Cup Final reached.

When it came to the crunch in the fourth meeting of the season, Sunderland's superiority told at Newcastle. Less than a quarter of an hour had gone when Gabbiadini and Owers combined for Eric Gates to score. For the rest of the match the visitors looked more likely to double their lead than the home side did to equalise and five minutes from time came Marco's moment.

Of all the goals 'Marco Goalo' discovered for Sunderland, the one he plundered five minutes from time in the Play-off at Newcastle is the one that provides supporters with the most iconic image of him decades later. Beating their nearest rivals on their own turf ranks for many fans as the greatest moment since the 1973 Cup Final, coming as it did in a match of such magnitude. The goal epitomised the G-Force. Gabbiadini had received the ball from young Warren Hawke. Looking up, he played the ball to Gates and then thundered through, knowing that little Eric would slide a perfectly weighted ball into his path. 'Eric was a master,' says Marco. 'Whenever I got that split second to look up, he would always be available. I went past one and he came off his markers a yard, so I played it for him. He'd always put it into a space for me to run on to. He did so this time, but I was wider than I thought and on my weaker side, although I always thought I was pretty decent on my left foot…I caught it nice, didn't blast it. I knew Burridge couldn't get near it. I was only about nine or 10 yards from the touchline but the angle was a good 15 yards across goal. It seemed to take an age to go in. I remember wheeling away, thinking, "Is it going in or what?" There was just that split second as I was turning away to celebrate when I thought it might hit the post. It was a perfect goal though.'

Unable to cope with the harsh reality that they had been beaten fair and square, home fans came on to the pitch as the away section celebrated. It took 20 minutes to clear the pitch after which the final few minutes were played out and Sunderland began making plans for the Play-off Final at Wembley.

Marco challenging for the ball in the 1990 Play-off Final.

The Final proved as damp a squib as the Milk Cup Final appearance of five years earlier – another disappointing performance and another 1–0 defeat to a deflected goal. But Sunderland were still promoted when opponents Swindon were subsequently punished for financial irregularities.

Just three years after the darkest day in the club's entire history Sunderland were back in the top flight. Marco had become the first man to score over 20 goals a season for three years running since Sunderland's all-time record goalscorer Bobby Gurney in the 1930s and his retention of the Player of the Year award was never in doubt.

'There's a lot of work goes into becoming Player of the Year,' says Marco. 'You have to make a large number of appearances and stay free of injury. You want there to be several players in contention if the club are to have had a decent season so to be voted Player of the Year is a nice accolade within a team sport. One of the great things at Sunderland is all the branches have their own award so you get to go around to places like Wingate and so on and meet the people who have voted for you, which makes it more personal. Most years the same player has pretty much a clean sweep of the awards but it's great the way that Sunderland supporters want to say well done.

'I won five Player of the Year awards in my career including the Young Player of the Year I won in my first year at Sunderland and then after the Player of the Year awards at Sunderland in 1988–89 and 1989–90 I won others at Derby and Darlington. I look on it as my greatest achievement in the game to be held in high esteem at more than one club. I have the awards on display in my house and they are something I'm immensely proud of.'

Marco Gabbiadini at Sunderland
Debut: 26 September 1987: Sunderland 0–2 Chester City
Last game: 21 September 1991: Sunderland 1–2 Grimsby Town
Total appearances (all competitions): 183+2 as sub / 87 goals

Season by season
1987–88	39 games / 22 goals
1988–89	43+1 games / 23 goals
1989–90	57 games / 26 goals
1990–91	34+1 games / 11 goals
1991–92	9 games / 5 goals

Other clubs
York City 1984–87
Crystal Palace 1991–92
Derby County 1992–97
Birmingham City (loan) 1996
Oxford United (loan) 1997
Stoke City 1997–98
York City 1998
Darlington 1998–2000
Northampton Town 2000–03
Hartlepool United 2003–04

Kevin Ball

Division One: 19th out of 20, relegated
FA Cup: Third round, lost to Arsenal
League Cup: Third round, lost to Derby County
Zenith Data Systems Cup: Third round, lost to Everton
Top scorer: Marco Gabbiadini, 11 goals, 9 League, 2 League Cup
Ever present: Gary Owers, 38 out of 38 League plus all four Cup ties
Player of the Year: Kevin Ball
SAFCSA Player of the Year: Kevin Ball

'He's bigger than that, isn't he?' These were manager Denis Smith's words when I suggested his new centre-half Kevin Ball must be a tremendous player to be a success in that position at only 5ft 9in. A centre-half by trade himself, Smith was used to dealing with the physical challenges and aerial combat that comes with the role.

Having taken Sunderland from Third Division to First in three seasons, the manager had spent the funds at his disposal on centre-back Ball (who for the record says: 'I'm five foot nine and a half and a little bit'), and former England forward Peter Davenport. At £300,000 and £350,000, this was not as much strengthening a side (which less than 100 League games before had been plying their trade in the third tier), as replacing ageing players.

Davenport had been signed to dovetail with the Player of the Year for the last two seasons, Marco Gabbiadini. Marco had enjoyed an almost telepathic understanding with Eric Gates. Veteran Gates possessed an astute football brain and had spent three seasons helping Gabbiadini make his name by providing the ammunition for Marco to make his mark. Smith had experimented with target men such as Billy Whitehurst and Thomas Hauser to provide flick-ons for Marco in the way Niall Quinn would for Kevin Phillips at the back end of the decade just starting. Gabbiadini, however, was at his best when running on to slide-rule passes that Gates measured out and Davenport seemed a wise choice to step into Gates' boots. The former Forest, Mancheser United and Boro man was renowned for his guile and craft. Like Gates he would look to feed his fellow front-man and chip in with a few goals himself.

Ball had been signed from Portsmouth where he had been Players' Player of the Year in 1987–88 before suffering a serious injury. He was acquired to replace John MacPhail. MacPhail had been one of the men with lower League experience that Smith had signed to get Sunderland out of the Third Division. He had done a fine job, being a resolute centre-half who offered the added bonus of being an efficient penalty-taker. MacPhail was 34 and not one of his 432 English League appearances had been in the First Division so Ball was signed to take over from him, and to partner Gary Bennett at the heart of the defence.

Rarely has a player had such a disappointing start at Sunderland, let alone one who would become Player of the Season at the first time of asking. Ball had a torrid time in pre-season and his performance against Torpedo Moscow resulted in him being left out of the side on Sunderland's return to the big League.

Having gained promotion through the back door having lost the Play-off Final, only to be elevated at Swindon's expense due to the Wiltshire club's punishment for financial irregularities, Sunderland found opening-day opposing Norwich fans only too willing to chant, 'You're in the wrong division'. A trademark of Sunderland under Denis Smith is that they

always tried to play good football. The new front partnership got off to a cracking start, Gabbiadini scoring a screamer and debutant Davenport getting straight off the mark. Unfortunately the game was lost 3–2. It would be a scoreline seen four times on the road as Sunderland became everyone's favourite visitors. Massive travelling support, enterprising attacking football and going away as gallant losers was a guarantee of being welcomed with open arms.

MacPhail's appearance at Carrow Road proved to be his final game for Sunderland and the only one of his career in the top flight. Recognising that while MacPhail had given the club terrific service, his decision to replace him for the rigours of the top level was right and Denis Smith decided to put his new signing Ball into the team. Despite his disappointing pre-season there was only one way to find out if the new man would sink or swim and that was to chuck him in at the deep end.

Ball was not as much thrown into that deep end as pushed off the highest level of the diving board. For his Sunderland debut, in front of a packed and expectant Roker Park as Sunderland hosted their first top-flight game in five years, the visitors were Tottenham Hotspur. This was straight after the World Cup of Italia '90 and Spurs included national hero Gary Lineker, whose goals had propelled England to the semi-final, they were unlucky not to win against eventual world champions Germany. The visitors also fielded Paul Gascoigne. Gazza had been England's trump card, but ultimately had shown his childish side when going snap in the semi and becoming a national celebrity when bursting into tears.

The former Newcastle man was given plenty of stick by the Sunderland crowd whereas Lineker was given a hero's welcome. As the teams lined up the man with the task of marking one of the world's top strikers was Kevin Ball. Come the final whistle after a pulsating, fast-paced match that finished goalless, Lineker was released from Ball's pocket. Many opposing players would disappear into that same pocket during Bally's Sunderland career.

'To be honest it never bothered me in the slightest,' says Kevin Ball, looking back at being left out for the opening game of the season after signing for Sunderland. 'Denis Smith pulled me to one side and although he didn't quite say to me that I'd had a beast in pre-season — even though I knew I did — he said he wanted to play Monty [John MacPhail] in the game because that would mean he'd played in all four divisions. Maybe he also felt that I wasn't ready for it and if he did feel that then he covered himself very well and I'll give him credit for it. I was obviously disappointed not to play but when I look back then yes, that pre-season was a very difficult one for me.

'It was a big change with a new club and it's only when you move that you appreciate the difficulties you have in travelling, sorting out accommodation and getting your family sorted out. Taking everything into account I'm not surprised I had a poor pre-season. I remember running around the woods at Maiden Castle and me and Dickie Ord were last. When we eventually crossed the line Smithy turned round to me and said, "Well I'm glad I didn't sign you for your cross-country running," and took the mick out of me a little bit. I'm not going to lie. It was a difficult pre-season for me. I scored an own-goal against Torpedo Moscow but I felt I was settling down as pre-season was coming to a close.'

Like an actor who does not look the part in rehearsal but becomes the star once the curtain goes up, Bally was happiest on stage. 'I remember it was on the Tuesday night in lovely conditions. Having not been in the team at Norwich for the first game I was then told I was playing. If there was pressure it was probably more in that match because it was the first home game. All the things to do with changing my environment affected me before then but I remember it was a fantastic game although it was 0–0. I played well and that set my stall out at my new club which is maybe one of the best things I've ever done because it raised expectations. It really did spur me on if you forgive the pun and I loved it after that. I did put in a lot of extra training because Sunderland played a slightly different way to the way I was used to and they were teaching me new things. I'd not come into pro football until I was 17 and maybe things hadn't sunk in enough with me when I was at Portsmouth. At Sunderland I did a lot of work with Denis [Smith] but more so with [assistant manager] Viv Busby and I really appreciated everything he did for me.'

Kevin Ball had found his natural home. Once the real stuff started Ball immediately made himself a vital member of the team and would remain so for a decade. He may have been all at sea against Torpedo Moscow but it was the realisation that Sunderland was on the coast that helped the southerner feel at home in the North East.

'I remember being sat in a car with Denis, his wife and my wife Sharon on the day I signed. We were picked up at the station. Denis was quite sarcastic but humorous with it and was taking the mickey out of me within 10 minutes of meeting him. One of the first things he said to me was: "Has your car got an alarm on it because if it hasn't you won't have it for very long once you move up here." I was thinking, "Oh dear" but then he said: "I'll take you down to the seaside for a coffee." I was surprised because I didn't know Sunderland was by the sea which was ignorance on my behalf but when he said that it was brilliant. I grew up by the sea and when I'd gone to Coventry as an apprentice it was right in the middle of the country and I didn't particularly enjoy living there so I felt at home as soon as I knew Sunderland was on the coast.'

From his debut in August 1990 until his transfer to Fulham in December 1999, almost 400 appearances later, Kevin Ball staked a claim to be regarded as SAFC's man of the decade. Bally became a massive hero. He would go on to become an outstanding captain and convert to a midfield anchorman but in that first season in the North East it was as a centre-back under the captaincy of Gary Bennett that Kevin Ball established himself as a favourite son of Sunderland.

Fellow SAFC Player of the Year and legend Gary Bennett says of Bally: 'Kevin is a great lad and someone any player would like to have on their team because he is an out and out winner. He's the kind of player who will pull you through if you're having a bad time because he'll always be there saying "Come on" and when you talk about team spirit that's what we always had when you had Kevin in the team, especially when you talk about other lads like Johnny Kay also being around. You didn't go out on the pitch thinking, "I wonder what we'll be like today?" because you knew with Bally around there was no way anyone would slack or be under the best level of performance they could manage without getting an earful from Kevin.'

Once in the side the only way Ball was going to be left out was through suspension. It would take a very bad injury to keep him out and loss of form did not come into the equation because Kevin quickly became so important to the team that even if he was not on top of his game his contribution to the team effort still made him a vital part of any line up.

The Saturday after Tottenham's midweek visit, Manchester United were in town and were beaten 2–1 with a brilliant last-minute winner from skipper Bennett. Sunderland would score two goals in each of the next three games but glean just two points before defeats by Second Division Bristol City (in the League Cup), Liverpool and Villa saw the goals dry up.

Kevin Ball got his first goal in an astonishing 6–1 away win that overturned Bristol City's one-goal League Cup first-leg win and when that was followed up with a second League win of the season, renewed optimism surfaced regarding Sunderland's ability to survive. For the third time both Gabbiadini and Davenport found the back of he net in the same match while at the back Ball was quickly establishing himself as a reliable defender who covered ground quickly, would launch himself into 50–50 tackles and played as if his life depended on it.

Nonetheless the harsh reality was that Sunderland were competing at the top level with a side barely strengthened since playing in the Third Division and survival was going to be a tall order. Promising local youngster Martin Smith came into the side but transfer activity was minimal despite this being way before transfer windows came into being.

Two narrow away defeats, two home draws and a 6–0 hammering in the League Cup at Derby were endured before the season's third League victory which came courtesy of a Gabbiadini brace in late November at Sheffield United. The three points lifted Sunderland four places to 14th.

A dismal December brought only one point from six games, Ball scoring the final goal of the year with a penalty at QPR, as Sunderland ended the calendar year one place off the bottom.

Another successful Ball spot kick brought New Year's Day victory over Southampton. It was the start of a decent two-month run of three wins, two draws and two defeats that surprisingly did not change the Lads' League position. The last of that run saw Bally put Sunderland 3–0 up away to fellow strugglers Derby only for a hat-trick by the Rams' Dean Saunders to deny Sunderland two vital points. That set in train a demoralising run of six defeats in seven games punctuated only by a youth-inspired home win over Crystal Palace.

With four games to go Sunderland were in deep trouble as they travelled to face relegation rivals Luton Town. The Hatters had a ban on away supporters in place but when Gordon Armstrong and Colin Pascoe scored the goals that secured an important away win, sizeable pockets of Sunderland fans were visible all around the stadium.

Victory failed to lift Sunderland higher than the second-bottom place they had occupied since the beginning of March but with only two to go down it did bring third-from-bottom Luton to within two points.

Next up were Wimbledon's Crazy Gang. While in years to come Wimbledon would move 'lock, stock and two smoking barrels' to Milton Keynes and change their name into the bargain, this was a halcyon period for the then London club. Three seasons earlier they had sensationally lifted the FA Cup and would finish this season in an extremely creditable seventh place, one position behind Manchester United.

When the team from Plough Lane came to Roker Park it was Sunderland who were the underdogs but they fought for a goalless draw, albeit seeing the game out after Bally was shown his second red card in five home games – he had also walked in a defeat by Sheffield United.

Bally would play his final game of the season in helping the Lads to earn a vital point from a goalless home draw with Arsenal before missing the final game of the season due to suspension. The Gunners' point on Wearside won them the League title although they would not realise it until Liverpool lost at Forest two days later.

While the top end of the table was sorted out, the relegation battle saw Sunderland have everything to play for in the last game of the season. The scenario was that Derby were down and it was between Sunderland and Luton as to who joined them. Sunderland had done the double over Luton and faced an away game at Manchester City while Luton had a home fixture to look forward to against dead-men Derby.

Going into the final day, Sunderland and Luton were both on 34 points but Sunderland had a marginally inferior goal difference of minus 21 to Luton's minus 20. Sunderland knew that they needed to win by two goals more than Luton could beat Derby by – two because if goal difference ended level, Luton had scored more.

It was always going to be a tall order with Luton seemingly sure to beat Derby but there was the hope that with nothing to play for against a potentially nervous Luton, Derby might relax and play as Sunderland had seen them do when sticking six past the Lads in the League Cup or fighting back from three down in the League.

The Red and White Army decamped en masse for Manchester. Having filled one end to bursting, Sunderland supporters were also given a sizeable section of the huge Kippax terracing that ran the length of the pitch at City's old Maine Road ground. The gate of 39,194 was 14,000 higher than any of City's previous three home gates and almost 3,000 more than their second-highest gate for their Manchester derby with United.

With some 14,000 Red and Whites hoping for a miracle, Sunderland led at Maine Road but eventually succumbed 3–2 to Peter Reid's City side for whom Niall Quinn netted twice. Luton, meanwhile, beat Derby 2–0 with the first goal being an own-goal by Sunderland-born but ex-Luton player Mick Harford, who would later come to his home-city club.

Once again Sunderland had endured a last-day cliffhanger. Sometimes these had proved successful such as at Anfield in 1981 and sometimes they had ended in tears – such as against Gillingham in 1987.

This was to be one of the latter occasions but it was not a day for hanging heads. Like the miners who had gone back to Wearmouth Colliery and elsewhere in 1985 after the miners' strike to the sound of brass bands and with heads held high in the knowledge that they had put up a hell of a fight, so Sunderland went down with a bang rather than a murmur. Surviving after two promotions in three seasons had been a step too far but Sunderland had given it their all and in Kevin Ball had found a man who completely fitted the identikit image of what Sunderland supporters expect of a player in terms of spirit, commitment and no little ability.

Unknown to anyone at the time, Sunderland had also laid the foundations for two people who would work alongside Bally at Sunderland and leave their own indelible mark on the club. It would take Sunderland five years to climb back to the top tier. When they did City manager Peter Reid would be in charge at Sunderland with Kevin Ball as his captain. Moreover, making his debut as the club's record signing in their next top-flight game would be the man who scored twice to relegate them – Niall Quinn. In time Quinn would enjoy an Indian summer to his playing career with Sunderland and would later return to take over the club, briefly managing it before becoming chairman. Quinn and Reid's era was still some way off but Ball's had begun and while he could not prevent Sunderland going down it would be Kevin who did as much as anyone to keep the faith alive until the good times came back.

Kevin Ball's first season at Sunderland was the only year he won the official club Player of the Year award but Bally was a deserving winner of no fewer than four Player of the Year awards from the Supporters' Association. Kevin did the double of both awards in 1990–91 and also collected the SAFCSA trophy in 1992–93, 1994–95 and 1996–97.

What this quartet of seasons have in common is they were bad ones: two relegations and two near misses. Sometimes in difficult campaigns people go missing. Bally never did. 'Maybe I could flip it on its head and think that when we were under pressure it brought the best out of me,' says Kevin when considering that his quartet of individual awards all came in seasons of struggle. 'The first year I played was in the top flight before the start of the Premiership and we were very unlucky to be relegated. We put in a bloody good effort and if we'd had a player or two more to strengthen us or maybe a bit of fortune in one or two games that went against us we'd have stayed up. I know I performed as well as I could have done that year.'

In 1990–91 the Lads fought to the last, in 1996–97 they did the same and went down with 40 points; 1992–93 saw Sunderland perform dismally a year after reaching the FA Cup Final. On the final day only Bristol City beating Brentford prevented Sunderland from a second relegation to the old Third Division. One of the worst performances in the club's history saw a pitiful 3–1 defeat at Notts County, who were below the Lads at kick-off. Bally scored Sunderland's goal and tried manfully to lift the team. The game epitomised Kevin Ball, who no matter what the circumstances were would fight as if his life depended on it. 'I remember being chaired off by the supporters that day but I was due to have a hernia operation and I promised the bloke carrying me he could have my shirt so long as he didn't squash my nuts,' says…er…Bally.

Sunderland were again threatened with the drop into the third tier in 1994–95. The arrival of Peter Reid as manager seven games from the end of the season steered Sunderland to safety, Bally scoring the winner in Reid's first away game to underline the captain's importance to the team. Kevin knew for many people their whole well-being depended on it and if ever a footballer

Bally lifts the Championship trophy in 1999.

played as if he was a supporter it was him. 'Sometimes I'd run 60 yards to put a last-ditch tackle in and people would ask, "How do you do it?" But the reason was simple – I wanted to do it and I wanted to win.'

Playing as a centre-back in the season he won his first Sunderland Player of the Year award, Kevin had been a defender throughout his career and played in the middle of the back four under his first two Sunderland managers. Both of those had been highly-respected centre-halves: Denis Smith and Terry Butcher. However, as soon as Butcher was replaced by Mick Buxton the one time Sunderland Boys full-back decided to switch Ball into midfield in his first League game, and he was a revelation.

'It was Mick Buxton who first moved me into the middle of the park. It was back at my old team Portsmouth. I played really well and decided I liked it especially because it meant I could get involved all over the pitch. My awareness wasn't as good as someone like Lee Clark showed in later years but my game progressed under Mick and then under Reidy and Sacko [Peter Reid and assistant manager Bobby Saxton]. I remember playing away to Luton once and I sprayed the ball out to John Mullin on the right and we scored. It was probably the longest pass I'd ever hit and people were raving about the pass afterwards. I remember Reidy saying to people: "I told you he could pass, you just didn't believe me." Sacko used to say: "Do what you're good at and that makes you a good player."

'I think people just saw me as this tough lad in the centre of the park who motivated people and when they talk to me people often end with, "But you weren't the best footballer in the world, were you?" I've got to the stage now where while I don't want to punch them anymore I look at them and say: "Can you quantify what you just said?" When they think about what makes a good footballer they often end up thinking I was better than they first thought because to start with they just think of me as a tackler. I think that comes from the fact I'd previously been a defender. As a centre-back I was bloody good in the air, there's no two ways about that, I could tackle and kick with both feet. At times my awareness needed to be better but I did well and enjoyed it there. That was the era of the old-fashioned centre-forward and I loved playing against them. Overall though I preferred playing in midfield because I was more involved there.'

Whatever Bally's attributes, and there are many, perhaps the most important is his ability to get the maximum out of every member of the team. This has been seen in recent years where in 2011 his Under-18 team won their League for the fourth time in five seasons. Ball was undoubtedly the best captain at Sunderland since the days of Player of the Century Charlie Hurley in the 1960s and Kevin knows the value of getting the best out of everyone in what is, after all, a team game:

'It's a massive strength as a player if you can get more out of your teammates. I loved being captain at Sunderland. When I went to Fulham Chris Coleman was captain and at Burnley Steve Davis, who I'm still big mates with now, was the captain. I said to both of them, "You're still the main man but if you ever need anything I'm here for you." When they didn't play I'd be captain but I never took it that I was doing the job for any longer than they were out of the side and I respected them immensely.

'At Fulham I played centre-midfield. I'd been injured when I went there and Fulham never saw the best of me. I then had two years at Burnley when I played centre-mid and centre-back. When I dropped back into the back four after playing in midfield I found it a piece of cake. To start with people at Burnley weren't sure about me but I know that they came to believe I was a big plus at the club. Three months after I left Stan Ternent even rang me up and asked me to go back but it was too late by then. I'd been Player of the Year at Portsmouth and at Sunderland but I wasn't at Fulham long enough and I didn't win one at Burnley. I know this is going to sound really conceited but how I didn't win it at Burnley I don't know. We had some good players but in my opinion if the award had been the manager's to give I believe I'd have won it both years. Maybe it's the recognition we all strive to get. I do look back on the trophies I've got and every one of them I've loved having. Whenever I've gone up to collect such an award, irrespective of what kind of season we've had, I've asked myself, "Have I done everything I could have done to help the team?" If I have then I've received the trophy with a tremendous amount of pride. If I hadn't done everything I could have done that would have been wrong but I can assure you that wasn't the case.'

Kevin Ball at Sunderland
Debut: 28 August 1990: Sunderland 0–0 Tottenham Hotspur
Last game: 27 November 1999: Watford 2–3 Sunderland
Total appearances (all competitions): 375+13 as sub / 27 goals

Season by season
1990–91	39 games / 5 goals
1991–92	39+2 games / 1 goal
1992–93	49 games / 4 goals
1993–94	41 games / 0 goals
1994–95	46 games / 2 goals
1995–96	40+1 games / 4 goals
1996–97	34+1 games / 4 goals
1997–98	34+3 games / 4 goals
1998–99	47 games / 2 goals
1999–2000	6+6 games / 1 goal

Other clubs
Coventry City 1981–82
Portsmouth 1982–90
Fulham 1999–2000
Burnley 2000–02

1991–92   John Byrne

Division Two: 18th out of 24
FA Cup: Finalists, lost to Liverpool
League Cup: Second round, lost to Huddersfield Town over two legs
Top scorer: John Byrne, 14 goals, 7 League, 7 FA Cup
Ever present: No one
Player of the Year: John Byrne
SAFCSA Player of the Year: John Kay

John Byrne made such an instant impression at Sunderland that he was named Player of the Year in a season when the FA Cup Final was reached even though he was not even at the club for the first 15 games of the season. Byrne actually scored at Roker Park against Sunderland three weeks before he signed for Sunderland. Manager Denis Smith had managed the young Byrne at Byrne's first club York in the 1980s and had long aimed to bring the striker to Wearside.

Byrne had worn the blue and white stripes of Brighton for the first 15 games of the campaign, scoring seven times. Two of those goals had come in the League (Rumbelows) Cup against Brentford, and it would be Cup goals that would ensure his place in Sunderland folklore and with it the official Player of the Year award.

However Byrne, now working as a podiatrist and assisting Brighton & Hove Albion, has doubts about which Player of the Year award he actually won that season! 'I actually should have been Brighton's Player of the Year in the same season, even though I left to join Sunderland in October. What happened was that so many Brighton supporters voted for me that apparently I won it hands down. There was a lot of trouble going on behind the scenes at Brighton at the time as the club was subject to a takeover. The club didn't want me to win it as having a Player of the Year being someone they'd sold didn't look good so they allegedly discarded the votes I'd received. I was gutted because I'd have won a colour telly!'

When it comes to the Sunderland award though, John is not so sure: 'I didn't realise I'd won it. I thought it was John Kay! I knew I'd won some award but was never sure about it. I suppose the different Player of the Year awards are a bit like the different belts in boxing! I'm very proud though to have been Player of the Year at Sunderland.'

In fact Byrne's award as the official Sunderland AFC Player of the Year in a competition run by the *Sunderland Echo* and sponsored by the North of England Building Society was announced in the *Roker Review* for the last home game of the season against Cambridge United, but John understandably had other things on his mind with the Lads due to play in the FA Cup Final the following Saturday. Sadly on that day, the deserving SAFCSA Player of the Year Kay missed out on what would have been one of the highlights of his career through injury. Perhaps had 'the Red and White tractor' Kaysie been fit the Man of the Match – young winger Steve McManaman – might have been 'slowed down' somewhat and perhaps the outcome of the Final might have been different.

Byrne himself might have changed the Final which Sunderland lost 2–0 to Liverpool. He had been the single biggest influence on the Lads reaching Wembley. John had scored in every round of the Cup run including the winner in the semi-final against Norwich but he missed a good chance to give Sunderland the lead in the Final. It is a miss which still haunts him:

'Most footballers beat themselves up about the things they got wrong and for me, despite the goals along the way, my miss in the Final is a massive tarnish on the memory. It grates on

John Byrne of Sunderland takes on David Burrows and Michael Thomas of Liverpool during the 1992 FA Cup Final.

me. We'll never know if we'd have been able to hang on or whether Liverpool would have come back to win anyway but it would have been nice to find out. I still think about that miss every day and I think I always will.'

Like Roy Keane, who would always recall the things that failed to satisfy him but moved on quickly from successes – not wanting a parade when winning the Championship in 2007 for instance – or Clive Walker, who scored key goals to take Sunderland to their previous Cup Final (League Cup) in 1985 but only really recalls the penalty he missed in the Final, John Byrne feels that Sunderland supporters remember him for his miss rather than his magic and has to be reassured of the esteem in which he is held on Wearside.

'He was a great finisher,' says teammate and fellow Mancunian Gary Bennett. 'You are talking about someone who could find the back of the net and he was tremendous for us on the run to the FA Cup Final. He was unlucky not to score in every round especially when you look back on the opportunity he had in the Final. He did very well for us and if you look back at his career his finishing was brilliant and that was something Sunderland needed at that time.'

Sunderland certainly did need him, struggling as they were at the time. Having made his final appearance for Brighton at Charlton on 19 October, a week later Byrne lined up at Roker Park against Bristol Rovers, where a Gary Bennett goal gave Sunderland a one-all Second Division draw in the last season before the Leagues were restructured and the newfangled Premier League came into being.

Sunderland had been relegated the previous season but were suffering something of a hangover. The point from Byrne's debut lifted the Lads to 16th place. Early-season results had seen four goals put past Byrne's Brighton and Charlton but also a 5–3 defeat at Swindon, who Sunderland had lost to at Wembley 16 months earlier. The handsome win at Charlton had included a blistering six-minute hat-trick from the 1988–89 and 1989–90 Player of the Year Marco Gabbiadini, but his £1.8 million transfer to Crystal Palace left Sunderland in need of a striker. Byrne was that man, soon followed by big-money buy Don Goodman from West Bromwich Albion.

Other than the fact that Byrne was more like Gabbiadini's great strike partner Eric Gates and Goodman was more a replacement for Gabbiadini himself, there was one big difference between the front-running newcomers: Goodman was Cup-tied while Byrne was not. The consequence was that as the season progressed, a partnership between the pair had difficulty in blossoming because as Sunderland would enjoy their best Cup run since winning the trophy in 1973 Byrne found himself playing alongside Goodman in the League but Peter Davenport in the Cup. 'Peter and Don were both good players and I was happy playing with either,' says John, but the Cup unavailability of Goodman led to constant chopping and changing.

However, there was a fair amount of water to pass under the bridge before Cup football would come around, not least the sacking of manager Smith who spent the Gabbiadini money in bringing Byrne and Goodman to the club.

Byrne immediately endeared himself to the Roker crowd. It was an open secret that Sunderland were interested in the Republic of Ireland international long before he signed so fans had monitored his October performance closely, leaving the ground happy with an exciting 4–2 win and impressed with the goalscoring performance of the transfer target. When Byrne subsequently marked his second appearance in red and white by scoring the 100th and 101st League goals of his career in a comfortable win over Watford, he had got off on the right foot with the fans who would subsequently vote him Player of the Year.

Despite an away win at Ipswich a week later, hopes of bouncing straight back with an immediate promotion to become founder members of the new-look Premiership dwindled as the side struggled. A home draw with a Newcastle side managed by Argentinian Ossie Ardiles – who had been in charge of Swindon when they had beaten Sunderland at Wembley the previous calendar year – proved to be the only point taken in a run of four games. Byrne was displaying some nice touches up front but the team lacked a cutting edge. Having tried local youngsters David Rush and Craig Russell up front, Sunderland recognised that a major purchase was required and thus invested a club record £900,000 in West Brom's Don Goodman.

Goodman must have wondered what he had let himself in for when within 10 minutes of his debut away to Wolves he found his striker partner Byrne and midfielder Gordon Armstrong sent off. A week later Goodman marked his home debut with the only goal of the game against Leicester before Byrne's suspension kicked in. With Armstrong and Byrne missing the next two games when the only goal for was an own-goal, the new-look front pairing of Byrne and Goodman completed only their second 90 minutes together in a dismal 3–0 defeat at bottom-of-the-table Oxford in the last game of 1991, only to find that the man who had brought them to the club, Denis Smith, had been unceremoniously sacked.

Sunderland were 17th in the Second Division, had scored only four goals including an own-goal in their last nine games, and far from being at the negotiating table considering the carve-up of the future of football, the prospect of a return to the Third Division loomed menacingly. Chairman Bob Murray knew that the club had done well to immediately escape the clutches of the lower Leagues just five years earlier and the prospect of Sunderland being a club who would flirt with such an ignominious fall from grace a second time was something he was not prepared to contemplate; thus the axe swung for Smith, who having been in charge for 237 games, had survived longer than any boss since Alan Brown's first spell at the club between 1957 and '64.

With three home games in a row to come, opportunity beckoned for the caretaker manager Malcolm Crosby. A former player of Smith's at York, South Shields-born Crosby had been brought in as youth-team coach at Sunderland in the summer of 1988 and had moved up to look after the reserves a year later. Following Smith's dismissal of his long-term right-hand man Viv Busby, shortly before his own sacking, Crosby suddenly found himself in the right place at the right time when Bob Murray needed a caretaker manager. Despite having played over 400 League games, 'Crossa' was almost unheard of in the game, having spent the bulk of his playing days with Aldershot. Crosby would shoot to stardom however, winning the divisional Manager of the Month award in his first month in the job and by May he was a household name as he led out Sunderland at Wembley for the FA Cup Final, Byrne having become the talisman for the Cup team.

The New Year and new era started well enough with a 2–0 League win over Barnsley. Goodman was on the score sheet but had to miss the Cup visit of Port Vale three days later. Goodman's previous club West Brom were in the Third Division. Consequently on the same weekend Sunderland had met Newcastle in November, Don had played – and scored – in an FA Cup first-round meeting with non-League Marlow. Subsequently the Baggies went out of the Cup at Leyton Orient in the second round a couple of days after Goodman debuted for Sunderland. Oddly, Don's strike partner at West Brom had been Colin West, who had controversially been left out of Sunderland's last Cup Final side in the League Cup in 1985. However, whereas West was left out at Wembley having scored three times in the semi-final, Goodman was destined to watch his new teammates progress through a thrilling Cup run knowing all the while that he was not a part of it.

Peter Davenport was a similar player to Byrne. Both were intelligent international footballers whose natural inclination was to feed their strike partner as much as they were likely to go for goal themselves. Each was a good forward in his own right but best used as a foil for an out-and-out striker like Gabbiadini or Goodman. Nonetheless, they dovetailed admirably when used up front together and both scored in the 3–0 FA Cup third-round win over Port Vale that sent 15,500 fans home pleased but oblivious to the fact that when the Cup Final came round, and demand for tickets had tens of thousands claiming to have been there at the start of the Cup run, they would be the ones telling the truth.

Byrne and Davenport were on the mark in the next game too but were upstaged by the returning Goodman, who blasted a hat-trick in a 6–2 thrashing of Millwall. A week later Byrne and Goodman were on the score sheet again as Crosby's first away game, at Derby, brought a

2–0 win to end a run of five successive defeats on the road. Moreover, Sunderland had won four in a row, were up to 12th and in the fourth round of the Cup. Things were looking up.

Port Vale took a point from Roker, where they had lost in the Cup, four days before Sunderland travelled to Oxford for an FA Cup fourth-round tie. Oxford had convincingly beaten Sunderland in the League less than six weeks earlier but despite a United fightback, Sunderland won 3–2 with Byrne opening the scoring.

Goodman was restored to the team for the return to League action but despite another Byrne goal – his fourth in five games – defeat at Bristol Rovers was followed by a disappointing home draw with Tranmere. Sunderland had lost momentum ahead of an eagerly-awaited home fifth-round tie with top-flight strugglers West Ham.

Preceded by a minute's silence for two miners killed in an accident at Wearmouth Colliery, where the Stadium of Light stands now, the West Ham game was ruined by strong winds whipping in off the North Sea. Byrne managed Sunderland's second-half equaliser in the scrappiest of draws. Left-back Anton Rogan – who had made his debut against Byrne and Brighton earlier in the season – began the move. The ex-Celtic man found Davenport, whose perfect cross invited Byrne's header. Defender Julian Dicks stopped the effort on the line but without the need for a penalty Byrne reacted first to net the rebound at the Fulwell End. Fired up by the goal, Byrne twice went close to a winner. With just seven minutes to go he flicked the ball over his shoulder and volleyed the dropping ball, only to be thwarted by 'keeper Tony Parks with the custodian diving full-length to deny Byrne in the final minute.

A dismal 2–0 defeat at Southend, where future Sunderland man Brett Angell scored, meant Sunderland had gone five games without a win since the initial burst after Crosby took over. Essex locals watching the lads at Roots Hall ahead of the Upton Park replay would not have seen too much for West Ham to worry about.

The Hammers did not help themselves. With just six minutes gone Byrne intercepted a back pass from the on-loan Ray Atteveld and coolly slotted the ball past Tony Parks to give Sunderland the lead. Sunderland had not won an FA Cup tie in the capital since beating Leeds in the Final at Wembley in 1973. Nor had they knocked out top-flight opposition since 1979, but this was the perfect start. Halfway through the first half Byrne doubled the lead, leaving two defenders on their backsides as he latched on to a peach of a Davenport through ball before slamming the ball past Parks. In the fourth round at Oxford Sunderland had let the home side back into the game with two late goals which threatened a 3–0 advantage and again here they took their foot off the pedal. Two long-range strikes from Martin Allen brought the Hammers level and with 'keeper Tony Norman needing to produce a wonderful save from Tim Breacker, Sunderland burst the home side's bubbles with a winner 12 minutes from time. This time Byrne turned provider, flicking on substitute Kieron Brady's centre into the path of David Rush, who took Sunderland into the quarter-final.

Byrne's only penalty goal for Sunderland to beat Wolves earned what would be a solitary League win in 10 attempts, but by now the Cup run was gathering momentum with a Monday night quarter-final at Chelsea live on television. Managed by Sunderland's 1973 FA Cup Final goalscorer Ian Porterfield, the Londoners were seventh in the top flight but Byrne's second-half equaliser at Stamford Bridge earned Sunderland a replay.

Chelsea had lost to Sunderland in the semi-final of the run to the League Cup Final seven years earlier and were undone at Roker after another immense display by goalkeeper Norman and a dramatic last-minute header from Gordon Armstrong on one of the great Roker Park Cup nights.

Victory over Chelsea in the 1985 semi had led to a Cup Final showdown with Norwich and it was the Canaries who were next in store for the first FA Cup semi-final to be held at Sheffield

Wednesday's ground since the awful Hillsborough disaster of three years earlier. In the absence of any notable official tribute to the 96 dead, the huge Sunderland following preceded the game with the most poignant rendition of the Anfielders' anthem 'You'll Never Walk Alone'. It was a moment that showed the true spirit of football and Norwich's always superb supporters were at their best too. They took defeat with the same grace that the Red and White Army had shown when it had been Norwich's day at Wembley in 1985 at what became known as 'the Friendly Final'.

Norwich lost to a goal made by Young Player of the Year Brian Atkinson and headed home by Player of the Year John Byrne as Sunderland reached Wembley from a similar starting point to that of 1973. Unlike that day, just short of two decades earlier, however, there was to be no fairy-tale ending. A fixture pile-up which saw Sunderland play 10 times in April eventually eked out a position of League safety, although the Cup Final turned out to be a tale of what might have been.

'The whole Cup run is the highlight of my time at Sunderland although the thing that stands out is the chance that I missed at Wembley. It was good at Sunderland and I really enjoyed my time there,' says John, who also adds: 'As I live at the other end of the country I rarely get back there but the Sunderland Former Players' Association is fantastic and keeps me in touch. What struck me when I joined was that I didn't realise how big a club Sunderland is. I'd played at QPR but the amount of interest from the press in Sunderland caught me by surprise but they had to feed the level of interest from the fans. The passion for the club is unbelievable, and remember I'm from Manchester and am used to United and City.'

John Byrne at Sunderland
Debut: 26 October 1991: Sunderland 1–1 Bristol Rovers
Last game: 29 September 1992: Watford 2–1 Sunderland
Total appearances (all competitions): 43 / 15 goals

Season by season
1991–92   35 games / 14 goals
1992–93   8 games / 1 goal

Other clubs
York City 1977–84
Queen's Park Rangers 1984–88
Le Havre 1988–90
Brighton & Hove Albion 1990–91
Millwall 1992–93
Brighton & Hove Albion (loan) 1993
Oxford United 1993–95
Brighton & Hove Albion 1995–96
Crawley Town 1996–97
Shoreham FC 1997 (from March as a player, from August as joint manager)

Don Goodman

Division Two: 21st out of 24
FA Cup: Fourth round, lost to Sheffield Wednesday
League Cup: First round, lost to Huddersfield Town on away goals after extra-time over two legs
Anglo-Italian Cup: Eliminated at group stage
Top scorer: Don Goodman 17 goals, 16 League, 1 FA Cup
Ever present: No one
Player of the Year: Don Goodman
SAFCSA Player of the Year: Kevin Ball

Don Goodman's first full season at Sunderland was 1992–93, having become the club's record signing when bought for £900,000 from West Brom midway through the previous campaign. Rarely can a player have been so pleased to be involved in pre-season training as Don, who had missed out on an FA Cup Final appearance the previous season. Goodman had arrived on Wearside Cup-tied, having played for the Baggies against non-League Marlow Town in the first round before arriving at Sunderland, where under Malcolm Crosby the Lads had upset the odds to reach the Twin Towers in a season in which relegation to the Third Division had been flirted with. Indeed, Sunderland had been the lowest-placed club to reach the Cup Final since 1949.

Three seasons earlier Sunderland had found themselves in Division One despite losing the Play-off Final on their previous trip to Wembley. As the 1992–93 campaign kicked-off Sunderland again found themselves in Division One despite finishing in the lower reaches of Division Two. This was because as Sunderland started with a sloppy single-goal defeat away to 1990 Play-off Final opponents Swindon, the all-singing, all-dancing, newly-created FA Premier League was taking the first steps into a new world.

The changing face of football is illustrated by the fact that although Manchester United were the first champions of the new-look League Norwich finished third, QPR fifth, Sheffield Wednesday seventh, Wimbledon 12th and not one of the bottom nine in what was then a 22-team League would be in the top flight in 2011. One of those clubs falling from grace was Middlesbrough, relegated in the Premiership's first year. Quick to take their place were 'New Division One' champions Newcastle, to maintain a North East presence in the top flight. But as for Sunderland?

The Wearsiders had finished 18th out of 24 the year before but slumped to fourth from bottom, missing relegation by a single point courtesy of Bristol City saving their bacon on the final day. In the first year of the Sunderland Player of the Year award (1976–77) Bristol City had been involved in the infamous and allegedly underhand shenanigans at Coventry, but on this occasion the Bristolians would save Sunderland. The Robins' manager was Russell Osman, former centre-back partner of Sunderland boss Terry Butcher in their Ipswich days. Fortunately for Butcher, Osman's team saved Sunderland from the chop by beating Brentford on the final day, thereby leaving the Bees a point adrift of Sunderland. The Lads were unable to help themselves, losing woefully on the final day to Notts County, whose win secured their own safety.

Captain Kevin Ball, who scored Sunderland's goal in the 3–1 defeat, remembers the day: 'After the game Butch [player/manager Terry Butcher] was distraught and it was [assistant manager] Bobby Ferguson and myself that spoke. Butch was gone and it was a pity because I loved Butch. I wanted him to slam the door behind us and tear into the team because we hadn't been good enough. I wanted him to grab us as a team that day because I think it would have helped us the following year if he'd put us in our place but it didn't happen.'

Perhaps Butcher felt he couldn't rip into his underachieving team because he had played himself and as a veteran of 77 England caps, a player renowned for his fighting spirit had seen his side offer a meek surrender. Butcher had only been in charge of the team for three months and the upheaval that had seen off manager Malcolm Crosby must have left Goodman wondering why he had come to the North East.

From the day of his debut in December 1991 when within 10 minutes he had seen two of his teammates sent off, Goodman often seemed to find circumstances conspiring against him. Despite scoring a winner on his home debut, he found the man who signed him (Denis Smith) sacked within a month of investing a record fee in him. Then came the Cup run he could not be a part of followed by a season of struggle that brought the downfall of Smith's successor Malcolm Crosby.

That Sunderland did not drop into the Third Division – or 'New Division Two', as it now was – was due in no small part to Goodman. Top-scoring with 16 League goals in a struggling side, it was more than twice as many as second-top scorer Shaun Cunnington. 'The Don' actually took a dozen games to notch his first goal and only had five to his name by Christmas despite playing virtually every game.

It was a dismal period in Sunderland's history. In the previous two seasons the Lads had been relegated and had finished 18th in the Second Division, which was the position Sunderland fans found themselves in at Christmas with memories of a run to that year's FA Cup Final completely out of keeping with a run of 52 defeats in the previous 106 League games.

Manager Malcolm Crosby was sacked after a home defeat by mid-table Watford in January. Crossa's Cup formula had vanished. His penultimate game saw fourth-round elimination after an uncharacteristic last-minute error by 'keeper Tony Norman at Sheffield Wednesday on the same ground that was the venue of the manager's greatest day in the previous season's semi-final.

Crosby was replaced by a man he had brought to the club: Terry Butcher, who became the club's first 'permanent' player-manager. Butcher had been one of the country's top defenders and had endeared himself to the crowd by playing to the gallery on the five occasions Sunderland had won at Roker Park with him in the side. Whenever three points had been secured 'Butch' had shared his delight with the vociferous Fulwell End conducting the victory songs in a display of chest-beating pride. Goodman had scored in three of those five home wins to date with another of the victories sparked by a home debut goal from local youngster Michael Gray who would go on to top 400 appearances for his home-town club and be capped by England.

If the board hoped that a change of manager would bring a change of fortune they would be as disappointed as the fans. Defeat at home to Swindon did not augur well but penalties in successive games were both converted by Goodman to give the new boss back-to-back wins followed by three consecutive goalless draws which gave hope that Sunderland were becoming better organised.

It remained a season of struggle. Goodman was the only forward likely to score but he could not do it on his own. John Colquhoun never found the net in 20 appearances that season, former England man Peter Davenport scored four in 34 games and the previous season's Cup talisman John Byrne had left after one goal in six games; local youngster David Rush fared better with six goals from his 18 appearances. To his credit, Terry Butcher tried to bring in some help for Goodman by signing two locally-born target men: Mick Harford and Lee Howey.

Tough nut Mick Harford had been the villain of the piece on the day of Sunderland's relegation in 1990. His own-goal to the benefit of his former club Luton had helped to seal Sunderland's fate. Now 34 and a veteran of seven clubs including Newcastle, Harford was signed from Chelsea, where he had done so well that he remained their top scorer at the end of the season. Despite 11 goals for the Londoners, Harford was discarded in favour of Sunderland's 1987 Play-off adversary Tony Cascarino. Sunderland's 1973 FA Cup Final goalscorer Ian Porterfield had just been sacked as Chelsea manager, thereby becoming the first manager dismissed in the newly-formed FA Premier League. With a 1970s Cup hero of Chelsea's own in David Webb taking over at Stamford Bridge, Harford did not fit the bill.

Harford was quickly off the mark, scoring in his third and fourth games, the latter seeing Goodman join him on the score sheet – but both of these matches were yet more defeats. The latter was a demoralising 4–2 home reverse to Southend for whom both Stan Collymore and future Sunderland man Brett Angell were on the mark as Sunderland lost having led at half-time. Such was Sunderland's stature in this period that this was the second in a run of four successive seasons that the Shrimpers won at Sunderland.

A hard-working player who always grafted for the team, Goodman continued to be Sunderland's best hope of a goal. Sometimes Don's willingness to forage for possession was arguably to the team's benefit if not his own. Often he would be the man working the channels, particularly down the right, and he would regularly put in good crosses that ideally he would have been on the end of. Whereas some strikers in the Greaves and Lineker mould let everyone else do the graft and simply focus on being in the right place at the right time to finish moves off and claim the glory, Don Goodman was the sort of player – like Wayne Rooney, although obviously not as good – who always wanted to be involved and doing everything he could for the cause. It was this attitude allied to his goals that secured him the Player of the Year award.

Goodman's goals earned Sunderland's next two points – a draw at Brentford and a brace only good enough for a point at home to Luton – either side of two more defeats, the latter of which had seen Harford, now on a barren run that would extend to the end of the season, sent off at Grimsby.

With four games to go Sunderland were 18th with the teams beneath them snapping at their heels and relegation haunting the corridors of Roker Park. As if that was not bad enough the next game was away to high-riding Newcastle where the Magpies were flying off into the promised land of the Premier League while the Black Cats struggled badly and Sunderland boss Butcher admitted pre-match: 'If you look at the League form and table, we should be in for a right stuffing.' The Sunday high noon kick-off was the first game between the clubs to be broadcast live on TV.

Just six years later a resurgent Sunderland would gloriously win at St James' in torrential rain. On this occasion the heavens opened every bit as much and to make matters worse Sunderland were behind after just 10 minutes, a Scott Sellars free-kick skidding in off the post after being conceded by the player-manager. There would be no further scoring but the result put Kevin Keegan's Magpies on the perch at the top of the table while sinking Sunderland to fourth from bottom. Five of the Newcastle team that day were either ex or future Sunderland players: Barry Venison, Paul Bracewell, Andy Cole, David Kelly and Lee Clark, while a sixth was the brother of a man who would debut for Sunderland a week later.

That debutant was Lee Howey, brother of Newcastle's Steve. Lee had been brought in by Terry Butcher in March and got his chance to debut for Sunderland as a sub in the absence of the other striker brought in with him, Harford, who was suspended having been sent off in the defeat at Grimsby. Newcastle's title rivals Portsmouth were the visitors. Managed by Jim Smith, who had been Newcastle's boss when the Tynesiders lost to Sunderland in the Play-offs three years earlier, the 'Bald Eagle' brought his team to Wearside on the back of 11 wins and a draw, a spell which had seen them concede a mere three goals. As well as a mean defence Pompey also possessed a striker who already had 40 League goals to his name, Guy Whittingham, who would duly register at Roker.

In contrast Sunderland had won just two of their last 15 games following the back-to-back victories in Butcher's second and third matches. Nonetheless, football being football and Sunderland being Sunderland the lads romped to their biggest win since a Goodman hat-trick in a 6–2 thrashing of Millwall 16 months earlier. This time Goodman scored twice in a stunning 4–1 win.

The game turned on a first-half penalty that saw visiting defender Guy Butters sent off for handball on the line. Goodman converted the spot kick and Sunderland were one up against 10 men. Don doubled the lead with a second penalty early in the second half, this time after he had been brought down by Kit Symons. Suddenly full of confidence against a team who were in shock, Sunderland produced easily their performance of the season. The goal of the game came from right-back Martin Gray. It was his only goal for the club and climaxed a free-flowing move that had Sunderland looking like the team at the top of the table. Portsmouth had lost their heads by now and were reduced to nine men with the dismissal of former Liverpool and Spurs man Paul Walsh for an off-the-ball incident with the scorer of the third goal. It was soon four courtesy of Gordon Armstrong and although goal machine Whittingham grabbed a late consolation for Pompey the three points lifted the Lads three places.

That was just as well as it proved to be the only victory from the final 10 games, seven of which were defeats, including the two remaining fixtures. Kevin Ball was sent off at promotion-chasing Tranmere but fortunately was still available for the final match at Notts County when, despite the magnitude of a match that could relegate the Red and Whites into the third tier, Sunderland 'didn't turn up' and only escaped the drop thanks to results elsewhere. The away support which almost doubled County's previous home gate deserved better yet again.

When the dust settled Sunderland had finished fourth from bottom of the Second Division. It may have been called 'New Division One' now but for a support better educated in football than to be conned by new branding, the fans knew that Sunderland had been perilously close to a second visit to the third tier. The previous time they had been there they had come straight back up thanks largely to long since discarded manager Denis Smith. Had Sunderland dropped down again it does not bear thinking about what might have happened. Look at that great club Sheffield Wednesday for a warning.

As Sunderland drew breath from their escape, Wednesday were finishing seventh in the newfangled FA Premier League in a season when they reached Wembley in both Cup Finals. The Owls' demise and the Black Cats' rise illustrate the changing fortunes of football. Had it not been for the invaluable goals of Player of the Year Don Goodman and the never-say-die commitment of captain Kevin Ball, who took the Supporters' Association award, then the largely forgotten 1992–93 season may have proved to be the most catastrophic in club history, worse even than 1957–58 or 1986–87.

Almost two decades on supporters still appreciate Don Goodman's part in the Sunderland story. Now a familiar and much respected analyst on Sky TV and an accomplished after dinner speaker, Don says: 'I often get people coming up to me and saying they've met a Sunderland fan who couldn't believe I knew you. They always sing your praises and that doesn't happen rarely. It's a frequent thing and that amazes me because Sunderland fans put me on a pedestal and that is priceless. I'll never ever forget that and I love them for it. Still to this day I never fail to look for Sunderland's result and I always want to know what's going on at the club and I always will until the day I die. They are just amazing supporters through thick and thin. Unfortunately for me Sunderland were a club I played for at a time that wasn't a successful time in the club's history and I am so, so pleased that Sunderland have gone on from that time and have progressed to the Stadium of Light and the Premier League.'

Don Goodman at Sunderland
Debut: 7 December 1991: Wolverhampton Wanderers 1–0 Sunderland
Last game: 29 November 1994: Port Vale 0–0 Sunderland
Total appearances (all competitions): 126+4 as sub / 47 goals

Season by season
1991–92   20+2 games / 11 goals
1992–93   45 games / 17 goals
1993–94   42+1 games / 16 goals
1994–95   19+1 games / 3 goals

Other clubs
Bradford City 1983–87
West Bromwich Albion 1987–91
Wolverhampton Wanderers 1994–98
Sanfrecce Hiroshima 1998–99
Barnsley (loan) 1998–99
Motherwell 1999–2001
Walsall 2001–02
Exeter City 2002–03
Doncaster Rovers (loan) 2003
Stafford Rangers 2003–04

1993-94   Gary Bennett

Division Two: 12th out of 24
FA Cup: Fourth round, lost to Wimbledon
League Cup: Third round, lost to Aston Villa
Anglo-Italian Cup: Eliminated at group stage
Top scorer: Phil Gray, 17 goals, 14 League, 3 League Cup
Ever present: No one
Player of the Year: Gary Bennett
SAFCSA Player of the Year: Phil Gray

Gary Bennett had seen two promotions, relegation and a Cup Final in the six seasons since he had been the 1986–87 Player of the Year. Former England centre-back Terry Butcher was Gary's sixth manager in his time at Sunderland but as 1993–94 kicked-off as Butcher's first in charge from the start of the season, stalwart Bennett found himself in an unusual situation.

'It was a new challenge for me because the new manager had had his first close season to bring his own men in and all of a sudden I found myself not in the team. Terry Butcher had brought in five new players and wanted to go in a different direction. I found myself out of the comfort zone because I'd been one of those who was mainly picked year in year out and I found myself not in the starting line up and just a squad player. It was a case of "What do I do now?" because I'd never been in that position.'

With former SAFC Player of the Year Ian Atkins as his assistant, Butcher's new-look side got off to a desperate start. Several of the new signings had been involved in a car crash on the eve of the campaign when new midfielder Derek Ferguson allegedly went the wrong way round a roundabout. Nonetheless, having been given more money to spend than any manager in the club's history as Bob Murray tried to propel Sunderland into the Premiership, the team collapsed to their heaviest ever opening-day defeat, losing 5–0 at Derby.

Although Butcher had decided to concentrate on managing the side, his team could have used his experience on the pitch but, like Bennett, he was not in the team that day, preferring new signing Andy Melville. The Wales international played with the relatively inexperienced Ian Sampson in central defence. The Rams had a field day, two-time Sunderland Player of the Year Marco Gabbiadini being among the scorers.

'Getting beat 5–0 on the first day of the season was a disappointing day for the football club although from my point of view I thought it might be an opportunity for me to get a chance to get back into the team and show him what I could do,' remembers Gary, who justified his reinstatement as Chester were swept aside in the League Cup after the Lads trailed at half-time and Charlton were thumped 4–0 in the opening home League game. Bennett was Man of the Match against the Addicks and given an outstanding '9 out of 10' by the *Sunderland Echo*.

Butcher had been brought to the club by Malcolm Crosby at the start of the previous season. As nice a guy as there is in the game, Crossa had been warned that in installing the veteran England pivot into his squad Sunderland had a ready-made replacement if they decided a change of manager was needed, particularly as Butcher had gained managerial experience already at Coventry. In due course, when Crosby was relieved of his duties in January, Butcher was handed the keys to the manager's office. Initially he continued as a player and Bennett, who had barely played all season, found his opportunities limited: 'I didn't play much alongside Terry in the heart of the defence although I had a few games at full-back,' says Benno of that period. 'When

Terry was manager of the team I wasn't playing regularly shall we say, and we all know that when Terry was player-manager he wanted to play himself. He did reach a point where he took himself out of the team and started to manage but obviously when he was still a player it was a case of picking himself or picking me so there was only going to be one winner there. I wouldn't say it was the best of times.'

Having decided to give up playing in the summer of 1993–94, Butcher found more use for Bennett. Following a poor start that saw them bottom after six matches and win just one of the first seven in the League, the side started to look as if it was clicking into gear with a decent run of five wins in six. The defeat in that sequence, however, brought a disappointing 4–1 loss at Middlesbrough live on TV, which meant that even allowing for an exciting League Cup victory over Leeds – who at the time were third in the Premiership – the crowd were never really convinced that the manager could take Sunderland back to the top level.

It was a bad time in the club's history. Just one of the last nine years had been spent in the top flight and that had seen Sunderland relegated. The same period had seen Sunderland drop into the third tier for a year. The re-energised top flight looked a million miles away as Butcher's team nosedived into a run of six defeats in a row. Meanwhile, cranking up the pressure on the Wearsiders, Butcher's old England teammate Kevin Keegan simultaneously sparked his Newcastle side into a run of four Premier League wins in a row that lifted them to third in the table, their fans enjoying the sight of Liverpool being beaten 3–0 with an Andy Cole hat-trick while the Red and White hard core trooped home having seen a home defeat to Southend United. Inevitably, Butcher got the chop six days later.

Once again Roker Park was the scene of massive upheaval as with the club contemplating a move away from Roker to a proposed new stadium adjacent to the Nissan car plant, chairman Bob Murray stepped away from the figurehead position. John Featherstone took over while Murray retained his position as the club's major shareholder.

Fifty-year-old Mick Buxton was already on the coaching staff and stepped into the manager's shoes. A former Sunderland Boys player, Buxton had managed Huddersfield and Scunthorpe and was not looking to come back into management, being seemingly content in a coaching role. 'Mick was from the old school. He was a Sunderland lad who had grown up in Ryhope,' says Bennett. 'He loved the club and knew the ins and outs and he concentrated on doing the basics. He got us set up and we did a lot of shadow play. We used a 4–4–2 and we all knew our individual jobs. At times in training it was boring because of the drills we went through week in week out but what he did do was steady the ship.'

A day into the job, Buxton saw his new charges lose at home. However, there was noticeably more fight in the side as they went down by the odd goal in five to Nottingham Forest. Managed by Sunderland's 1980 promotion-winning assistant manager Frank Clark, Forest were just embarking on a run that would take them from mid-table to promotion with two of their goals at Roker coming from Stan Collymore, who had scored in Southend's big win on Wearside the previous season.

Buxton quickly had a positive effect. Bennett produced another Man of the Match performance on his 32nd birthday as the new manager enjoyed his first win at Portsmouth. A win in the city which houses HMS *Victory* began a run of 19 points from eight games, culminating in a turning of the tables on Middlesbrough who lost to a bullet header from Lee Howey scored in front of a delirious Fulwell End. The run lifted the Lads from a relegation place to 14th. It was not until Buxton had been in the job for over three months that he was able to bring a player in but as a full-back himself, his acquisition of experienced Poland international right-back Dariusz Kubicki – who would be the next season's Player of the Year – showed promising judgement.

Under Buxton, Bennett was doing what he had been doing for the best part of a decade: being a strong, determined character at the heart of the defence. An integral part of Gary's game was to storm out of defence leaving opponents in his wake and he usually chipped in with the occasional goal, but in 1993–94 Gary Bennett would become only the second outfield player to win the Player of the Year award at Sunderland without claiming a goal throughout the season.

Unusually for Sunderland, who only once since 1978 – in 1988–89 – had had a season where the closing games were not a nail-biting battle to go up or stay up, Buxton had guided the club, who still sported a ship on their club badge, into safer waters. 'It was a rarity for Sunderland to be in mid-table,' recalls Bennett, 'and from my point of view having been there so long I knew that we always seemed to leave it until the last one or two games of the season, so to find ourselves halfway up the table with four or five games left was strange. We seemed lost, we had nothing to fight for as we couldn't go up or down. The season was over and it was over for the supporters as well. The supporters were used to biting their fingernails on the last day of the season and maybe wondering about other results as well as our own. It was good that we found that security but, as a player, I missed being involved in drama right through to the end, so it was something new.'

The curtain came down on the season with the reverse fixture to Buxton's first. A year earlier the final day of the season on the other side of the River Trent at Notts County had seen Sunderland as lucky as they ever have been not to drop into the third tier. At Forest they were up against a side already promoted into the big League but came up with two goals in the last 10 minutes to dampen Forest's promotion party and show that Mick Buxton had instilled some grit into the side.

As anyone who watched Benno in his time at Sunderland knows, regardless of how the team were faring, the Mancunian was always the sort of grafter supporters love. His sending-off in 1990 for just about beating up Coventry's David Speedie – never the most popular team or individual on Wearside – had cemented his status with the fans. Not a naturally dirty player, Gary could mix it with the hard men of the game when he had to…sometimes even when he didn't have to! Watford's visit in March was a case in point as Benno stung Hornet Paul Furlong in front of the main stand leaving visiting boss (and former Newcastle man) Glenn Roeder to protest vociferously to referee John Key of Sheffield that Bennett should have been sent off. He should have been, too, and while no one condones violence on the football field the fact was that if someone wanted to treat the Lads to the rough stuff they would have Benno (and Kevin Ball) to reckon with. It was the quality of his play allied to his always evident commitment that made Gary such a crowd favourite.

As with so many real darlings of the crowd, Gary recognised the value of the fans as much as they appreciated him. 'I think it's massive to win the Player of the Year award, especially at Sunderland which is such a big club,' he says. 'To win a Player of the Year award at Sunderland is a big achievement and something people can't take away from you especially as it's voted for by the supporters and because of the calibre of the players you are competing with. Having the crowd on your side makes it easier for anyone. Every player who goes out in any game does so with the intention of giving 100 per cent. They'll always want to win a game of football and to do their best but sometimes it doesn't happen that way but as long as you are seen to be giving 100 per cent the supporters will accept that and forgive you if you make mistakes. You're not going to go 10 years or however long you're at a football club for without making a mistake and it's how you react to it that is the important thing. You try to do the best you can and if it doesn't work out and you don't let it stop you then supporters will warm to you. When I was at

Scarborough later in my career I ended up winning Player of the Year there. I had two tremendous seasons there which was excellent and in my early days I won the Young Player of the Year award at Cardiff but to be Player of the year at Sunderland was extra special.'

No Sunderland Player of the Year has played as many games for the club as Gary Bennett and in his role as Sunderland summariser for the local BBC radio commentary, listeners can still feel Benno's passion for the Lads. He remains a player looked up to by all those who saw him and one of a select band of men to be Player of the Year more than once.

Gary Bennett at Sunderland
Debut: 25 August 1984: Sunderland 3–1 Southampton (scored)
Last game: 15 April 1995: Sunderland 1–1 Luton Town
Total appearances (all competitions): 434+9 as sub / 25 goals

Season by season

1984–85	46 games / 3 goals
1985–86	33 games / 4 goals
1986–87	48 games / 5 goals
1987–88	43 games / 2 goals
1988–89	44+3 games / 3 goals
1989–90	7 games / 3 goals
1990–91	43 games / 2 goals
1991–92	44+2 games / 3 goals
1992–93	16+1 games / 0 goals
1993–94	46+2 games / 0 goals
1994–95	23+1 games / 0 goals

Other clubs
Ashton United 1979
Manchester City 1979–81
Cardiff City 1981–84
Carlisle United 1995–96
Scarborough 1996–98 (player/coach)
Darlington 1998–2000
Darlington 2000–01 (manager)
Worksop Town 2001
Scarborough 2001

Dariusz Kubicki

Division Two: 20th out of 24
FA Cup: Fourth round, lost to Tottenham Hotspur
League Cup: Second round, lost to Millwall over two legs
Top scorer: Phil Gray, 15 goals, 12 League, 2 FA Cup, 1 League Cup
Ever present: Dariusz Kubicki 46 out of 46 League plus all five Cup ties
Player of the Year: Dariusz Kubicki
SAFCSA Player of the Year: Kevin Ball
Sunderland Echo Player of the Year: Martin Smith

In 1994–95 Sunderland had three different Players of the Year. The indefatigable Kevin Ball won the third of his four SAFCSA Player of the Year awards and young Sunderland-born forward Martin Smith was voted the *Sunderland Echo*'s man of the season, which would normally have been the club's official award. But in 1994–95 the official SAFC Player of the Year as judged by voters in the club's own matchday programme was the ever dependable Poland international full-back Dariusz Kubicki, with Smith named as the club's official Young Player of the Year.

Under Mick Buxton an eight-game pre-season build-up included a 9–0 win in Norway and the visit of Porto for Gordon Armstrong's testimonial match. Once the real stuff got underway the Lads enjoyed their longest unbeaten start for 84 years but a succession of draws meant that only two of the first eight games were won. In fairness to the manager there had been little money to invest after a season in which the Lads had finished 12th, Buxton having taken over with six games to go. He had, though, spent £100,000 on permanently signing Kubicki, the Pole having initially arrived in March on loan from Aston Villa, who had paid twice as much to buy him from Legia Warsaw in the summer of 1991.

ROKER REVIEW PLAYER OF THE SEASON

First of all may we thank all Roker Review reader who sent in their votes for "Player of the Season". The response was tremendous with hundreds of entries pouring in. *The results of the competition are as follows:*

PLAYER OF THE SEASON
DARIUSZ KUBICKI
2nd - Phil Gray
3rd - Kevin Ball

The winner of this section is **Philip Cheshire** from Whitburn in Sunderland. Philip wins Dariusz's *original* autographed 1994-95 first team shirt.

YOUNG PLAYER OF THE SEASON
MARTIN SMITH
2nd - Craig Russell
3rd - David Mawson

The winner of this section is **Kathryn Traynor** of Washington. Kathryn wins a 1994-95 shirt which is autographed by all of the players.

GOAL OF THE YEAR
CRAIG RUSSELL -v- SHEFFIELD UTD (h)
2nd - Martin Smith -v- Swindon (h)
3rd - Phil Gray -v- Wolves (h)

The winner of this final section is **Karen Parkinson** from Pallion in Sunderland. Karen wins an autographed football.
All three winners have also won two Main Stand tickets and two Executive Lounge Passes each for today's game

ROKER REVIEW WOULD LIKE TO CONGRATULATE ALL OF TODAY'S WINNERS

Dariusz Kubicki

Martin Smith

Craig Russell

Sunderland had a squad that included several stalwarts including Kevin Ball, Richard Ord, Don Goodman and Gary Bennett, all of whom were previous or future Players of the Year, although Bennett was in his last season at Roker and would be used sparingly while Goodman was sold before Christmas. There was also a smattering of good local youngsters such as Smith, Mickey Gray and Craig Russell, seasoned pros like Andy Melville and Phil Gray, plus two excellent 'keepers in Alec Chamberlain and Tony Norman.

Kubicki would play in all 76 of Buxton's games in charge. Consistency could have been Kubicki's middle name. The longer you watch football the more you realise that when you use the term 'on his day' to describe the attributes of a player, you are discussing a footballer who probably will not go far in the game. Lots of players can be good 'on their day' and look brilliant on the highlights DVD their agent compiles but if you look at the top clubs, their players perform to a high standard in eight games out of 10 or more. Even the best can have an off day but the off days of top players are few and far between. Kubicki was a player who did not do off days.

The holder of 47 caps for his country, Dariusz was simply a class act. Football is a simple game and he kept it that way. He would not try the 'Hollywood' ball, he would just play it nice and easy, retain possession and immediately look to make himself available for a pass. The possessor of fine positional sense, Kubicki was reliability personified. He would not win games for the team – he was a full-back after all – but he would not lose them either. If in later years Tore Andre Flo became nicknamed Tore Andre Four because that is how many marks he usually got in the paper then you could add the appendage seven to Dariusz. Consistently good, game in and game out.

From his debut, Dariusz made 123 consecutive appearances between March 1994 and September 1996 when Buxton's successor Peter Reid controversially dropped him for newcomer Gareth Hall when Kubicki was on the cusp of a club record. Kubicki prided himself on always being available to play. As reigning Player of the Year in December 1995 he suffered a horrific gash to his ankle early on in a game against Crystal Palace but did not let on until after the final whistle. He knew that if he had taken his shin pad off at half-time to inspect it the chances were he would have to come off so he kept quiet, helped to win the game with a clean sheet, and six days later was again in action as another clean sheet was kept in another win. Dariusz would deserve the medal he won that year as a Division One champion when he was an ever present in the side for the second successive season.

In 1994–95 Kubicki was the only man to play every match. Starting the season at left-back for the first five games, he switched to his favoured right in a hard-fought draw at Middlesbrough and remained in that berth for the rest of the season. 'I don't mind where I play, the most important thing is to be in the team,' was typical of his attitude. Despite the unbeaten start it was to prove a difficult campaign. Many games became stalemates as Sunderland lacked the cutting edge to create victories but had the experience at the back to give little away.

Despite finishing fifth from bottom, Sunderland conceded less than a goal a game, a record bettered only by the top two. The Lads were the League's lowest scorers though, with home fans never seeing their side score more than twice. Inevitably there were a lot of draws – 18 of them – equalling the club record set exactly 40 years earlier.

Buxton brought in a sizeable fee for striker Don Goodman, got a month out of talented midfielder Ian Snodin on loan from Everton and at Christmas traded the long-serving Gary Owers plus £450,000 to bring in left-back Martin Scott from Bristol City. Scott debuted in a Boxing Day Roker draw with promotion-bound Bolton and would prove a sound investment. In January another quarter of a million of the Goodman money was spent on midfielder Steve Agnew, but Sunderland could not escape the lower reaches of the division.

Since relegation four years earlier, Sunderland had barely been out of the bottom half of the second tier. There was little hope of a return to the top flight while up the road a Newcastle team that included two former Sunderland Wembley captains (Barry Venison and Paul Bracewell) were disappointed to finish sixth in the Premiership after being runaway leaders until November.

In contrast, Sunderland welcomed Premiership opposition to Roker in the form of Tottenham Hotspur. Jurgen Klinsmann highlighted the star quality Sunderland were missing and the German World Cup superstar helped himself to two goals as Spurs won easily by 4–1. It was a depressing time on Wearside. Three successive gates of 12,000 showed that the club were down to the real hard core of support.

Whereas nowadays clubs have to cope with transfer windows in January and the close season, prior to their introduction players could be bought and sold up to the third Thursday in March. With Sunderland looking over their shoulders at the haunting spectre of relegation once again, chairman Bob Murray sanctioned two acquisitions. If Mick Buxton had excelled in his choice of full-backs in Kubicki and Scott, it is hard to imagine a double signing that went so horribly wrong as the pair brought in as transfer deadline day arrived. £750,000 was spent on striker Brett Angell, who would start the remaining eight games without breaking his duck. After three games and a solitary League Cup goal the following season he was eventually discarded for a fee reported to be less than a sixth of what had been paid for him. Angell was one of those players who had a good record against Sunderland but did not deliver the goods once Sunderland signed them. Angell had scored against the Lads four times in the previous three seasons. However, he was the better of Sunderland's pair of acquisitions.

Dominic Matteo was an up-and-coming 20-year-old brought in on loan from Liverpool who went on to become a full international with Scotland. Like Angell, Matteo debuted at Barnsley on a cold and windy Friday night at Oakwell. Matteo was not a bad player but administrative inefficiency meant Sunderland had not correctly registered him to play. With every point vital there was a possibility of the club having points deducted but a Football League commission met a week after the game and imposed a £2,500 fine. In his days in Poland Dariusz had seen Cup semi-final opponents Olimpia Poznan have a 2–0 first-leg scoreline awarded 3–0 to his club Legia after Poznan fielded a suspended player, but Sunderland escaped serious punishment.

Had Sunderland not lost the game at Barnsley, any points that were gleaned may have been taken away. Matteo returned immediately to Anfield and Angell was left to wonder. In his first minute as a Sunderland player he found the back of the net, glancing home a Kubicki throw-in only for referee Mr Allison to disallow the 'goal', saying that Angell had not touched the ball which had entered the goal directly from Dariusz's throw. 'I definitely got a touch,' claimed Angell afterwards.

The match was to prove Buxton's last as he was sacked the following Wednesday to be replaced by Peter Reid. Having been in charge of Manchester City when they relegated Sunderland at the start of the decade, Reid had seven games to keep Sunderland up. Immediately sparking back-to-back wins for only the second time in the season, he guided Sunderland to safety, young player of the year Martin Smith scoring in all of the last three games including a vital winner over Swindon.

Reid would resurrect Sunderland, guiding them to the title a year later with Kubicki again a mainstay of the side. The bad times were over for now at long last but it is in the bad times that you most need people you can depend on and Sunderland's favourite Pole proved to be a deserving Player of the Year.

Dariusz Kubicki at Sunderland
Debut: 5 March 1993: Sunderland 2–0 Notts County
Last game: 13 April 1997: Sunderland 1–2 Liverpool
Total appearances (all competitions): 149+1 as sub / 0 goals

Season by season
1993–94   15 games / 0 goals
1994–95   51 games / 0 goals
1995–96   52 games / 0 goals
1996–97   31+1 games / 0 goals

Other clubs
Zastal
Stal Mielec 1981–83
Legia Warsaw 1983–91
Aston Villa 1991–94
Wolverhampton Wanderers 1997–98
Tranmere Rovers (loan) 1998
Carlisle United 1998
Darlington 1998–99

As manager
Legia Warsaw 1999
Polonia Warsaw 2003–04
Lechia Gdansk 2007–08
Znicz Pruszkow 2008–09
Wisla Plock 2009–10
Dolcan Zabki 2010–

Richard Ord

Division One: First, promoted
FA Cup: Third round, lost to Manchester United in a replay
League Cup: Second round, lost to Liverpool over two legs
Top scorer: Craig Russell, 14 goals, 13 League, 1 FA Cup
Ever presents: Dariusz Kubicki and Michael Gray, 46 out of 46 League
and both played all six Cup ties
Player of the Year: Richard Ord
SAFCSA Player of the Year: Richard Ord

'I never got praise off my dad but at the end of the season when we'd won the League I walked in with so many Player of the Year trophies from all the branches that I couldn't carry them all. He just looked at me and said, "Aye, you've had a canny season, son." It was a big thing for my dad to say and my mam was crying. It really stands out for me.'

Richard Ord became a cult hero at Sunderland and his achievement in being the Player of the Year in a title-winning season when the standards were high and the team was sprinkled with popular players illustrates just how canny a season the miner's son had enjoyed.

Having made his debut as a 17-year-old in a thumping 7–0 victory over Southend in the year spent in the Third Division in 1987–88 and been Young Player of the Year the following season, by the time the 1995–96 campaign came around Richard Ord had 182 games under his belt. Just under 19,000 were at Roker Park for the visit of Leicester City, who won 2–1 to put a dampener on Peter Reid's first game as 'permanent' manager.

Reid had rescued Sunderland from a threatened return to the third tier. Coming in near the end of the previous season, he had overseen a change in fortunes and avoided the drop. During that spell five players including former record signing Tony Norman and two-time Player of the Year Gary Bennett had played their final games for the club. Two games into the new season Gordon Armstrong joined Gary Bennett in being another man with over 400 games to his name for the Lads to play for the club for the final time, leaving Ord as the club's longest-serving player.

Hanging around in the lower reaches of the old Second Division fighting relegation battles left Sunderland what seemed a million miles away from the new-found riches and glamour of the three-year-old Premiership. Reid re-introduced his old Everton midfield partner Paul Bracewell into the Roker ranks for a third spell as a player. Now assistant manager as well, Brace's last game for the club had been as captain in the 1992 FA Cup Final. Since then he had been part of the Keegan revolution on Tyneside and returned to help Sunderland reach the top flight again too.

Before long Reid made another former Magpie the Wearsiders' first £1 million signing when he persuaded David Kelly to return to the North East…before informing vice-chairman John Fickling that he had set up the deal and a big fee would be required. Fickling then had the task of raising the subject with chairman Bob Murray. After the years of struggle the club did not have the cash but to their credit Messrs Fickling and Murray personally backed the deal.

Two years later – after promotion in 1996 followed by immediate relegation – Reidy's Red and Whites would find 90 points were not enough to finish in the top two while 83 points would make them champions this time. Then, as in this campaign, the team would come good with a tremendous run after a slow start. Former Manchester City boss Reid had been given the job

after a 'trial' spell in which only one game in seven was lost as relegation was avoided. In contrast, as the new season got going, only one of the first five League games was won.

Dickie Ord started only the opening two of those, and may not have even been involved had rumoured summer interest from Ipswich Town materialised, but he was restored for the visit of the club he had debuted against almost eight years earlier. Winning that game – despite being reduced to 10 men by the dismissal of Kevin Ball – kicked-off a nine-game unbeaten run.

Ord and Andy Melville soon developed a solid central defensive partnership. 'We are quite alike in that we aren't boisterous, in fact we don't talk to each other a lot on the pitch but we seem to have a good understanding. This is the first time since I was 18 that I've had a settled run in the side as a central defender. People have seen me as a bit of a utility player in the past, but I've always regarded a central defensive role as my best position,' said Dickie at the time.

They were ably supported by reigning Player of the Year Dariusz Kubicki at right-back and the impressive Martin Scott in his first full season at left-back. Sunderland were getting into their stride. With the back four screened by Kevin Ball, and Bracewell asserting his calming influence in the centre of the park, Sunderland were becoming a compact and well-drilled unit basing their game plan on a sound defence in which Ord was an integral part.

In the final analysis Sunderland comfortably won the League although only nine of the division's 24 sides scored fewer goals and even relegated Watford scored more. The defence, though, was as watertight as the ships for which Sunderland had been famous. The side with the second-best defence conceded a dozen more goals than Sunderland's 33 from 46 games, a figure that included a club record 26 clean sheets.

Having been in the familiar territory of 19th after five games, Sunderland hit the top of the table before Christmas in style with a 6–0 thrashing of Millwall, who went into the match top of the tree. Craig Russell had the match of his life that afternoon, scoring four times, but manager Reid pointed out: 'Richard Ord was exceptional.'

At the time Ordy was in top form and had won the November Player of the Month award. It was a good time for Richard to be enjoying his testimonial season and December brought race nights and dinners following on from a successful golf day in late September. Sadly, when his own testimonial match against Steaua Bucharest came around at the start of the following season, Ord had the frustration of being unable to play through injury.

Reaching the summit of the table made Sunderland draw breath. A run of just one win in the next nine League games saw them slip to fifth. That oasis of a victory came courtesy of Richard's only goal of the season, a winner against Grimsby remembered more for the celebration than the strike. 'Everybody remembers it,' says Ord with the same resignation as Bolo Zenden sheepishly recalling his 'Dad dance' when attempting to join in with Asamoah Gyan at Chelsea in 2010. 'It was a dour game and we were struggling a little bit at the time,' Richard recalls. 'Scotty put a cross in which I took down with what wasn't a bad touch on my right and slotted it in with my left. I went berserk after scoring and ran so far and so fast that I couldn't run for about the next 10 minutes.'

The goal celebration illustrated the passion Ord had for the red and white stripes and the lad was in the form of his life. A week earlier he had been Man of the Match in a Cup replay against Man Utd with Ryan Giggs collecting the visitors' award. Eric Cantona played in the game. For all the Frenchman's iconic status with Manchester United fans, he did not overly impress the Red and White Army who came up with a song that went: 'Who needs Cantona when we've got Dickie Ord?' and included the lines, 'The great thing is and it makes us proud, if he wasn't on the pitch he'd be with us in the crowd.' Recorded by a group of fans calling themselves Simply Red and White, it made the lower reaches of the charts.

Richard himself recollects: 'It started off as a bit of a p***take. I first remember hearing it at Watford one cold Tuesday night. At the time I did the odd turn even though I was playing at the back because I was full of confidence. As a Sunderland supporter it was a dream to even have a song sung about me at Roker Park but to have it recorded on to a CD and for there to be T-shirts with it on, and so on was just unbelievable.'

By the time that cold Tuesday night at Vicarage Road arrived the massed ranks of the Red and White Army were in fine voice. The Lads were well and truly on the road into the Premier League for the first time as some of the most dismal years of SAFC's history receded into the memory. Sunderland drew 3–3 at Watford on the night 'The Dickie Ord Song' was aired for the first time. The draw ended a superb run of nine straight victories that had lifted the Lads to the top of the table. The first eight of those wins had seen just one goal conceded.

Programme cover of Richard Ord's testimonial match

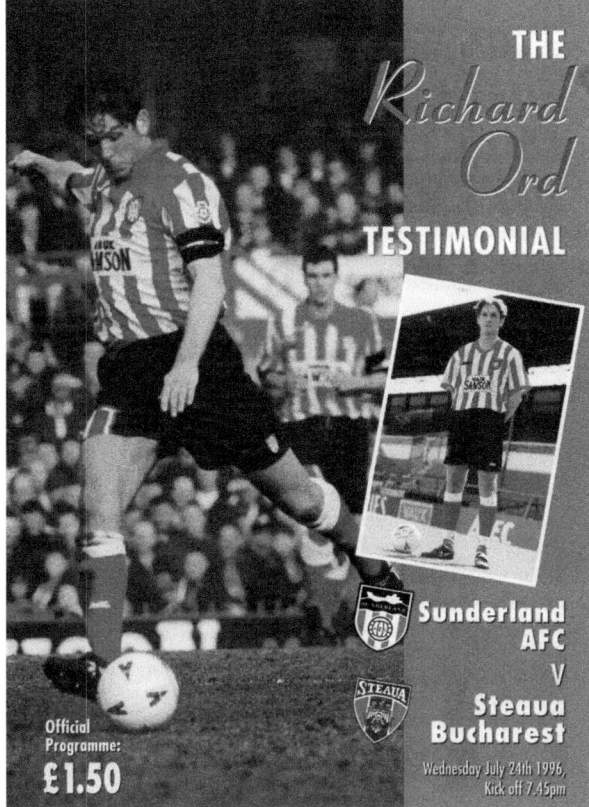

Peter Reid had shown his willingness to take a tough decision by dropping reliable goalkeeper Alec Chamberlain in favour of a teenager brought in on loan from Blackburn. That youngster was Shay Given, who would later spurn Sunderland's attempts to sign him in favour of joining his childhood hero Kenny Dalglish who was manager of Newcastle. At least he won a winners' medal in his 17 games on Wearside. Given would spend almost 12 years on Tyneside but only add losers' medals to the collection started on Wearside during a spell when he also won the first of over 100 caps for the Republic of Ireland.

Given's final game was the next one after the Watford draw as an injury sustained at Barnsley let Chamberlain back into the side. Unperturbed by being left out, Chamberlain returned with five successive clean sheets, not conceding until after promotion was sewn up. Peter Reid was at Darlington watching his brother Shaun's club Bury on the day Sunderland's elevation was secured. Peter Reid had ended his own playing career by turning out for the Shakers the previous season. Eventual runners-up Derby's draw with Birmingham mathematically guaranteed promotion with an emotional Reid declaring, 'I've won a lot in football but this is the highest on the list,' as his brother added: 'He's overjoyed because he loves it at Sunderland. He's always going on about the fans.'

Sunderland still had two games to go and played out a goalless draw at home to West Brom before party time in the final fixture away to Tranmere. The touring Roker Roar added over 10,000 to Rovers' previous home gate against Ipswich to give them easily their largest attendance of the season.

Meanwhile, rivals Newcastle at one stage had been 12 points clear at the top of the Premiership that Sunderland were about to make their bow in. On the day of Richard's son Liam's first birthday and a day after Ord celebrated his own 26th birthday by playing in a 4–0 win at Grimsby on 3 March, the Magpies had lost a crucial home game with title chasers Manchester United. As Sunderland partied at Prenton Park, the Black and Whites still had a chance of winning their first title since the 1920s and ears were glued to radios as the match unfolded at Tranmere. In a surreal moment just as player-manager John Aldridge converted a penalty to make it 2–0 to Tranmere, the enormous travelling support burst into ecstatic cheers.

News had come in of Manchester United wrapping up their game and the Premiership title at Middlesbrough, thereby denying Newcastle. The date was 5 May, 23 years to the day since Sunderland had gloriously won the FA Cup, so as well as now having the old Football League Championship trophy in the North East's only operative trophy cabinet, Sunderland were still the last team from the region to be champions of either League or Cup. Supporters had suffered jibe after jibe in recent years and the journey back from Tranmere was simply a time to sharpen the barbs that were to be sent in the opposite direction at the first and every opportunity.

It had been a great season. In 1992, for all the excitement of the trip to Wembley, the Cup Final had been lost in a very poor year in the League. In 1990 promotion had been won through the back door despite Wembley defeat to Swindon in the Play-off Final. In 1988 the Third Division had been won and enjoyed, but after all it was the Third Division, while in 1985 Wembley had again been a let-down in the League Cup Final and there was relegation to go with it. Consequently you had to go back to 1980 and the promotion-winning match over West Ham to have experienced the joy of 1995–96. Peter Reid had well and truly cheered up everyone and his Player of the Year Richard Ord had enjoyed a magnificent campaign, doubly enjoyable because the player himself was a lifetime Red and White.

Richard Ord at Sunderland
Debut: 3 November 1987: Sunderland 7–0 Southend United
Last game: 10 May 1998: Sheffield United 2–1 Sunderland
Total appearances (all competitions): 249+28 as sub / 7 goals

Season by season
1987–88	5+4 games / 0 goals
1988–89	34+5 games / 2 goals
1989–90	9+1 games / 1 goal
1990–91	12+5 games / 0 goals
1991–92	5+3 games / 0 goals
1992–93	24+3 games / 0 goals
1993–94	30+4 games / 2 goals
1994–95	35 games / 0 goals
1995–96	46+1 games / 0 goals
1996–97	36 games / 2 goals
1997–98	13+2 games / 0 goals

Other clubs
York City (loan) 1990
Queen's Park Rangers 1998–2000
Durham City

1996-97   Lionel Perez

Premiership: 18th out of 20, relegated
FA Cup: Third round, lost to Arsenal in a replay
League Cup: Third round, lost to Tottenham Hotspur
Top scorers: 4 goals, Craig Russell, all League. Paul Stewart, all League. Kevin Ball, 3 League, 1 League Cup. Michael Gray, 3 League, 1 FA Cup
Ever present: Paul Bracewell, 38 out of 38 League plus 3 out of 5 Cup ties
Player of the Year: Lionel Perez
SAFCSA Player of the Year: Kevin Ball

Rather like Belgian Simon Mignolet in 2010–11, Lionel Perez was a goalkeeper brought in from the Continent for a modest fee and expected to provide occasional back-up before being catapulted into the limelight after injury to the accepted number one. In Mignolet's case he won the SAFCSA Young Player of the Year after a terrific season deputising for Britain's costliest 'keeper Craig Gordon. For Perez he became Player of the Year after being thrust into the first team when veteran Tony Coton's career was ended by a leg break at Southampton.

Coton had made his own debut against Sunderland for Birmingham City in December 1980, saving a penalty in the first minute in a game Blues won with the help of goals from two players who would later come to Sunderland: Frank Worthington and Keith Bertschin. Sunderland's trip to the Dell in October 1996 would be Coton's 500th League game and his last. Making his 12th appearance for Sunderland, he shattered his leg in five places meaning that Peter Reid had to turn to Frenchman Perez. Unlike Mignolet, Perez was no untried youngster. Lionel was 29 and had played for many years in his home country and had numbered Zinedine Zidane among his teammates at Bordeaux.

An unconventional figure, Perez had an element of Cantona about him in terms of his flamboyance and his ability to become the darling of the crowd. Having impressed in a trial for the reserves at Gateshead, Perez gifted the visiting Aston Villa reserve side an equaliser when he trod on the ball in the last minute of his first appearance at Roker Park. Sporting long hair and short sleeves, Perez cut a strikingly different figure to any previous Sunderland goalkeeper.

Sunderland had had their fair share of great characters in goal but as the 68th custodian since the club entered the League over a century earlier, Perez was the first from outside the UK or Republic of Ireland, although Scottish cap Willie Fraser and England Under-21 international Iain Hesford had been born in Australia and Kenya respectively.

This was Sunderland's first season in the new Premiership and the last at Roker Park. It was an important campaign and not one for an erratic 'keeper. When Perez came into the team the side were beginning to slide down the table after a promising start. Coming off the back of a 3–0 defeat at the Dell, Perez enamoured himself to everyone with a clean sheet on his home debut as Villa were beaten with no clangers of the sort he had dropped against their second string.

The team of 1996–97 were a battling side. Manager Reid had had little money to invest after transforming a team that almost dropped into the third tier two years earlier into a top-flight side. Having seen two of his major recruits – Niall Quinn and Coton – suffer bad injuries, he coaxed his side every inch of the way as witnessed by the fly-on-the-wall TV series of the season, *Premier Passions*.

Wins were hard to come by but somehow the side, captained by SAFC Supporters' Association Player of the Year Kevin Ball, kept themselves out of the bottom three until the final

month of the campaign. The season brought highs – such as Perez's second clean sheet in a fabulous 3–0 trouncing of Chelsea – and lows, such as the 5–0 hammering at Manchester United the following week. United legend Eric Cantona scored one of his best goals in that game, exquisitely floating the ball over Perez from the edge of the box. It is a goal still frequently shown on TV in 2011 and one Perez had no chance at all with, although he would have known what Cantona was capable of having been teammates with him at Nimes.

Undaunted, Lionel would have simply rolled up his sleeves had they not already been permanently rolled up. Always able to pull off a spectacular save, he managed three clean sheets in the following five games and by the middle of January had played his part in helping newly-promoted Sunderland to a creditable 11th position.

The season, though, would gradually ebb away. Sunderland did not have a bad defence but they and Lionel were put under immense pressure by the team's toothless attack. With a joint top scorer for the year on a meagre four goals and a team that managed less than a goal a game, bad runs could come about too easily, such as the three consecutive 1–0 reverses that came in a run of six games with just one goal scored. Lionel only suffered from backache in a 4–0 home defeat by Spurs when everything went wrong and the side were three down very early, and when they conceded six at Chelsea.

There were good days though such as a home win over eventual champions Manchester United and a good draw at Newcastle in Perez's only derby. The French 'keeper rose to the challenge as Newcastle – the League's leading scorers – tried to get at Sunderland. There, like Christians being thrown to the lions in the year of the away fan ban, Perez excelled. Good early saves from Rob Lee and Les Ferdinand were overshadowed by a terrific save from Lionel's countryman David Ginola. After Michael Gray silenced the home crowd by putting Sunderland ahead, the Magpies had to wait until 13 minutes from time before they managed an equaliser but Perez was to have the last word with another stunning save to thwart Ginola and the Black and Whites and allow Sunderland to leave with their heads held high and a point better off into the bargain. It was one of Lionel's best matches of the season.

A fortnight later there would be a clean sheet for Lionel in another local derby as Sunderland won at Boro and he would keep his seventh shut-out when Everton came to Wearside for the final League match in Roker Park's 99-year history. Consequently the claim to have scored the last visitors' goal at the ground went to Southampton's Egil Ostenstad – the player involved when Tony Coton broke his leg.

Cruelly, Sunderland were relegated with 40 points after losing to Wimbledon on the last day of the season. Eight teams conceded more goals including sixth-placed Chelsea. The team had given it everything and Perez had let no one down having been called into action.

The thing about Perez though is you never knew what you would get with him. On one occasion after helping Sunderland to a draw in the Cup at Arsenal, the Gunners' manager Arsene Wenger was fulsome in his praise of his fellow Frenchman – who was then found having a crafty smoke behind a hot dog van outside the Highbury players' entrance. Later the same month Peter Reid extolled Lionel's virtues in a press conference after a brilliant display by the goalie helped earn a point at Leicester only for the manager to have a real *Premier Passions* pop at Perez when he found the 'keeper had missed the coach home. Reid was in his car and cancelled his plans to head to Merseyside in order to drive Perez all the way back to the North East, no doubt giving the Frenchman the non-stop 'hairdryer' treatment.

Having sported piratical long hair in his first season at Sunderland, Perez returned from his summer in France with a much shorter peroxide blond look. He looked completely different but was as eccentric as ever. The problem with Lionel as a goalkeeper was that his defenders did not know what he was going to do. Having an unpredictable striker like Asamoah Gyan can be a bonus because if his teammates do not know what he is going to do then neither can the opposition. With a goalkeeper, though, teammates need to be on the same wavelength. Complaints from the defenders of the time were that sometimes they would attack a ball coming into the box only to find the fearless Frenchman flying through the air to deal with it while the next time a cross came in they would look for the goalie coming to take it only to find him rooted to his line.

Perez's hot and cold moments were illustrated dramatically at the end of his second and last season at Sunderland, the first at the Stadium of Light. On what proved to be his final appearance at the new ground Perez produced the best save yet seen at the Stadium of Light, including Craig Gordon's Premier League save of the 2010–11 season from Bolton's Zat Knight. Lionel's moment came in a Play-off semi-final with Sheffield United. With a thrilling game in the balance he came up with a double save to rival Jimmy Montgomery's at Wembley a quarter of a century earlier. Firstly Lionel did superbly to stop a screamer from Paul Devlin – the man whose double blast had almost relegated Sunderland at Notts County in 1993 – but if that save was special the next one was even better as Perez somehow also stopped the follow-up shot from Dean Saunders.

The save sent Sunderland to Wembley, where with five minutes to go and Sunderland leading, he came rushing off his line for a ball that was never his, got nowhere near it and conceded a soft goal with Charlton eventually winning on penalties. It was a sad way for a player who gave so much to the club to be remembered. Perez, though, made so many friends among the supporters at Sunderland that it is the good times which they prefer to recall.

A goalkeeper needs the crowd on his side at Sunderland and Lionel certainly had that, summing up his relationship thus: 'I had a very good rapport with the public in France but not like I have had at Sunderland with 42,000 people. It was something very emotional and very special. I play with my heart, I give everything and people know and feel that. People in Sunderland are very proud and I am very proud as well.'

Lionel Perez did well for Sunderland. He could occasionally lose games as well as win them for the team but he had what people want to see in a Sunderland shirt – passion – and for that he can be proud to this day of his contribution at SAFC.

Lionel Perez at Sunderland
Debut: 19 October 1996: Southampton 3–0 Sunderland (sub)
Last game: 25 May 1998: Charlton 4–4 Sunderland (after extra-time – Charlton won 7–6 on penalties)
Total appearances (all competitions): 83+1 as sub

Season by season
1996–97   31+1 games
1997–98   52 games

Other clubs
Girondins de Bordeaux 1993–96
Nimes Olympique (loan) 1994–95
Stade Lavallois (loan) 1995–96
Newcastle United 1998–2000
Scunthorpe United (loan) 1999
Cambridge United 2000–02
Enfield 2002–03
Stevenage 2003–04 (coach from 2004–06)

Division One: Third out of 24, lost Play-off Final on penalties
FA Cup: Fourth round, lost to Tranmere Rovers
League Cup: Third round, lost to Middlesbrough
Top scorer: Kevin Phillips, 35 goals, 29 League, 2 Play-offs, 4 FA Cup
New post-World War Two record
Ever presents: Lionel Perez and Lee Clark, 46 out of 46 games in Division One. Perez and
Clark each played 6 of 8 knockout games
Player of the Year: Kevin Phillips
SAFCSA Player of the Year: Kevin Phillips

The first year at the Stadium of Light saw Sunderland re-energised despite relegation. The biggest and best football ground built in the country in the second half of the twentieth century did not have a seat spare for the opening game against Ajax and when Manchester City rolled up on a Friday night for the first competitive match the crowd of just under 39,000 was some 16,000 higher than the final capacity of a dilapidated Roker Park.

Making a scoring debut at the stadium's inaugural League game was a diminutive striker by the name of Kevin Phillips. He scored and simply did not stop. Phillips went on to become Sunderland's record post-World War Two scorer, his 130 goals in six years being 27 more than anyone else has managed since the pre-war days of Bobby Gurney and Raich Carter.

'Moving to the new stadium was a big move and to fill it in the way we did when we weren't even in the top flight showed what a big club Sunderland is,' said Phillips in 2011. 'The atmosphere was magnificent and to play in front of those supporters was a privilege because for me there are no better supporters in the country and I'm proud to have been their Player of the Year.'

If people thought the red and white goal machine was the best thing since sliced bread it was closer to the truth than they might have imagined. Earlier in the 1990s Phillips had been working for Mother's Pride while it would be a man named Allinson who would use his loaf and set Phillips on the path to success after Kevin's childhood dreams of being a footballer had been shattered by his release from Southampton with whom he had been associated for six years.

Drifting into non-League football, Kevin claimed his first Player of the Year award in 1991–92. As Sunderland were competing in that year's FA Cup Final at Wembley, Phillips was triumphing in the Herts Charity Cup with Baldock Town – for whom he had spent the season at right-back. It was Baldock's manager, the ex-Arsenal striker Ian Allinson, who thought that Kevin was worth trying as a striker.

Born in Hitchin, Phillips quickly became a hotshot as a striker and soon attracted the interest of Watford. It was 21 February 1995 when the Hornets gave Kevin his League debut at Vicarage Road – against Sunderland.

Back in 1981 then Sunderland manager Alan Durban had given a debut to a young striker who would become Rangers' all-time record scorer after not being persisted with on Wearside – Ally McCoist. In 1997 Durban was back at Sunderland as chief scout and turned the clock back to find another gem. Scoring his first goal in a pre-season friendly at Macclesfield the day after he turned 24, Phillips was forced to miss the opening day of the season at Sheffield United due to a suspension carried over from his Watford days but wasted no time in making a big impression. In his first five games Phillips scored as many goals as the club's top scorer had

managed in all of the previous season! The 'Hitchin Hotshot' scored in four of those five games and hit the post in the other.

Briefly dropping out of the side due to a problem with his abductor muscle gave people the chance to ponder whether this new lad's spectacular start was a flash in the pan or whether he was the real deal. His early strikes had indicated a poacher's instinct and while he was only 5ft 7in and possessed the low centre of gravity that went with it he had already notched one of his goals with a clinically-despatched glancing header.

There was room for the doubters to hold sway when Phillips failed to hit the back of the net in any of his first six games after returning as the team slipped to 11th. However, none of those half a dozen appearances had seen Kevin partnered with Niall Quinn. The Irish target man had been Sunderland's record signing when bought a year earlier but he had suffered horribly through injury and had not scored in over a year – not since his first start against the side who were the Lads' next opponents – Nottingham Forest. Quinn was even on the receiving end of a few boos when he came on as sub but this was the match that was to prove a turning point in Sunderland's history.

Phillips duly scored against Forest, Niall netted a week later in a big away win, Phillips pounced in the next two games, Quinn the one after and Phillips in the next six. In fact, from Forest's visit on 8 November it would be late January before Sunderland played a match in which neither 'Superkev' nor 'the Mighty Quinn' scored.

Sunderland had not enjoyed a strike partnership so in tune with each other since the 'G-Force' days of Gates and Gabbiadini that had come together almost exactly a decade earlier. That duo had powered the Lads into the top flight and the hope was the new partnership would do the same. 'It's superb! I feel I've settled in really well. The whole environment is pure class: the stadium, the supporters and the whole set-up is absolutely brilliant,' commented Kevin at the time, adding: 'I am enjoying it and I know Niall is enjoying his football again. The lads are all enjoying it and this is possibly as happy as I have been throughout my career. I am at a big club with a good manager, good coaching staff and good players.'

When the FA Cup came around Superkev slotted in four goals at Rotherham, Quinn grabbing the other as the Lads went nap. Elimination came in the fourth round but with the Lads on the march in the chase for promotion that was no bad thing. The disappointing start had given the front runners a head start – so much so that a 16-match unbeaten run had only taken Peter Reid's side to fourth.

Despite not being top of the table, Sunderland had a good claim to be the best team in the League. With Lee Clark contributing regular goals from midfield and Allan 'Magic' Johnston on the wing becoming the fourth member of the side to hit double figures for the season in the goals tally, Sunderland became the division's top scorers and outclassed table-toppers Forest on their own turf. A 3–0 win at the beginning of March with Phillips completing the scoring was a comprehensive victory over the Nottingham outfit who themselves had beaten second-placed Middlesbrough 4–0 three days earlier.

The following Saturday, with Superkev scoring again, it was Quinn's turn to become the third player in as many months to take home the match ball. Johnston had done the trick at Huddersfield and the Hatters of Stockport were the victims as Quinn scored the Stadium of Light's first hat-trick. The result took Sunderland into the automatic promotion places for the first time.

Back-to-back draws made it a temporary trip into the top two, the second of them being the second draw of the season against Charlton Athletic where Sunderland could not hold out after Phillips gave them the lead. Failure to finish off Charlton would come back to haunt the Black Cats.

Nonetheless, five wins and two draws from the next seven games – during which Superkev scored six more goals – had Sunderland second with two to play. Both were away from home at Play-off-chasing Ipswich and 1990 Play-off Final opponents Swindon.

Most Sunderland supporters are probably unaware of the importance to Sunderland of Manchester City's left-back in the first ever League game at the Stadium of Light. Tony Vaughan moved from Ipswich to his home city of Manchester in the summer and had it not been for that move Kevin Phillips would have almost certainly never played for the Lads.

Former Sunderland player George Burley was Ipswich's manager at the time and explains that Phillips, '...came into my office and we agreed everything about his contract. He was

Kevin Phillips in action in 1997–98.

dedicated to come but at the time we were waiting for money from a tribunal for Tony Vaughan and the club was not to go to a tribunal at the same time.'

Phillips concurs: 'I was all set to sign for Ipswich in the summer but the clubs couldn't agree a fee. I've got family and friends in the Norwich area and the move would have suited me. But I'm pleased now it didn't happen.'

As they watched Phillips rattle in the goals in the North East rather than East Anglia, Ipswich must have winced every time they saw Superkev score but they exacted some revenge. Inflicting Sunderland's first defeat in 13 games, despite Lionel Perez saving a penalty, allowed Middlesbrough to leapfrog the Wearsiders with a draw against Wolves 24 hours later.

A week before the Ipswich defeat Phillips had made his international bow for England at B level but there were now doubts as to whether the star striker and Sunderland were going to be able to test themselves against the best the following year.

Phillips did all he could with a brace – one the most spectacular of hooked overhead volleys – as Swindon were beaten. However with Boro beating Oxford on the same afternoon, Sunderland were destined to finish third despite having 90 points – seven more than had won them the title just two years, but what seemed like a world away, earlier.

The Play-offs paired Sunderland with Sheffield United. The Blades had beaten Sunderland at Bramall Lane on the opening day and would do so again in the first leg by a 2–1 margin. Their visit to Wearside in January had been the best game of the season beyond a shadow of a doubt. A pulsating game that left no one in any doubt that the famous Roker Roar had successfully made the transition to the new stadium had seen two goals from Phillips help secure a thrilling 4–2 win. Sunderland would need to win by two goals again.

In becoming the first side to visit the Stadium of Light twice, Sheffield United's second trip proved to be as exciting as their first. Phillips made it 2–0 and therefore 3–2 on aggregate before half-time after Nicky Marker had deflected an Allan Johnston shot past his own 'keeper. However, it was Sunderland's goalie Perez who would be the hero with one of the all-time great double saves to protect the lead.

And so to Wembley. The Play-off Final with Charlton saw Sunderland score 10 goals and still lose – no wonder the game is looked on as one of the national stadium's greatest ever matches. A four-all draw ended up with the Londoners winning 7–6 on penalties after each side scored their first six spot kicks. Sadly, Phillips was not on the pitch to take a penalty.

Trailing 1–0 at half-time, Sunderland led within fifteen minutes of the restart, Quinn having levelled and Phillips having put Sunderland ahead. It was Superkev's 35th goal of the season, taking him past Brian Clough's post-war record set in 1961–62. Phillips, though, was carrying an injury and had to go off, being replaced by striker Danny Dichio, who missed a good chance and did not take a penalty.

Denied promotion in cruel circumstances, Sunderland would smash records galore in storming to the title 12 months later with Phillips scoring 25 goals despite missing four months through injury! 'The way Kevin scores goals is priceless – you can't buy that off the street. You have to be born with it and coached into it,' said Niall Quinn of his strike partner. 'He has it and what I like about him is he is hungry for more. He is almost greedy which is a great way to be when you are a striker.'

Kevin Phillips' first season at Sunderland ended in Wembley disappointment but he had set down a marker that Sunderland had one of the greatest goalscorers in the club's history in their midst, and there was more to come.

Speaking in 2011, eight years after he pulled on a Sunderland shirt for the last time, Superkev summed up his thoughts on being SAFC Player of the Year.

'At whatever club you play for, to pick up a Player of the Year award voted for by supporters means a hell of a lot. They watch you week in, week out so for them to believe you have been the Player of the Season is an achievement which is right up there with whatever awards you win in your career.'

Kevin Phillips at Sunderland
Debut: 15 August 1997: Sunderland 3–1 Manchester City (scored)
Last game: 11 May 2003: Sunderland 0–4 Arsenal
Total appearances (all competitions): 233+2 as sub / 130 goals

Season by season
1997–98 47+1 games / 35 goals
1998–99 32 games / 25 goals
1999–2000 38 games / 30 goals
2000–01 41+1 games / 18 goals
2001–02 39 games / 13 goals
2002–03 36 games / 9 goals

Other clubs
Southampton 1987–91
Baldock Town 1991–94
Watford 1994–97
Southampton 2003–05
Aston Villa 2005–06
West Bromwich Albion 2006–08
Birmingham City 2008–11
Blackpool 2011–

Division One: First out of 24. Promoted with record 105 points tally
FA Cup: Fourth round, lost to Blackburn Rovers
League Cup: Semi-finalists, lost to Leicester City over two legs
Top scorer: Kevin Phillips, 25 goals, 23 League (in 26 games), 2 League Cup
Ever present: No one
Player of the Year: Niall Quinn
SAFCSA Player of the Year: Niall Quinn

Too many seasons covered in this book were disappointing years for the club and its supporters, sometimes the efforts of the Player of the Year being one of the few things that sustained faith in the thin times. 1998–99 was the kind of season that makes up for the worst of times.

The previous season had been one that ultimately was of glorious failure akin to 1976–77. Ninety points had not been enough for automatic promotion and the Lads had lost one of Wembley's classic matches on penalties in the Play-off Final. That disappointment would have seen teams of lesser men fade away but Sunderland, with immense characters like Niall Quinn, Kevin Ball, Bobby Saxton and Peter Reid had famously used the experience to galvanise themselves to come out fighting the following season.

That is exactly what they did. Sunderland had a good side that in 1998–99 became a great one. They had been better than Nottingham Forest and Middlesbrough who had gone up automatically the previous season. The problem then was they had given them a head start in the aftermath of Sunderland's own relegation. A home draw with Forest in November had seen the Wearsiders left in 12th place on a day when Niall Quinn was booed. Coming on as a sub after missing 13 games with injury, the record signing who had not reached double figures in games played in his first season up to that point had managed just one goal at home in his Sunderland career. The Mighty Quinn had returned to the starting line up the following week, however, scored the first goal in a 4–1 away win and ever since then had been truly magnificent.

With Quinn and Phillips up front, Sunderland had been the League's top scorers in the previous season and they would be again as they romped to the title, setting a new national record of 105 points. The difference was, whereas in 1997–98 they had conceded a half century of League goals, in the 105-point campaign a mere 28 were leaked in 46 League games and a club record 29 clean sheets clocked up. All but one of those were made by new goalie Thomas Sorensen, who marked his debut with an opening-day shut-out as QPR were beaten by a Phillips penalty. Even playmaker Lee Clark being stretchered off with a broken leg would not stop Sunderland.

'We had a great team spirit and they were good times,' says Niall, now of course as charismatic as Sunderland chairman as he was when leading the line as centre-forward. 'Whenever I meet any of that group of people now, we all say it was the highlight of our careers really. I'd been at big clubs in Arsenal and Man City but the enjoyment we got as a group at Sunderland was second to none I've ever experienced at any club.'

Quinn himself managed only the first two games before being ruled out for a month with injury but nine goals in the next two games set the tone and by the time Niall returned as a sub in a 7–0 win over Oxford, the Lads were sitting pretty at the top of the League. It was a position they would never relinquish despite the fact that Super Kevin Phillips was by now also out injured and would miss four months.

Returning to the starting line up, Niall notched as a point was taken at Norwich. After a goalless home draw with eventual runners-up Bradford City, the Wearsiders showed how strong their resolve was to make up for their Play-off near miss by battling back from 2–0 down at half-time away to West Brom to win 3–2. Soon they would embark on a run of five consecutive victories that left the rest of the division disappearing into their wake. Quinn spearheaded this run by scoring in six successive League games. The last of those saw Niall and an effervescent Michael Bridges each score twice in a 4–0 win over Sheffield United at Bramall Lane. It was a

Niall Quinn in action against Coventry City.

match that saw the Blades player-manager decide to hang up his boots after a career which featured 737 League games. Later appointed by Niall as Sunderland manager, the centre-back who Niall and young Bridges tortured that afternoon was none other than Steve Bruce.

In the midst of this scintillating League form, Peter Reid's side were progressing in the League Cup. An away win on penalties over Premier League Everton propelled Sunderland into the quarter-finals, where Luton were convincingly beaten.

As people took stock at Christmas, Sunderland were eight points clear of second-placed Ipswich and 13 ahead of the teams chasing an automatic promotion place. There was also the club's first Cup semi-final to look forward to since 1992. Quinn would score in that with a peach of a header as Sunderland unluckily were beaten over two legs by top-flight Leicester after a spirited fightback.

Boxing Day brought only the second defeat of the season in any competition, at Tranmere, but normal service would be resumed two days later with a routine home win over Crewe. There would only be one more League defeat to come in the second half of a season that saw fewer defeats than any other since the club entered the League in 1890.

As if things were not daunting enough for the rest of the division, the man who fed most off Niall Quinn – Kevin Phillips, who had broken SAFC's post-war scoring record the season before – returned in the next League game at QPR. Superkev marked his return with a stunning volley, with Niall also scoring, as another point was added to the tally as Sunderland simply went from strength to strength, Quinn hitting another purple patch with five goals in four games.

The 105-point team was a fabulously entertaining side. Very few Sunderland fans can reel off all of the regular line up of the promotion teams of 1976, 1980, 1988, 1990, 1996, 2005 or 2007 but the 1999 team, along with the 1973 Cup winners and the very first promotion winners of 1964, can be recited without hesitation by many a fan of the right age. The class of '99 were exceptional and for all the talent in the team centre-forward Niall Quinn was as much the kingpin as centre-half Charlie Hurley had been 35 years earlier, a couple of years before Quinn was born.

Putting gender to one side, Niall was more queen than king – and that had nothing to do with his disco pants. Quinn was like a queen bee that Peter Reid's willing workers buzzed around. Phillips was always on the move, looking to benefit from Niall's contribution as the focal point of the attack. Classic wingers Allan 'Magic' Johnston and Nicky Summerbee – one all jinky tricks, the other simply a stand and deliver winger – based their entire game on finding Niall. Each wide man had an almost telepathic understanding with their marauding full-backs Chris Makin and Mickey Gray. In the centre of midfield, Kevin Ball proved there was more than one 'Superkev' at Sunderland and along with Lee Clark supplied a constant stream of possession to the wide men. Both Ball and Clark missed chunks of the season through injury but whenever Alex Rae played he slotted in brilliantly. Meanwhile, at the heart of defence Paul Butler had a dominant first season alongside Wales cap Andy Melville with the versatile Darren Williams always ready to plug a gap. Given the absences through injury at times of Quinn and especially Phillips the contribution of back-up strikers Danny Dichio and Michael Bridges can be measured by the fact that both reached double figures for the season in the goals tally. With a strong squad that saw Martin Scott and newcomer Gavin McCann play a part it was a fine team that scored over 100 goals in all competitions.

What is noticeable about the really great teams is that no matter how good the star man, that man knows the value of his colleagues. Brazil in 1970 were more than Pelé, Liverpool in the 70s and 80s were more than Dalglish and the Barcelona who made Manchester United chase shadows at Wembley in 2011 were more than Messi. While Sunderland's promotion side of 1999 are not being claimed to be in that bracket, the point remains that in a team game the team is only as good as its weakest part and you could not find a weak link in a team that gained 105 points.

Niall takes exactly that view. Modest as ever, he shares the accolade of being Player of the Year when asked about winning the award: 'Straight away you think, "If it wasn't for Nicky Summerbee and Allan Johnston putting the ball in I wouldn't even be at the do, I'd probably have been dropped long ago." I know of course there was Kevin Phillips making the most of everything I managed to send his way and then you had Lee Clark and Bally, the great wing partnership of Chris Makin and Mickey Gray dovetailing immaculately with Summerbee and Johnston, two committed centre-backs in Paul Butler and Andy Melville and then Tommy Sorensen as a last line of defence. You have to realise how important it is to work as a team. It was a nice accolade for me as an individual but everybody knew the way the team had gelled together was so good that for anybody to go off boasting and think they were better than anyone else just wouldn't be true. Everybody knows that if you win an individual award in a team game that your teammates have had a lot to do with it.'

With Quinn and Phillips in tandem for the rest of the season after being reunited at QPR, Sunderland steamrollered the division. Of the 19 games left after the QPR fixture 15 were won with just one lost and one of the three draws came when both the regular front pair were absent. The Lads finished a massive 18 points ahead of runners-up Bradford.

Quinn's ability to behave like a comic book hero came to the fore in the away match at the second-best team in the division. Having put Sunderland in front with what proved to be the only goal of the game, Niall was later required to go in goal following an injury to Sorensen. Clad in blue, he ensured a clean sheet with a display as full of confidence as if he was up front.

Promotion, which would bring Premier League football to the Stadium of Light for the first time, was mathematically guaranteed with four games to spare. A five-goal romp away to eventually relegated Bury saw Quinn get one and Superkev rattle in four. Under the stands at ramshackle Gigg Lane that night Quinn literally kicked the Nationwide League signs out of the away dressing room in delight at not being part of that League any more. 'I had to write to the League and apologise for my exuberance,' he admitted years later.

As he showed in years to come when he returned to the club he grew to love at a low point in its history and took over as chairman (and briefly as manager including a horrible Cup defeat back at Bury), Niall never did anything by half. In 1998–99, just as he had scored twice on his full debut in Sunderland's first ever Premiership win, just as he'd claimed both the first goal and the first hat-trick at the Stadium of Light and become the first Sunderland player to score twice in a game at Wembley, so Niall had to have the final word. On a glorious afternoon at the

Niall Quinn with Mick Horswill and Duncan McKenzie.

Stadium of Light, when Republica had turned up to perform the Red and White 'Ready to Go' anthem, it was Niall who scored the winner as a half-time deficit against Birmingham was overturned and 105 points clocked up.

'There was a lot of hard work with a sprinkling of fun but above all else there was a feeling of unity,' says Niall of the season in which he was Player of the Year. Since becoming chairman in 2006 the Mighty Quinn has applied the same philosophy. It was a man from the Republic of Ireland who became Sunderland's first Player of the Century in the centenary year of 1979 in Cork-born Charlie Hurley. Come 2079, if anyone has a stronger claim to be the man of Sunderland's second century than Dubliner Niall then a stunning story of service to Sunderland is to be written in the years to come.

Niall Quinn at Sunderland
Debut: 17 August 1996: Sunderland 0–0 Leicester City (Sub)
Last game: 19 October 2002: Sunderland 0–1 West Ham United
Total appearances (all competitions): 183+37 as sub / 69 goals

Season by season
1996–97	9+4 games / 3 goals	
1997–98	37+2 games / 17 goals	
1998–99	42+4 games / 21 goals	
1999–2000	36+2 games / 14 goals	
2000–01	34+3 games / 8 goals	
2001–02	25+14 games / 6 goals	
2002–03	0+8 games / 0 goals	

Other clubs
Arsenal 1983–90
Manchester City 1990–96

Premiership: Seventh out of 20
FA Cup: Fourth round, lost to Tranmere Rovers
League Cup: Third round, lost to Wimbledon
Top scorer: Kevin Phillips, 30 goals, all League
Golden Shoe winner as Europe's top scorer
Ever present: No one
Player of the Year: Kevin Phillips
SAFCSA Player of the Year: Kevin Phillips

Since the introduction of a Player of the Year award in 1976–77, 1999–2000 is arguably the best season Sunderland have had to date. The seasons before and after run it close but not least because of the prowess of Kevin Phillips as Player of the Year. This first campaign in the Premiership since the opening of the Stadium of Light edges the previous wonderful 105-point season because in the final analysis that great campaign was not at the top level. Perhaps achieving seventh place again in the often difficult 'second season' could eclipse 1999–2000's seventh position but as one point less was managed and the Lads were four points behind sixth place as compared to level on points a year earlier, the case for 1999–2000 is strong.

Moreover, the achievement of Superkev in winning the Adidas Golden Shoe as Europe's top scorer, winning the Carling Premiership Player of the Year award and being runner-up (to future Sunderland manager Roy Keane) in both the PFA Player of the Year and Football Writers' Association award was simply magnificent. Only Player of the Century Charlie Hurley had done as well as the only previous Sunderland player to ever be runner-up as FWA Player of the Year, in the King's case as second to FA Cup-winning captain and future England World Cup-winning skipper Bobby Moore.

Most importantly of all, with Sunderland now installed in their much praised, state-of-the-art new home, the club burst into the top flight and proved that Wearside had a team to match its surroundings, a team that could hold its own with the best and a team that could make the entire nation believe what Sunderland supporters had never doubted – that the Lads had not just been a sleeping giant but that they were one of the biggest giants of all.

For Phillips, born in the year Sunderland last won a major trophy, Sunderland's success at the turn of the Millennium went hand in hand with the pinnacle of his own career: 'Sunderland supporters were fantastic to me for the six years I was at the club and I can't thank them enough. It was a golden period in my career and I was lucky enough to be there in what was a golden period in the club's history too. To finish seventh two seasons running as we did made it a great time to be at Sunderland.'

Following a promotion that smashed record after record, the Red and White Army could not wait to unleash their 105-point side on the top flight. It was an eventful summer with more change than anyone could have envisaged. Midfield dynamo Lee Clark was sold to Fulham for a club record £3 million 11 days after being pictured in two Sunday newspapers wearing a T-shirt bearing a derogatory message about Sunderland supporters while out with mates from his home of Newcastle at the FA Cup Final where the Tynesiders were well beaten. There was no coming back from that and Clark followed veteran centre-back Andy Melville in signing for Paul Bracewell at Craven Cottage.

The fee Sunderland received for Clark was only a record for 16 days until Michael Bridges was sold to Leeds for a reported £5 million. Young striker Bridges was a rare talent but had not been able to command a place when Phillips was fit. Along with winger Allan Johnston, Bridges had refused to sign a new contract and with the pair entering the final year of their existing deals in these new days of 'Bosman' moves, Peter Reid took the decision that they were not mentally fully committed to the club and decided they would not play. In addition the scorer of Roker Park's final goal, John Mullin, former SAFCSA Player of the Year Martin Smith and one-time record signing Martin Scott were all released.

Coming through the 'in door' were Steve Bould, Stefan Schwarz, Thomas Helmer, Carsten Fredgaard, John Oster and soon Eric Roy. Veteran Bould was a colossus in helping Sunderland establish themselves although injury restricted him to half a season. Schwarz, a record signing at £4 million from Valencia, proved to be a top-class midfielder who ensured Clark was quickly forgotten and when Roy arrived he would only start half the League games but would prove to be at the heart of several outstanding performances.

One thing about former Sunderland man Brian Clough when he became one of the all-time great managers was that when he realised he made a mistake he did not keep digging in order to make the hole he had got himself into bigger: he just got rid of a player he realised was a mistake to sign. Reid took a leaf out of Cloughie's book when it came to Fredgaard and Helmer and although Oster never convinced and got a few games off the bench he never started a Premiership game in his first year.

Completing a summer of change that brought a new club sponsor in car dealer Reg Vardy, coach Adrian Heath left to become manager of Sheffield United while Peter Reid himself had a new job. In addition to managing Sunderland, Reidy accepted a post as coach to the England Under-21 team, where he would work closely with the FA technical director Howard Wilkinson – the man who would eventually replace him at Sunderland.

Regardless of the summer merry-go-round the first game at Chelsea was relished but Sunderland were brought down to Earth with a mighty bump. With Gianfranco Zola and Gus Poyet in irresistible form, Sunderland were very lucky to only lose 4–0 as the Cockney crowd taunted the visitors with choruses of 'Welcome to the Premiership.' Eight of the starting line up at Stamford Bridge had started the final game of the previous season; Clark, Melville and Johnston had been replaced by Bould, Alex Rae and youngster Chris Lumsdon. The latter, like sub Fredgaard, found it his only League game of the season.

Sunderland had just three days to get over the shock. The club had put a ceiling on 36,000 season tickets to enable some match-to-match sales and an expectant crowd were ready for the first top-flight game at the Stadium of Light. Opponents Watford were Phillips' old club who had been promoted via the Play-offs. Superkev got both goals in a 2–0 win, a penalty and a superb curling long-range shot. It was the kind of goal that had become his trademark. 'I'd been practising that a lot in training,' he explained. 'When I got the ball I knew I was just going to have a go. I struck it well and then thought it was going to be one of those that hits the bar and comes out.'

The three points won against Watford were gratefully put on the board but following the hammering at Chelsea the prospect of a visit from Arsenal was daunting and Reid shut up shop, changing from the 4–4–2 that had seen Sunderland score 101 goals in the 47 League games played at home since the Stadium of Light opened. Leaving Quinn on the bench, Phillips was suddenly asked to play up front on his own and it was the same at Leeds a week later. 'I won't be getting many tap-ins this season, that's for sure, so I've got to try and make things happen out of nothing,' said Kevin after Sunderland took a point from a goalless home draw and lost by the odd goal in three at Elland Road where Phillips notched a spot kick.

In between the two games Kevin had launched his autobiography *Second Time Around*, written in conjunction with an old schoolfriend who was now features editor at *Shoot* magazine, but the best chapter was about to be written. After four games, Sunderland had four points and Phillips had scored all three of their goals. Three of the points had come from a home game against the side that had come up through the Play-offs, though, and only one of the goals had not been a penalty.

Sunderland's last three seasons in the top flight had all ended in relegation and they were already in the bottom five. Next up was a trip to local rivals Newcastle United. Throughout the mid to late 1990s the Magpies had managed to win precisely nothing, although they had become media darlings while their fans had constantly dished out endless stick to Sunderland supporters during the bleak years on Wearside. Derby games in the North East have a special intensity. It is not like the Manchester, Merseyside, London, Birmingham, Sheffield, Nottingham or Bristol showdowns – it is a fixture between two rival cities 10 miles apart. What is more, it is a match between two cities that have been rivals for centuries going back to the civil war and despite attempts to join them by the creation of the county of Tyne and Wear, to most it is still the contest between the counties of County Durham and Northumberland.

For a match of such magnitude a rainstorm of biblical proportions engulfed St James' Park. With building work underway, large sections of the ground had no cover, including the directors' box. With Quinn restored to the starting line up the visitors had the better of the early exchanges, Phillips hitting the target with a scissors kick but it was Newcastle who led at half-time through a 28th-minute Kieron Dyer goal created by Paul Robinson, the man keeping home favourite Alan Shearer on the bench.

Sunderland have a history of many great victories on Tyneside turf and this match was about to join the list. Warnings were posted and ignored. Soon after the restart Phillips was only stopped by a last-ditch tackle after latching on to a Quinn flick-on. Before long Quinn headed the equaliser with a perfect glancing effort from a Nick Summerbee free-kick. Newcastle tried to stem the red and white tide coming towards them by bringing on Shearer but by now Sunderland were dominant. This was the 105-point team announcing their arrival. They had had a look at the Premiership, they had responded to the opening-day lesson and now they were handing one out themselves.

Kevin Phillips scored 130 goals for Sunderland: many were important and many spectacular. The one he scored on this night of nights is one Sunderland supporters who saw it will relive until their dying day. Seventy-four minutes had gone when expert provider Summerbee found Phillips with a raking pass. Goalkeeper Wright made a fine save but Superkev was not done. Racing on to the loose ball, he turned and floated a shot that seemed to move in slow motion as it tantalisingly arced over the goalie and into the net. In the second or two it took for the ball to leave Phillips' foot and shake the raindrops off the St James' net the sands in North East football shifted. The Magpies had crowed long enough, now it was the Black Cats' turn to be top dogs once again and Kevin Phillips had added his name indelibly to the pantheon of Wearside heroes.

Only 800 Sunderland supporters had been allowed tickets and they were going mental, as were the 16,000 watching a beam-back at the Stadium of Light and the thousands listening on the radio. As the *Sunderland Echo* headline said: 'Stuffed 'em!'

Derby glory had come in the fifth game of the season. By the time five more were played Sunderland were second in the table. In the meantime Phillips had claimed a hat-trick as Sunderland won 5–0 away from home in the top flight for the first time in over half a century.

Sunderland did not have a game the following Saturday but Kevin Phillips and the Stadium of Light did as England played Belgium. 'Playing for England at the Stadium of Light has to be one of the proudest moments of my career,' said Kevin. 'I enjoyed the occasion, which was one

Scoring the first of three at Pride Park.

of the best days of my life. My mum came up for the game [his father Ray had died four years earlier], my wife Julie and baby daughter were there and the reception I received from our supporters was brilliant. It felt a bit weird actually, running out in an England shirt when it felt like a home game with all the noise.'

Subbed by Michael Owen in the 57th minute, Phillips nonetheless walked off with two Man of the Match awards as England won 2–1 in their first international on Wearside since 1950.

Resuming club service with both goals as Aston Villa left empty-handed, Superkev was proving a national sensation. Two goals against Southampton – the club that rejected him as a youngster when former Sunderland assistant manager Dave Merrington coached a youth team that had Phillips at right-back – meant that with 19 goals in 18 games Superkev had scored more before Christmas than anyone else in the country had managed in a full season for the last three years!

Had it not been for seeing a penalty saved by sub 'keeper Neil Moss, Kevin could have had a hat-trick against the Saints. It was his second spot kick miss of the season, the first at Boro having been scored on the rebound by youngster Michael Reddy.

Phillips gave the rest of the country's strikers a chance to catch up in the scoring stakes by missing the two games over Christmas but he had already given supporters an early Christmas box. The beginning of December had seen the reverse of the opening-day fixtures when pre-match chants of '4–0' from visiting Chelsea fans were silenced as Sunderland raced into a 4–0 lead against the men from Stamford Bridge. The match was the peak of the Peter Reid and Superkev years. One up in 44 seconds, it was four with still seven minutes to go before half-time, both Quinn and Phillips netting twice as they terrorised Chelsea. Niall was unplayable and Kevin was unstoppable, the first of his two goals being a 30-yarder that featured every week for a year in the title sequence of the weekly ITV highlights show that at the time was keeping *Match of the Day* off TV screens.

Sunderland certainly missed Superkev as they were hammered 5–0 at Everton without him. With Kevin the Lads might have beaten Manchester United rather than drawing a great game two-all but the season had taken an enormous turn for the worse. Having returned to make his 100th appearance in the first game of the new millennium in a defeat away to Wimbledon where only the crossbar denied him what would have been his 81st goal for the club, there was worse to come.

Signalling that if anything could go wrong it would do, Sunderland were dumped out of the FA Cup at Tranmere where the Division One side got away with bringing on a substitute for a player who had been sent off! This would be the fourth of a 12-game run without a win, a sequence that included conceding five for the second time in five League games at Leicester.

Astonishingly the Lads dropped just five places by mid-March despite not winning since before Christmas. Phillips had kept scoring, a run of six goals in as many games towards the end of that run including a brace in the return match with Newcastle that rescued a point after the visitors thought revenge was theirs when racing into a two-goal lead. Magpies defender Nikos Dabizas had claimed pre-match that Quinn and Phillips were predictable. He was right, everyone knew what Quinn and Phillips did – however, knowing about it and being able to stop it were two different things as the Greek discovered. A few days before the fixture, Phillips had been named Northern Rock Sports Personality of the Year for 1999 and the personal awards just kept coming.

The winless run ended with three victories in a row. A typical Superkev curled shot from distance secured three points against Everton before Kevin had the satisfaction of returning to Southampton and scoring the winner. Following a home win over League Cup conquerors Wimbledon, the revival was halted in its tracks by champions elect Manchester United at Old Trafford, but two late goals from Superkev at Sheffield Wednesday kept Sunderland in contention for a European place. 'My first against Sheffield Wednesday was a bit special,' said Kevin of another spectacular effort on a day when his brace broke Charlie 'Cannonball' Fleming's post-war club record of top-flight goals set in 1956.

The record that Kevin wanted was to rack up 30 Premiership goals for the season, and the Stadium of Light had the chance to acclaim that fantastic achievement in the last home game of the season when a neat first-half finish was enough to secure a win against West Ham. Despite defeat at Spurs in the remaining game where Chris 'Shoot' Makin scored his only goal for the club, Sunderland finished seventh with 58 points, having scored 57 goals – over half of them courtesy of the Hitchin Hotshot.

'This year will definitely be the best of my career and will take some beating,' noted Kevin, who was a golden shoe-in as Sunderland's Player of the Year to add to a host of awards in addition to being named in the PFA's Premiership team of the season.

Having also played for England during the season, Superkev, as the continent's top scorer, had every reason to believe he could wreak havoc at international level too, and he was not alone. England's second-top scorer of all time and leading scorer at the 1986 World Cup Gary Lineker knew a good striker when he saw one, declaring: 'I think he's a top goalscorer, his movement is fantastic and I think he's got a chance of making the team never mind the squad.' Lineker though was only half right: Phillips made Kevin Keegan's squad for Euro 2000 but never got even a minute's worth of action as England came home, tails between legs, after going out at the group stage.

England felt they could do without Superkev but Sunderland could not. As the national side toiled there was plenty of effort being put in at the Stadium of Light which was being extended by having a new top tier and 6,000 extra seats put in at the North Stand. Superkev and co. had literally raised the roof.

The only post-war player to make it into Sunderland's all-time goalscorers top 10 (he is sixth) Phillips deserves legendary status not just for this season but for his overall contribution to the club. But as Europe's top scorer and with 30 top-flight goals in just 36 games, 1999–2000 has to go down as his best year.

'I came to Sunderland as an unknown player and I left as an England international, a Golden Boot winner and a household name. I owe a lot of that to the supporters at Sunderland who made me known as Superkev and as far as I'm concerned they are superfans,' said Phillips after playing what almost certainly will prove to be his last ever game against the Lads in 2011. On that occasion at Birmingham City the Blues player was cheered to the rafters by the Red and White Army who recognised they were paying tribute to a player that in half a century some of them will be telling their grandchildren about. 'I couldn't thank them enough,' added Kevin. 'Sunderland supporters have always been great to me when I've played against them and for them to sing my name, especially at a difficult time, was top class of them but I've always known Sunderland supporters are top class. They sang my name after about five minutes of the game and again when I went off and I want to thank them and wish them all the best.'

Kevin Phillips at Sunderland
Debut: 15 August 1997: Sunderland 3–1 Manchester City (scored)
Last game: 11 May 2003: Sunderland 0–4 Arsenal
Total appearances (all competitions): 233+2 as sub / 130 goals

Season by season
1997–98	47+1 games / 35 goals
1998–99	32 games / 25 goals
1999–2000	38 games / 30 goals
2000–01	41+1 games / 18 goals
2001–02	39 games / 13 goals
2002–03	36 games / 9 goals

Other clubs
Southampton 1987–91
Baldock Town 1991–94
Watford 1994–97
Southampton 2003–05
Aston Villa 2005–06
West Bromwich Albion 2006–08
Birmingham City 2008–11
Blackpool 2011–

Don Hutchison

Premiership: Seventh out of 20
FA Cup: Fifth round, lost to West Ham United
League Cup: Fifth round, lost to Crystal Palace
Top scorer: Kevin Phillips, 18 goals, 14 League, 2 FA Cup, 2 League Cup
Ever present: No one
Player of the Year: Don Hutchison
SAFCSA Player of the Year: Don Hutchison

In one respect at least Don Hutchison was perhaps the most appropriate Player of the Year ever – if only because he was only a player at Sunderland for just a year. Hutchison had an excellent first season on Wearside, but soon he wanted to be away. Although from the North East and a ready-made hero at the Stadium of Light as a goalscoring midfielder in a successful team, he left for the bright lights of London. Reportedly, Hutchison doubled his money in moving to West Ham but the club doubled their dough as well, apparently receiving the Hammers' club record fee of £5 million compared to the £2.5 million paid to Everton a year earlier.

The Gateshead-born former Redheugh Boys player had learned his trade at Hartlepool, made his name with Liverpool, had a two-year spell with West Ham in the mid-nineties and then twice was signed by Howard Kendall. The Ryton-born boss first took him to Sheffield United and then to Everton where Don was Player of the Year in 1998–99 and scored 10 Premiership goals in 75 games in a two and a half year spell before Peter Reid stepped in. Hutchison had scored twice against Sunderland on Reid's return to Goodison in what was Sunderland's heaviest defeat of what otherwise was an excellent 1999–2000 season, and Reid signed him in July.

'Once Sunderland were after me that was it,' said Don. 'Charlton and Coventry offered me great deals, probably better than Sunderland, but this is the club I want to play for.' Cynics might suggest that given his nomadic career and the haste in which he left Wearside Hutchison was merely typical of the kind of player who simply hawks his wares to the highest bidder, but it was a good time to come back to the North East. The first season following promotion had been an exciting one and after a seventh-placed finish Reid was looking to build. Literally.

The season kicked-off in front of the newly-extended Stadium of Light. The first three seasons at the ground had seen the initial 42,000 capacity prove insufficient to meet the demand with Sunderland flying. Over the summer an extension to the North Stand saw the capacity climb to almost 49,000 and a sell-out crowd saw Arsenal beaten on the opening day with a trademark goal from their old boy Niall Quinn. The game also witnessed one of the all-time great debuts; Slovakian centre-half Stanislav Varga giving a Hurleyesque performance as the Gunners were repelled. In goal the excellent Sorensen had to go off injured leaving another newcomer, Austrian Jurgen Macho, to debut, and he too left the pitch having impressed. Hutchison, however, had been forced to sit out the game as a result of a suspension carried over after being sent off against Leeds in his penultimate game for the Toffees.

So it was that the second home game saw Sunderland unveil £10 million worth of new signings in front of an expectant crowd for a floodlit game with West Ham. New record signing Emerson Thome, future favourite Julio Arca and Hutchison were all in the starting line up, Arca marking his debut with a goal in a 1–1 draw.

Hutchison had already played twice, debuting in a defeat at newly-promoted Man City, where new man Varga had sustained a serious injury and veteran Steve Bould played the 500th

and final game of a distinguished career. A second defeat at another newly-promoted club in Ipswich – where Titus Bramble had burst from his own half to spectacularly score the only goal of the game – had made it a bad start. Another defeat followed at Manchester United a few days later before the Lads got into their stride.

Sunderland put together an eight-match unbeaten run and climbed to ninth place after beating Hutchison's pursuers Coventry in late October at a time when Don pondered: 'When I first came to the club I thought I was trying too hard and getting into positions too early. I wanted to get on the end of Niall Quinn's flick-ons but then I decided to sit back and try and dictate play more. As a midfield player I think you have to mix it up. Some midfield players are quite happy to just sit in and mark players but if they get forward they're not happy tracking back.'

He need not have worried about his lack of goals. He had found the back of the net as a Sunderland player on Scotland duty already and three days later he scored his first goals in a

Sunderland shirt with two belters in a League Cup win away to a spirited Bristol Rovers. That duck was broken on Halloween 2000. Sunderland could have done with that kind of performance a decade later to the day when they were hammered at Newcastle. Hutchison had found his shooting boots, however, and would score at Newcastle just over a fortnight later, by which time he was on fire.

His strike at St James' would be his fifth in four games, having scored at Spurs and in front of his home fans against Southampton in the meantime. It was the goal at Newcastle though that burned his name into the hearts of the fans, although his own badge-kissing as he celebrated the goal smacked more of a winding up of the natives by the lad from just over the water than the actions of someone who had Sunderland under his skin, unlike his fellow scorer Quinn.

Historically the North East's top club, at no time have the Magpies had more League titles to their name than the Black Cats. Sunderland had spent the mid-1990s in Newcastle's shadow as the Tynesiders under Kevin Keegan became the darlings of the media, if not Duraglit manufacturers. Sunderland, though, had been to Newcastle the previous season and won, the shock waves signalling United manager Ruud Gullit's departure. The Black and Whites had waited over a year to get Sunderland back on home turf and were determined to beat the Wearsiders.

With just four minutes gone the home side were ahead through Gary Speed, who pounced to net a ball that rebounded to him off Hutchison's back. Sunderland were undaunted. This was a side full of characters and they battled to stay in the game before eventually beginning to gain a foothold. An early Newcastle lead at St James' had been overturned the previous season and would be again. In 1999 the Red and Whites had scored in the 64th and 74th minutes, this time it would the 67th and 75th. Hutchison was responsible for the turning point. Bearing in mind his earlier comment about not getting into positions too early, he ghosted in late at the far post to convincingly finish a Kevin Phillips cross from six yards. Quinn soon put the visitors ahead and 'keeper Sorensen secured another famous victory with a late penalty save from Alan Shearer.

The Magpies had been put to the sword again, Don had scored and was finding the back of the net regularly. From then on he could do no wrong and was increasingly seen as a key member of the side. A win over the local rivals serves as a great confidence booster and the Lads duly won their next four games, climbing to fourth along with knocking Manchester United out of the League Cup.

Despite defeat at Leeds and League Cup elimination at Crystal Palace, the mood was still buoyant. Playing as a striker, due to Superkev being suspended, Hutchison showed his opportunism in scoring the only goal of Manchester City's visit with a cheeky quick free-kick as the visitors lined up their wall. Three of the next four League games were won with a terrific draw at Arsenal in the other.

Another quick Hutchison free-kick sealed a win at West Ham that took the Lads to second two days before Don's wife Debbie gave birth to son Max, things got better and better. After another goal against another former club in a home draw with Liverpool, a new peak was scaled as Don scored twice in a thrilling 4–2 win away at Chelsea.

Sunderland had been lucky to only lose 4–0 on their previous visit to Stamford Bridge in the first game of the previous season as the Lads returned to the top flight. Since then they had put four past the Londoners when they came to the North East and had beaten them again on Wearside in 2000–01. At the Bridge revenge was in the air as Claudio Ranieri's side twice took the lead. Both times Don supplied the equaliser: the first was a brilliant volley from an Arca free-kick. Sunderland went on to win 4–2 with Hutchison's goals taking him into double figures. They would, however, be his last goals in a Sunderland shirt.

Don Hutchison in action.

Fourth in the table after winning at Chelsea, only two points would be taken from the next five games before seven points from the last three fixtures secured a second successive seventh place. They were the club's two highest finishes since the fifties but they marked a high point rather than base camp. The loss of Hutchison after three games of the following season, Hutch's last appearance being back at St James' in a 1–1 draw, was a key factor in the team tailing off.

Back at West Ham, where he became their record signing for a second time, Don scored on his second home debut in a 3–0 win over Newcastle but it would prove to be his only goal of the season. Nonetheless, in 2001–02 it would be the Hammers that took seventh position while Sunderland finished one place above the relegated teams.

Don Hutchison at Sunderland
Debut: 23 August 2000: Manchester City 4–2 Sunderland
Last game: 26 August 2001: Newcastle United 1–1 Sunderland
Total appearances (all competitions): 37+2 as sub / 10 goals

Season by season
2000–01   35+2 games / 10 goals
2001–02   2 games / 0 goals

Other clubs
Hartlepool United 1989–90
Liverpool 1990–94
West Ham United 1994–96
Sheffield United 1996–98
Everton 1998–2000
West Ham United 2001–05
Millwall 2005
Coventry City 2005–07
Luton Town 2007–08

Jody Craddock

Premiership: 17th out of 20
FA Cup: Third round, lost to Arsenal
League Cup: Second round, lost to Sheffield Wednesday after extra-time
Top scorer: Kevin Phillips, 13 goals, 11 League, 1 FA Cup, 1 League Cup
Ever present: No one
Player of the Year: Jody Craddock
SAFCSA Player of the Year: Jody Craddock

Centre-back Jody Craddock won the Player of the Year award for 2001–02 despite missing two months in the middle of the season. 2001–02 was the morning after the night before. Wearside was dizzy after four splendid seasons at the new Stadium of Light which had opened on the day Craddock signed in 1997. An exciting but ultimately anticlimactic first season had ended in penalty shoot-out heartbreak at Wembley. The halcyon days under Peter Reid with Niall Quinn and Superkev at the spearhead saw a record 105-point promotion followed up with Sunderland's only two finishes in the top half of the top flight in a spell of over half a century. Crowds swelled, as did the stadium which had been extended.

Unlike Roker Park, which had witnessed grim years as well as glorious ones, the new stadium was all-seater and even had decent catering points and toilets. It was a world away from the Bovril and prehistoric loos in the Roker End and a new breed of fan joined those who had always kept the faith. The new fan was there to be entertained. In the first four years at Wearmouth 63 games had been won, 24 drawn and only 11 lost with 176 goals scored – just at home! Phillips had broken Brian Clough's post-war scoring record and followed it up by becoming the first, and to date only, Englishman to win the European Golden Shoe as the continent's top scorer.

These were the days Sunderland supporters had longed for. These were the sorts of days people's grandads had told them about, days when the Lads wiped the floor with any upstarts ready to challenge a club who from the first decade of League football had become renowned as the 'Team of All the Talents'.

It proved to be no more than a glimpse into what it was like to watch the boys of the 1890s: Johnny Campbell, Jimmy Millar and co., or the near double-winning side of Charlie Buchan and George Holley in 1912–13, or Raich Carter and Bobby Gurney in the great days of the thirties. In a blink, after the most glorious of promotions and two seventh-place finishes, the days that got under Niall Quinn's skin disappeared as quickly as they had arrived. Just as after the 1973 Cup triumph of Monty and Stokoe it took three years to win promotion only to be followed by instant relegation and the disintegration of what was left of the Cup team, so it transpired that Sunderland fell away. Badly. It was in this season that a centre-back missing throughout most of the winter was Player of the Year.

Since he had walked through the door at Sunderland the club had soared so did the slump to fourth from bottom come as a shock to Jody? 'It's a tough, tough division that gets harder every year. In the two previous years we had been seventh both times but then we finished fourth from bottom. We were safe but it was tough and the season after we were relegated. Even when you've finished seventh that's no guarantee that you'll be safe the following year because the League is so tough. You can never take anything for granted at this level because every year needs a lot of hard work because of how strong the League is. The danger is that if you drop into the Championship that is really difficult to get out of.'

Like all managers, Peter Reid's record largely depended on the success of his signings. Phillips, Quinn and Craddock between them with all the add-ons thrown in came to less than £2.5 million but the manager's shopping in the summer of 2001 had the distinct feeling of the purchases of someone who had not read the *Which?* reports. It was not a case that Reid spent fortunes, because fortunes were not there to be spent by a club that had built and extended a new stadium and were looking to move to a fabulous new training ground. Having had tremendous success with young Argentinian Julio Arca, Sunderland signed Arca's World Youth

Cup-winning teammate Nicolas Medina. Swiss right-back Bernt Haas came in, leaving wags to wish the Iranian midfielder Karim Bagheri who had played for Charlton the previous season was next on the manager's wish list so Sunderland could sport a 'Bagheri–Haas' combination. Sunderland had had a few of them in the past! Knowing that Quinn could not go on for ever, Reid looked to French international Lilian Laslandes to take over leading the line and recruited another French striker in the shape of speed merchant David Bellion to give him another option.

The season began quite well. By the time Craddock got on the score sheet on the same day Kevin Phillips became the first man to chalk up a century of post-war League goals in a 2–0 win at Bolton, Sunderland were fifth after eight games. It was not unusual for the Lads to be in the upper reaches of the Premiership at the time. People were getting used to it but there were clues that the good ship Sunderland was not surging through the waters at full steam. The win at Bolton was only the third of the season, defeats against Fulham and Spurs had been tame and Craddock was the first man apart from Phillips and Quinn to net in the League.

New man Laslandes was struggling. His only goal had come in a League Cup defeat at First Division Sheffield Wednesday. That night Laslandes also hit the underside of the bar with the sort of spectacular scissors kick that had been a trademark of his in France. Had it gone in and Sunderland had gone on to win a game they lost in extra-time with a rookie 'keeper in Michael Ingham, perhaps Laslandes' career on this side of the Channel might have taken off. As it was, his solitary strike at Hillsborough proved to be his only goal in red and white and he was soon discarded, having cut an unhappy figure. A bit like Johnny Cash's 'Boy named Sue', being a centre-forward called Lilian in Sunderland meant Laslandes really had to deliver quickly.

Of the other new signings, Bellion would not get a start in the League all season, Haas did moderately at right-back but his ability on the ball was no substitute for the sturdy Chris Makin, and as for Medina, he finally got what turned out to be his only game in English football more than a year and a half after signing.

Effectively, none of the new signings had added anything to a side that lost its reigning Player of the Year Don Hutchison at the end of the August transfer window with fellow midfielder Alex Rae making his last appearance in the game after Hutchison's farewell. After a decent enough start the team began to struggle for the first time since a blip almost exactly four years earlier. Following Craddock's contribution to the victory at Bolton, Sunderland would take only one point from the next 12 available as the side slid from fifth to 15th.

The slump coincided with Craddock limping out of Sunderland's last ever visit to Leicester City's old Filbert Street ground. 'A stud went into the back of my heel and I had to have an operation. I've still got the scar to show for it,' Jody recalls. Inevitably he was a big miss although the ever willing and versatile Darren Williams stepped in and helped the team concede just one goal in the four games Craddock missed. Looking to pick things up, Peter Reid paid a club record £4.5 million to bring in Claudio Reyna from Rangers. The USA international midfielder's debut coincided with Craddock's return to the side but Jody clearly was not right in a 2–0 defeat at Southampton and was again immediately sidelined for a further four games.

Sunderland impressed in the first two of these, Reyna hitting the winner on his home debut against Everton and Quinn – still being relied upon with Laslandes having already played his last game for the club – notching a couple in a handsome Boxing Day win at Blackburn. That lifted Sunderland back into the top half of the table with those back-to-back wins based on clean sheets, the defence having tightened up and enjoying a run of five shut-outs in seven games.

The turning point came in the last game of 2001. Just three days after a convincing win at Blackburn, Sunderland found themselves four down by half-time at struggling Ipswich, eventually losing 5–0. The injured Craddock was still missing. Between being on the receiving end of a 4–0 defeat away to Manchester United in April 2000 and going down 4–1 at the same ground in February 2002, Jody played 56 games for Sunderland without the team conceding more than three goals. Just as the defence leaked five goals at Portman Road when Jody was missing, similarly they let in four at Sheffield Wednesday, Manchester City and in a friendly at Dutch outfit NAC Breda when Craddock was absent. Despite these blips Sunderland had been able to bounce back from bad defeats but the hammering at Portman Road signalled a steep decline.

From being ninth at the halfway point going into the game at Ipswich, Sunderland slumped horrendously. Only three victories would come in the second half of the campaign as the Lads plummeted to just a single place above the drop zone. Craddock returned as sub in a home FA Cup defeat to First Division West Brom and to the starting line up at Everton a week later. From then to the end of the season Craddock would not miss a single minute.

Having had four and a half years where the side were used to winning, losing became a bitter pill to swallow. The fans kept turning up with the gate never dipping below 43,000 in a miserable second half of the season. When the chips were down as results deteriorated only Jody and Niall Quinn appeared in every game, although Niall was often limited to coming off the bench. It is when times are tough that supporters rely on strong characters and Craddock was exactly that.

At 6ft 2in he was big but not the biggest, and his 12st 4lb made him neither a powerhouse like Sam Allardyce nor a svelte figure like Shaun Elliott. If there was a single word to describe Jody the footballer it would be dependable. Craddock is not a name you would expect to find in too many teams of supporters' best XIs but he certainly would not be far off. Jody never let the team down, always gave his all and chipped in with the occasional goal. One of his greatest assets was that he was a tremendous team player who could adapt his game to the benefit of the side. Speaking of his 2001–02 teammates at the time Jody explained: 'They're all great players, it's just a case of adjusting to each partnership and hopefully it works out whatever the combination. Sometimes whoever is playing alongside me can alter my role depending on who we are playing against. George [McCartney] is naturally left-sided and I'm naturally right-sided so we tend to stick to our sides. If I'm partnering George I tend to go for more headers but if I'm alongside Emo [Emerson Thome] or Stan [Varga] I might tend to sweep up a bit more, which is fine by me either way.'

The very fact that Craddock had several central defensive partners indicates a side not at ease with itself. In the second half of the season Jody was paired with newcomer Joachim Bjorklund, a Swedish international, but an absence of goals – Sunderland scored twice in only two games in the second half of the season – put added pressure on the back four.

As the campaign came to a close, three successive defeats left the Lads looking over their shoulders at the wrong end of the table. Hopes of pushing on after two seventh-place finishes were in ruins and after a hard-fought draw at Charlton, Sunderland went into the final match at home to already-doomed Derby County not quite safe from relegation themselves. Unable to beat the Rams, the point gained was not needed as it turned out as Ipswich – who had been good enough to wallop Sunderland – were hammered themselves by Liverpool at Anfield and so the Black Cats used one of their nine lives.

It had been far from a vintage season. Rather, it had been one that reminded the new generation of the trials and tribulations with which Roker Park had become associated. Jody Craddock was a deserving Player of the Year and had the good news of the birth of a baby boy, Jake, as the season drew to a close. Tragically Jake would live to be only four months old, becoming a victim of cot death in August. Such a sad loss to a young family put footballing ups and downs firmly into perspective, reminding people that for all the passion and obsession, it is just a game after all. At the end of the 2001–02 season Jody played in Niall Quinn's benefit match, which raised money for children's hospitals in Sunderland and Dublin. Little did anyone know that night how soon the importance of children's services would be highlighted by a tragedy so close to a sporting hero.

Jody Craddock is one of the game's good guys. A talented painter, he found solace in his art which helped him to cope mentally with the loss of Jake. He now has three delightful sons in Joseph, Luke and Toby, and on a professional level went on to play over 200 games for Wolverhampton Wanderers, many of them as captain, scoring a crucial goal in old gold at Sunderland in May 2011.

Reflecting on his award on Wearside almost a decade later, Jody remains rightly proud of his place in the list of Red and White heroes, noting: 'It is a big personal achievement because it basically means you've had a successful season. A lot of work goes into it and winning a Player of the Year award is the icing in the cake. It's a pat on the back and it means a lot. I won the Player of the Year award at Cambridge and was Player of the Year at Wolves in 2009–10 so I've won it at all three of the clubs I've been with.' In his days in the North East, Jody's Player of the Year trophy had pride of place in the grand entrance in his home at Wynyard and he explains: 'Ever since I was a little kid even a certificate meant a lot to me and it's the same now if one of my children get a certificate or a trophy for football or anything. I think if you've worked hard to earn something it's nice to be rewarded and in turn that encourages you to keep doing your best.'

When Sunderland were relegated in 2003 after the most awful of seasons, the squad broke up with the club needing to get high earners off the wage bill. Craddock survived the cull until just before a pre-season friendly at Hearts. Manager Mick McCarthy (later to be reunited with Craddock at Molineux) was devastated at the news that he had to lose Craddock, even more so

Jody Craddock scores a crucial early goal for Wolves to put his relegation threatened side ahead against Sunderland at the Stadium of Light.

after watching his defence torn apart by Hearts' Marc De Vries that evening. McCarthy knew how important Jody was to his team. Craddock was a solid player and a man of character. Sunderland supporters may well have wanted the Lads to sign Bagheri to partner Haas but no one ever even suggested that Craddock's nickname could be Fanny Craddock and knowing how football supporters latch on to such things that is praise indeed.

Jody Craddock at Sunderland
Debut: 16 September 1997: Sunderland 2–1 Bury
Last game: 11 May 2003: Sunderland 0–4 Arsenal
Total appearances (all competitions): 158+10 as sub / 2 goals

Season by season
1997–98 39+1 games / 0 goals
1998–99 6+5 games / 0 goals
1999–2000 18+2 games / 0 goals
2000–01 35+1 games / 0 goals
2001–02 30+1 games / 1 goal
2002–03 30 games / 1 goal

Other clubs
Christchurch 1992–93
Cambridge United 1993–97
Sheffield United (loan) 1999
Wolverhampton Wanderers 2003–
Stoke City (loan) 2007

Premiership: 20th out of 20 (relegated)
FA Cup: Fifth round, lost to Watford
League Cup: Fourth round, lost to Sheffield United
Top scorer: Kevin Phillips, 9 goals, 6 League, 3 FA Cup
Ever present: No one
Player of the Year: Sean Thornton
SAFCSA Player of the Year: Not awarded

The rest of the team were not best pleased when a skinny 17-year-old Michael Bridges walked off with the Man of the Match award when he debuted with just 28 minutes to go in a goalless draw with Port Vale in 1996, so imagine how the rest of the squad felt when Sean Thornton was voted Sunderland's Player of the Year in 2002–03 having not made his debut until 14 January!

It was a season when the wheels well and truly came off. Having finished fourth from bottom the previous year following four wonderful seasons at the Stadium of Light, Sunderland spent megabucks. While the big-money signings failed to pay off, a teenage summer recruit for a tribunal-set figure of £225,000 from Tranmere offered a flicker of hope in the second half of a season that could not have been worse.

Indeed, Thornton was on the losing side in every one of his 11 Premiership appearances, but that was hardly surprising as Sunderland lost every single one of the final 15 League games of the season. They would lose the first two of the following campaign as well before Sean scored the opener in the victory that finally brought the run to a long overdue end.

Setting a record low points tally of a meagre 15 for the season – 14 of which had been claimed before Christmas – resulted in the Sunderland Supporters' Association not awarding their Player of the Year trophy for the season although Thornton topped the vote in the official poll.

Long-serving manager Peter Reid, who had brought the great days, had been sacked 10 games into the season with the club just outside the relegation zone but having astonishingly won 7–0 away to Cambridge in the League Cup in his penultimate game. His two deadline signings – Tore Andre Flo and Marcus Stewart – had scored twice each in that match, one less than they would score between them in the League all season. In fairness to Stewart he was terribly underused and ended the campaign with fewer League starts than Thornton but after a sensational debut goal against Manchester United, record signing Flo was to prove a massive disappointment as a replacement for Niall Quinn, who retired after one game under new manager Howard Wilkinson.

By the time of Thornton's debut the Lads were yet to hit the foot of the table. The occasion was an FA Cup third-round replay with fellow Premiership outfit Bolton Wanderers. A Kevin Phillips equaliser 10 days earlier had earned a replay but Superkev was not involved in the replay as Wilkinson had an eye on the following weekend's League fixture at Everton.

Lining up alongside Sean in midfield was another debutant, Nicolas Medina, an Argentinian. Sunderland won the game in extra-time with goals from Medina's Under-20 World Cup-winning teammate Julio Arca and local lad Michael Proctor but while Medina played the full 120 minutes and did well he never got another chance. However, after an eye-catching debut on the right of midfield, Thornton found himself in the starting line up at Goodison a few days later.

Sean Thornton sat on his staircase at home.

It was an ideal place for Shaun to make his Premiership bow. Having spent three years with Everton's near neighbours Tranmere he had plenty of mates at the match but a few on Merseyside were less than enamoured with him following his decision to leave and come to Sunderland.

Having previously played twice as a sub, Sean had started nine of Rovers' last 11 games of the season, scoring his first goal in a win over Wigan and becoming the club's Young Player of the Year. Drogheda-born, it had always been Thornton's aim to start at a club where he could make an early first-team impression. He had always been a star performer. After spending five years with Boyne Rovers from the age of seven he joined Bohemians and then a team called St Kevins along with his brother Kevin who subsequently made a name for himself with Coventry. Sean represented the Republic of Ireland from Under-15 level upwards and in 2002–03 added his country's Under-19 Player of the Year award to his Sunderland Player of the Year accolade.

You could not miss him at Sunderland. With bleached blond hair matching his bright yellow boots this was a lad not short of confidence. The team's struggles were nothing to do with him and he was totally unaffected by the way in which defeat after defeat sucked the confidence out of some of his teammates. For Thornton the Premiership was a stage to strut upon and for supporters starved of anything to cheer the sight of a young lad in red and white, ready to try anything, was something they quickly latched on to.

The defeats kept coming with Thornton scoring one of the two goals the team managed in the last 10 games. It was a brilliant free-kick that gave Sunderland an early lead against Champions League chasing Chelsea. After the Londoners emerged as 2–1 winners in what was a spirited game there was an unexpected knock on the dressing-room door. Standing outside requesting an exchange of shirts with young Sean was one of the finest footballers and sportsmen ever to grace the Premiership – Gianfranco Zola. The Sardinian maestro recognised the teenager's contribution to the game and wanted to mark it. Thornton obliged but with as crafty an approach as he had brought to the match he accepted the Italian legend's shirt as well as keeping the one he'd scored his free-kick in. 'He's a great player and for him to want to swap shirts with me was amazing,' said Sean of Gianfranco's gesture. 'But I gave him the one I wore in the second half because I'd put a clean one on at half-time!'

For all Sunderland's losing run, being heralded by one of the top flight's top stars was a far cry to Sean's experience in the first half of the season. It had started well with a medal after beating no less a side than Barcelona in the Final of the Lloyds TSB Reserve Team Trophy in Jersey where Sean had scored in a 3–1 win over Sporting Lisbon. He had then made a Stadium of Light debut as a sub in a reserve-team win over Newcastle but had soon gone on a disastrous loan to Blackpool: 'It was terrible. I wanted to go there to get games and Blackpool's manager Steve McMahon was the brother of my old Tranmere youth coach John McMahon but when I went to Blackpool I was only on the bench. I couldn't wait to get back to Sunderland but what it did give me was a hunger because not getting in the Blackpool team made me all the more determined to come back to Sunderland and do well.'

Sean succeeded in doing well at Sunderland and in the latter part of a truly terrible season acted as a beacon of hope to fans starved of success, hence his achievement as being Player of the Year having played far fewer games than any other winner in the season of their award. Unfortunately for both Sean and the club his ability was not maximised and the following season he polled less than 3 per cent in the Player of the Year vote. Having taken over as Sunderland's third boss of the season in the relegation year, Mick McCarthy began to mould a hard-working team to get Sunderland back into the top flight. Frustrated by Thornton's inability to consistently get the best out of himself, the manager put him through a special training routine including one to one sessions and made strenuous efforts to help the player with his lifestyle choices. Long-term success, though, was not to come Sean Thornton's way at Sunderland but for a five-month period his talent shone as golden as his hairdo.

Sean Thornton at Sunderland
Debut: 14 January 2003: Sunderland 2–0 Bolton Wanderers (after extra-time)
Last game: 16 April 2005: Ipswich Town 2–2 Sunderland
Total appearances (all competitions): 38+26 as sub / 9 goals

Season by season
2002–03   14 games / 1 goal
2003–04   17+13 games / 4 goals
2004–05   7+13 games / 4 goals

Other clubs
Tranmere Rovers 2001–02
Blackpool (loan) 2002
Doncaster Rovers 2005–07
Leyton Orient 2007–10
Shrewsbury Town (loan) 2008
FC Metalist Kharkiv (Ukraine) 2011–

Division One: Third out of 24. Lost Play-off semi-final on penalties
FA Cup: Semi-finalists, lost to Millwall
League Cup: Second round, lost to Huddersfield Town
Top scorer: Marcus Stewart, 16 goals, 14 League, 2 Play-offs
Kevin Kyle, 16 goals, 10 League, 2 Play-offs, 1 FA Cup, 3 League Cup
Ever present: No one
Player of the Year: Julio Arca
SAFCSA Player of the Year: Julio Arca

Following the incredibly disappointing relegation season of 2002–03 over 20 players left the club. Among the departures were former Players of the Year Kevin Phillips and Jody Craddock and big players such as Thomas Sorensen and Gavin McCann. One player who remained was crowd favourite Julio Arca.

'Basically, the year before I hardly played because for some reason the manager didn't seem to like me, and so I hardly got the chance to play which was very frustrating because I wanted to help the club which was struggling. In the summer the manager [by now Mick McCarthy] asked me to stay and said I was in his plans,' says Julio in explaining why he was not part of the exodus following relegation. 'I started at left-back and then was moved on to the left wing where I played a lot for Sunderland. I had a good year and played well for Mick McCarthy. My first year at Sunderland under Peter Reid was pretty good too and I had a few really good years at the club.'

The Argentinian had been taken to the hearts of Sunderland supporters ever since he arrived as a teenager in the summer of 2000. A young lad who had travelled to the other side of the world, Julio immediately impressed with his close control, willingness to get stuck in as if he was from Boldon rather than Buenos Aires and his ability to chip in with the odd goal, as he did on his debut.

Arca became as enamoured with Sunderland supporters as they were with him. Julio realised he was loved by the fans and, despite now being on the other side of the world, evidently felt at home on Wearside. To begin with he leaned on Brazilian Emerson Thome, who he could converse with and who could speak English. Thome had been a former record signing and was a solid defender but after Thome's departure Arca's own English improved and he increasingly embraced the region.

During the relegation season, Arca had been incredibly underused. Peter Reid started him in his final three games as boss, one of them seeing Julio score in a 7–0 away win at Cambridge in the League Cup. Reid's replacement Howard Wilkinson took three months to even give Arca an appearance as sub while the third manager of the season, Mick McCarthy, gave Julio just two starts in the nine games he oversaw. It is painful to look back on but 2002–03 saw just a single point taken after Christmas!

Arca was missing again at the start of McCarthy's first full season as defeats at Forest and at home to Millwall extended the shocking run to 17 consecutive defeats. The turning point came at Deepdale, home of Preston. With players of non-League Darwen in attendance expecting to see Sunderland lose and equal the all-time run of successive losses set by their club set in 1898–99, Julio's return coincided with Sunderland finally winning a game!

Julio Arca (in white) in his early days on Wearside with Emerson Thome.

First-half goals from Sean Thornton and Marcus Stewart rewarded the faithful who still travelled for a live TV game despite not having taken a point in over seven months! Having broken their duck, the Lads suddenly made winning a habit, notching four in a row.

In the third of them at Bradford a 4–0 triumph was capped by a goal that remains one of the indelible memories Sunderland supporters have of their favourite Argentinian. Playing at left-back, Julio gained possession in his own half and waltzed, if not tangoed his way through a bantamweight defence until he reached the edge of the box. Looking up, Julio saw his path to goal blocked by 6ft 5in goalkeeper Mark Paston. Arca's appeal was always partly because he looked like a David taking on Goliaths and this moment epitomised that. Having left the City defence in his wake, Julio produced the most sublime chip to arc the ball over the giant 'keeper and float it serenely into the net. Julio had begun his career at the home of his hero Diego Maradona and this was a goal of such magnificence that the great man himself would have been proud to have scored it.

'It probably has to be the best goal I've ever scored,' says Julio. 'I tackled a guy on the edge of our box and burst forward. As I was running I realised no one was coming with me so I just kept going. When I got to the edge of their box I saw their 'keeper coming out and he was a big guy but I thought I'd try to chip him and it went in.'

With Arca and the whole team now bursting with confidence and the fans making the most of the return of the good days after sticking with the club through the worst of the bad times, the Lads had climbed from second from bottom to fourth from top by Bonfire Night, with crowds up 50 per cent from the start of the season as belief returned.

Arca's popularity at Sunderland was so high that in a season where the Lads finished third in the table, reached the semi-finals of the FA Cup and only lost the semi-finals of the Play-offs on penalties, he still won the Player of the Season accolade despite injury restricting him to playing in less than half of the League games in the second half of the season. Indeed, Julio was such a favourite that non-football backroom staff used to joke that he would win the sponsors' Man of the Match awards even if he was not playing! In my role as programme editor I used to claim at the time that Julio to me was like Lady Di to the *Daily Express* in that if I put him on the cover I would print extra copies as I would expect to sell more.

A dodgy autumn spell of half a dozen games without a win dropped Sunderland back down to 10th before a run of five successive victories had the Black Cats' tails up once again. Julio scored the only goals in the last two of those wins. The first settled an FA Cup tie with lower League neighbours Hartlepool who brought a record 9,000 away fans – well above the capacity of their normally half-full ground – and a week later Arca wrapped up the points in a League win over Nottingham Forest that kept the Lads in the promotion reckoning.

Julio was missing when the winning run came to an end away to Millwall, the team who would eventually extinguish the Cup dreams that were blossoming after a fourth-round win at Ipswich where Arca scored for the third time in as many appearances.

The fifth round paired Sunderland with Premiership opposition for the first time since relegation with a record low number of points. The previous season had ended with 15 consecutive defeats with the drop made mathematically certain against Birmingham City, who now stood between Sunderland and a first FA Cup quarter-final since 1992 when the Lads had gone all the way to Wembley. Managed by future Sunderland boss Steve Bruce, Blues were in good form and in the top half of the top flight.

On 1 February the man who had led Sunderland the last time they had won the Cup in 1973 died. Bob Stokoe was a man who transformed Sunderland from a side near to the bottom of the Second Division and had them running round Wembley with the Cup within six months, having seen off three of the biggest, best and most glamorous teams in the country. His statue now stands outside the Stadium of Light, framed in time as he ran on to the Wembley turf at the final whistle.

Stokoe's passing gave some poignancy to Sunderland's next home game being in the FA Cup, when with over six million people watching the match live on BBC1 Sunderland held the higher-division club. Before the replay the heaviest defeat of the season was suffered at Cardiff where Sunderland were reduced to 10 men in the first half but it was all smiles at St Andrew's, where Sunderland beat Birmingham in extra-time. Tommy Smith was the hero with two well-taken goals.

Julio Arca at Doncaster in 2004.

Julio was on the score sheet again himself in an away win at Walsall before Sheffield United came to Wearside in the Cup, where again Smith's prowess in front of goal saw Sunderland progress.

Form was good going into the Old Trafford semi-final with fellow Division One team Millwall. With the other semi-finalists Arsenal and Manchester United nailed on for Champions League football the following year, the Black Cats and the Lions knew that just reaching the Cup Final would bring with it a passport into European football, something Sunderland had longed for since their solitary foray exactly three decades earlier courtesy of winning the Cup under Stokoe.

Sunderland's wait for another Cup Final and a place in Europe was to continue as Millwall edged a poor game 1–0 but there would be more semi-final heartbreak to come against another south London club.

Just two days after playing the semi-final at Old Trafford it was back to League action in the strange surroundings of the National Hockey Stadium against MK Dons, where there was no Cup hangover and another three points followed by three more against Cup victims Sheffield United made it 15 out of 15 as third-placed Sunderland tried to put pressure on the top two, Norwich and West Brom. In truth though, the leaders were well ahead and the results tailed off with just two taken from the next available 15. Completing their League programme with back-to-back wins, including one over champions Norwich, saw Sunderland finish third and facing a Play-off with Crystal Palace.

A 3–2 Friday night defeat at Selhurst Park was a game where, despite five goals, it was a bad night for football let alone Sunderland as the violence directed towards Sunderland's travelling support was shocking and appeared to be badly handled by the authorities. Three days later Sunderland led 2–0 and therefore 4–3 on aggregate in the dying seconds when Palace scored at the South End of the Stadium of Light. As sub Darren Powell put the ball into the net it was one of those occasions when you do not even glance at the referee to see if he is giving the goal as Sunderland 'keeper Mart Poom was blatantly held down by centre-forward Neil Shipperley and a free-kick seemed certain. Incredibly the goal was given, Palace survived extra-time with 10 men having had a player sent off and as in 1998 Sunderland lost a crucial Play-off game on penalties.

Third in the League, semi-finalists in the FA Cup, and missing out on a Play-off Final place on penalties meant it was a season that condemned the club to another year out of the top flight but after the horrors of the year before, 2003–04 was nonetheless a year when the rot was stopped and the good ship Sunderland turned around and headed back in the right direction.

Perhaps the Lads might have made it back into the top flight had Arca seen out the season. Julio's last game was against Palace in the mid-April League visit after which he missed the last six games due to a troublesome knee injury.

Having missed the start of the season and only started 11 League games after Christmas, Julio ended up outside the top six appearance makers and still took the Player of the Year award. And yet it was no more than he deserved. The Argentinian did not become a massive cult hero to Sunderland fans without reason. Julio had adhesive feet but got stuck in as well. He was one of those rare players who applied both guile and graft while in addition to that it became more and more known that he was – and is – an absolutely sound bloke. Julio always deeply appreciated the way Sunderland supporters took him to their hearts and is immensely proud of being the Player of the Year.

'It was very exciting and a great achievement for me at a club where many players had done well that season. Everything was good about the season other than missing out in the semi-finals

Julio Arca with Neill Collins.

of the Play-offs and the Cup and I was also selected for the PFA team of the season and that meant a lot too.'

Manager McCarthy summed up the feelings of everyone at the club regarding Julio. 'I was pleased that Julio Arca was chosen by his fellow professionals in the PFA Division One team...the lad deserves it. He wasn't in the side for the first couple of games but once he got in he proved his worth. I know the fans love him and he does things that excite but unlike some of the game's entertainers he puts his full share of graft in as well. He loves his football and has consistently impressed.'

A year later, when he contributed nine goals as Sunderland stormed to the Championship title, Arca was unfortunate to miss out on joining Marco Gabbiadini in retaining the Player of the Year award when he missed out by the narrowest of margins to his left-flank partner George McCartney. The pair had terrorised the division with their left-wing link-ups that created so many goals and produced a tremendous amount of exciting, attractive football.

Sadly 12 months further on and Sunderland were back in the second tier, this time having managed four fewer points than the record low they had set on their previous season in with the big boys. With the club in a state of upheaval as Bob Murray, the longest-serving chairman in history, sold the club to a consortium headed by former Player of the Year Niall Quinn, Julio decided it was time to put his career first, having stuck with the club the last time it had gone down.

'I'd been at Sunderland for a long time and knew it was time to move on because we had been relegated again and I

Julio Arca in2007.

didn't want to play in the Championship again. Niall was just coming in and I like Niall and have always got on well with him but I didn't know who the manager was going to be or anything and at the time Middlesbrough were doing well. I was happy to stay in the North East but didn't want to go to Newcastle out of respect for Sunderland supporters, who I knew it would hurt if I went to Newcastle. I knew that some fans would be unhappy if I signed for Middlesbrough but it would be a lot different than if it had been to Newcastle. I know there is a lot of hate between some Sunderland and Newcastle supporters but Sunderland v Middlesbrough is a derby but more of a friendly derby.'

As professional and committed as ever, Julio found the back of the net for his new club Middlesbrough against Sunderland just over a year later after the Wearsiders had bounced back into the top flight but Julio refused to celebrate the goal. 'After that it was 100 per cent clear to everyone how much Sunderland meant to me. Luckily enough I scored for Middlesbrough in the game but I showed respect to the Sunderland supporters by not celebrating the goal and supporters always talk to me about that. They understood why I didn't celebrate but I would never celebrate a goal against the club and the supporters who gave me so much.'

Sunderland and its supporters may well have given a lot to the boy from Buenos Aires but there is no doubt that he gave back so much more and that he will be revered by the Red and White Army for many, many years to come.

Julio Arca at Sunderland
Debut: 5 September 2000: Sunderland 1–1 West Ham United (scored)
Last game: 22 April 2006: Portsmouth 2–1 Sunderland
Total appearances: 165+12 as sub / 23 goals

Season by season
2000–01	29+1 games / 3 goals
2001–02	22+2 games / 1 goal
2002–03	12+6 games / 2 goals
2003–04	37 games / 6 goals
2004–05	41+1 games / 9 goals
2005–06	24+2 games / 2 goals

Other clubs
Argentinos Juniors 1998–2000
Middlesbrough 2006–

George McCartney

Division One: First out of 24, promoted
FA Cup: Fourth round, lost to Everton
League Cup: Second round, lost to Crewe Alexandra on penalties
Top scorer: Marcus Stewart, 17 goals, 16 League, 1 FA Cup
Ever present: No one
Player of the Year: George McCartney
SAFCSA Player of the Year: Julio Arca

When Sunderland played the football of the gods in 1998–99, winning the Championship with a record 105 points, it was with a team brimming with partnerships all over the pitch. The next promotion side after the 105 boys of '99 came in 2004–05. It was a team good enough to win the League by seven points but in years to come will not be remembered with the same reverence as the 1999 players. Just as the line up of the 1964 runners-up are rattled off by many more fans than can tell you the 1976 Division Two champions – even by Jimmy Montgomery who was the goalkeeper in both teams – so the 1999 side was a special team.

During that season a young left-back from Northern Ireland by the name of George McCartney was making a name for himself as the star man in a superb Under-19 team while also totting up 11 games for the reserves, who won the Pontins League Premier Division. While accepting the 1999 promotion team as exceptional, nothing should be taken away from the 2005 champions. Mick McCarthy had turned around a ship sinking under the embarrassment of breaking the club's own national low points tally just two years earlier. They had lost the Play-off semi-final on penalties and reached the FA Cup semi-final in 2004 and responded to those disappointments with style by marching to the title despite a bad start which saw them 16th after six games.

When you look at the previous promotion year it was like a Noah's Ark of a team in that the names came at you two by two: Phillips & Quinn, Gray & Johnston, Makin & Summerbee, Ball & Clark and Melville & Butler. In 2004–05, however, one partnership stood out above all others – that of McCartney & Arca.

This left-flank pairing with Argentinian Arca on the wing and

George McCartney in 1999.

McCartney steaming past him overlapping from full-back took the team on to another level. The match programme at one point revealed a statistic that illustrated the team took on average 0.4 of a point more per game when this partnership was paired compared to when one or both of them were missing. 'I think with me and Julio something just clicked straight away,' George observed. 'As soon as we formed that partnership it more or less came together. The two of us had a really good understanding. We're good friends and we understood each other's game. We brought the best out of each other because I knew what he was going to do and he knew what I was going to do. It seemed to just click and it certainly went a long way to helping the team to win promotion.'

Arca himself had come to Sunderland as a left-back so instinctively filled in for McCartney whenever he had released the overlapping full-back with a ball slid down the flank for George to race on to and deliver into the box. Equally having been brought through the ranks by coach Pop Robson, who had developed the attacking side of the full-back's game, McCartney never needed a second invitation to join the attack. He would either give the ball to Arca or see him receive possession. Before the ball was even at Julio's feet George would be on his bike. He knew that Arca's first thought was, "Where does George want it?" With such an accurate passer as Arca, McCartney knew that endless runs up and down the wings were not energy wasted because more often than not Arca would have played a beautifully weighted ball right into his path. Simple but sublime: the way football is supposed to be played.

After the bad start that brought just a single win and three defeats from the opening six games the turning point came with a handsome 4–0 away win at Gillingham, where Marcus Stewart took home the match ball after hitting a clinical hat-trick. Someone who just got quietly back on the coach after that game with no souvenir trinket, just the satisfaction of a job well done, was George McCartney, who had had a hand in three of the afternoon's goals. His influence had been missed during the slow start to the season; the Gills game was just his third start.

The season was the 125th in the history of the club. The anniversary would be celebrated with a trophy with the winning of the newly-named Coca-Cola Championship. The summer had seen Sunderland PLC withdraw from the stock market it had entered in 1996 while the constant change that surrounds a football club had seen former captain Jason McAteer depart along with experienced defenders Phil Babb and Joachim Bjorklund plus the home-produced Paul Thirlwell. New faces arriving included Dean Whitehead, Liam Lawrence, Stephen Elliott, Steve Caldwell, Mark Lynch and Carl Robinson, who had previously been on loan.

Ten days after the big win at Gillingham, Darren Williams played his 238th and final game for the club in a Cup tie at Crewe that was lost on penalties. Following Williams' departure McCartney was surprised to find himself Sunderland's longest-serving player. 'I know it's strange to be the club's longest-serving player at the age of 23,' he noted at the time, notwithstanding the return of Michael Bridges, whose career at Sunderland pre-dated George but who had been away from the club for much of the intervening period. 'I've seen so many players come and go here that it's hard to take in,' said George. 'For me to still be here after eight years [he had joined on 8 July 1997 and made his first-team debut on 19 September 2000] and playing in the first team is pleasing for me. I would never have expected to be the club's longest-serving player at such a young age.'

In time to come McCartney would emulate Bridges in leaving Sunderland only to return for a second spell. George would be sold to West Ham by Niall Quinn in 2006, only to be bought back by Roy Keane two years later for a reported fee of £6 million, meaning that at the time the biggest fee paid for a player produced by the Sunderland Academy had been paid by…Sunderland. George had excelled at West Ham, playing 71 times in two years and being runner-up as Hammer of the Year to goalkeeper Rob Green in 2007–08.

It was his form in his first spell at the Stadium of Light that attracted other clubs to him in the first place. As the 2004–05 season settled down the Lads clicked into gear. Having turned the tide with the 4–0 away win at Gillingham in McCartney's second start after injury, Sunderland won the next four League games and would not lose a game in which both George and Julio played until Boxing Day, having climbed from 16th to third in that spell.

From Boxing Day to a season's worst performance at Brighton, in mid-February results were mixed, Everton comfortably disposing of Sunderland's FA Cup challenge along the way. Always a particular thorn in Sunderland's side, Tim Cahill wrapped up a 3–0 scoreline at Goodison. The Aussie had scored Millwall's goal that beat Sunderland in the FA Cup semi-final less than a year earlier on a day when McCartney captained the side but had a disastrous afternoon on what was his 100th appearance: 'You could say the game was partly the best and partly the worst of my football memories,' recalls George. 'It's not every day you get to the semi-final of the FA Cup with the chance to go to the Final but as it turned out on the day I made the mistake for their goal and it cost us a place in the Final but you have to move on from that. Probably for a couple of months after that it was always in my head but everyone makes mistakes and you have to get on with things and forget about it.'

To some extent McCartney's redemption mirrored that of Mickey Gray, the man in the same position in the previous promotion team. Gray had failed to score with the deciding penalty in the 1998 Play-off Final but had bounced back up again, excelling in the promotion year which followed during which he became a full England international. In George's case international football had long been part of his regular experience since making a goalscoring debut for Northern Ireland in 2001. Like Gray he managed to put his costly moment behind him and look to the future.

Returning to the North East after losing to struggling Brighton – who had had a man sent off in the first half – you could hear a pin drop on the flight. Barely a word was said. The team knew they had had a very bad day at the office and had let down the supporters who had followed them all the way to the south coast only to be afforded a terrible view of a terrible game. Stuck behind one of the goals at the not at all missed Withdean Stadium – with an athletics track between them and the pitch – the only thing the fans had a good view of was the entrance to the dressing rooms, which was adjacent to them. The fans let the players know it was not good enough – just as they had done at the 'Nightmare at Elm Park' at Reading in 1997 – and now as then, the response was emphatic.

Eight games in a row were won beginning with four being put past Rotherham and including the season's best victory of 5–1 against Plymouth on a night of five different scorers. Among them was Arca, who with nine goals from the left wing was third in the scorers' list behind the regular front two of Marcus Stewart and Kevin Kyle, the latter a former youth team colleague of McCartney's who benefitted from many a George cross. 'I'd played with big Kev throughout the years and when you play with someone for so long you know their game. He scored a few goals that year and it was probably the best year he had at Sunderland,' notes McCartney.

Not dropping a point from 24 jettisoned Sunderland from being members of the promotion pack to front runners. The last of the sequence brought an evening away victory at nearest rivals Wigan, where a sell-out away following of 7,400 filled not the stand Wigan normally give opponents but the bigger stand that runs the full length of the pitch. The travelling support alone was almost a thousand more than the total gate at Brighton less than seven weeks earlier.

Almost across the finishing line, the Lads led against Play-off hopefuls Reading only to lose at home in a game where regular 'keeper Thomas Myhre had to be substituted by youngster Michael Ingham. A trip to third-placed Ipswich looked to have brought three points only for an 89th-minute equaliser from future Sunderland Player of the Year Darren Bent to keep the party on hold but promotion was secured in the penultimate home match with Leicester.

Ingham having failed to impress, manager McCarthy gave a debut to untried 17-year-old Ben Alnwick. Within five minutes he was picking the ball out of the back of his net but soon came up with a wonder save and after goals from Stewart and Steve Caldwell, he found himself part of a promotion-winning team after his first 90 minutes' experience.

For McCartney and his teammates who had put in a full season to earn the return to the top flight, it was fabulous to be part of the first team to secure promotion in a home game since 1980. Finishing the job off in style, the Championship was won on McCartney's 24th birthday with a superb performance at West Ham, who would gain their own promotion via the Play-offs before the trophy was lifted in front of a full house and another win over Stoke.

Sunderland were about to face a season when even their lowest ever points tally set in their previous top-flight campaign was beyond them, but for now it was a time of celebration. McCartney, Arca and skipper Gary Breen were all named in the PFA Championship team of the season. Arca retained his SAFC Supporters' Association Player of the Year accolade and striker Stephen Elliott was a convincing winner of the club's Young Player of the Year award, but the votes for the Players' Player of the Year and official club Player of the Year awards were as close as they ever have been. McCartney was edged out by midfielder Dean Whitehead in the Players'

George McCartney away at Doncaster in 2004.

Player award but came out on top (slightly ahead of his left flank partner Arca) to take the club's official Player of the Year trophy. George was a deserving winner but the fact that he and Julio were so close was indicative of the way in which the pair bonded as one unit in the title-winning season to bring the best out of each other.

'Looking back now, when Mick McCarthy came in the previous year we got to the semi-finals of the FA Cup and the Play-offs but it wasn't our year. After those disappointments we set out determined to win promotion and we had a really good bunch of lads in the squad. The team that year had a bit of everything and we reached our goal,' comments George, who retains a refreshing attitude when it comes to sharing the individual accolade he achieved. 'To be recognised throughout the whole season as the most consistent and one of the best players is a great achievement for any player and for me personally it is what you strive for. It's something that gives you confidence because it makes you recognise that you've had a really good year. Winning a Player of the Year award gets put down as one of your greatest achievements throughout your football career. It is hard to single out any one player, especially in a season when the whole team has done well, because it is a team game and everyone in the squad plays their part throughout a long season. For me to be voted the top player in that season was a great achievement and something I'll always remember throughout the rest of my life but it took all of us to win the League because there are 11 players out there.'

George McCartney at Sunderland
Debut: 19 September 2000: Sunderland 3–0 Luton Town
Last game: Still on books to date
Total appearances: 175+28 as sub / 0 goals (to summer 2011)

Season by season
2000–01   3+3 games / 0 goals
2001–02   14+6 games / 0 goals
2002–03   19+11 games / 0 goals
2003–04   49+1 games / 0 goals
2004–05   37+1 games / 0 goals
2005–06   13 games / 0 goals
2008–09   17+1 games / 0 goals
2009–10   23+5 games / 0 goals
2010–11   0 games

Other clubs
West Ham United 2006–08
Leeds United (loan) 2010–11
West Ham United (season loan) 2011–12

Dean Whitehead

FA Barclaycard Premiership: 20th out of 20, relegated
FA Cup: Fourth round, lost to Brentford
League Cup: Third round, lost to Arsenal
Top scorer: Anthony le Tallec, 5 goals, 3 League, 1 FA Cup, 1 League Cup
Ever present: No one (Dean Whitehead missed one game due to suspension)
Player of the Year: Dean Whitehead
SAFCSA Player of the Year: Not awarded

Just three years after setting the record for the lowest number of points since the creation of the Premiership, Sunderland broke their own unwanted record. Just 15 points were garnered from 38 games with the solitary home victory coming at the 20th time of asking despite there only being 19 Wearside fixtures. That long-overdue win in front of incredibly loyal home fans came courtesy of a replayed match with Fulham, who had been leading when the original fixture became the first ever game in the history of the Premier League to be abandoned due to weather conditions.

Had Sunderland doubled their points tally for the season they would have still finished bottom of the pile. They were that far off the pace and yet allegations that the class of 2005–06 was Sunderland's worst ever are well wide of the mark. Self evidently they were not good enough but unlike the side of 1986–87 who were relegated into the Third Division when they started the season believing they could win the League – or the Bank of England team who got Sunderland relegated for the first ever time in 1958 – the 2005–06 team did not underperform. The plain fact is that they simply were not good enough for the top flight but to their eternal credit they deserve to have pointed out that they never lost by more than three goals.

If you have ever played football at any level you will know how dispiriting it can be to lose. To lose game after game can see heads go down, people go 'missing' and in the end scorelines become embarrassing. In 2005–06, 29 of 38 games were lost but there were no absolute hammerings as the towel was never thrown in by a bunch of honest, hard-working players, many of whom had come from the lower Leagues.

In just his second season at Sunderland since joining from Oxford United, Dean Whitehead typified the team. Not the easiest on the eye when considering top-flight midfielders, 'Deano' nonetheless deserved his Player of the Year accolade. There was no knocking this lad down. No matter how many setbacks Sunderland suffered Whitehead would never be found slacking. Never failing to contribute 100 per cent effort to the cause, 'Deano' was the classic modern 'box to box' midfield man. Supremely fit and always ready

Dean Whitehead – front row third from left – in 1993 with the Vale of White Horse Primary Schools FA. Matthew Taylor who went to play for Portsmouth, Bolton and West Ham is immediately behind him.

to chase people down and hurry opponents even if he could not get the ball, Whitehead did as much as anyone to prevent an awful season being unimaginably even worse.

Frequently the player to top the statistics of most blocks, most tackles, most passes etc, Whitehead commented, 'It's nice because I like to get involved in everything. I like a tackle and I like a pass.' That attitude had made him the Players' Player of the Year the season before as Sunderland won the Championship in his first year since his transfer north. Having helped the Lads to promotion, though, he found himself part of a team strengthened modestly for the start of the new campaign with £1.8 million buy Jon Stead the most expensive purchase.

Five years later Darren Bent would score very nearly as many goals for Sunderland as the entire team managed in 2005–06 and Bent marked the start of the season with two goals at the Stadium of Light as 10-man Charlton easily won 3–1. It was the first of five successive defeats that followed promotion. In the sixth game captain Gary Breen gave the Lads an early lead at home to West Brom only for the Baggies to steal an equaliser four minutes into injury time. That blow left players and supporters with a sickening feeling that would rarely go away for long but after struggling past fourth-tier Cheltenham after extra-time in the Carling Cup, Sunderland went and won handsomely at Middlesbrough before taking another point against West Ham on the first day of October as things briefly looked up. Indeed, that night's League table showed Sunderland in 17th place.

It was the only table all season that had Sunderland not in a relegation position. All 10 games from then until Christmas were lost, including a 3–0 runaround at home by Arsenal's youngsters in the Carling Cup. During this spell Whitehead took over as penalty taker, converting spot kicks against Portsmouth and Villa, but it was from a brilliant free-kick at Tottenham that Deano enjoyed his personal highlight of the season. A regular dead-ball taker, too many of Whitehead's free-kicks hit the wall but at White Hart Lane he beat England 'keeper Paul Robinson all ends up with an immaculately placed free-kick. Getting goals from midfield was never the player's forte but on this occasion he netted with a shot even David Beckham would have been proud of.

Although the team were struggling, Deano had adapted well to the top flight and at this point in early December he had just been offered an improved contract. 'It's nice to have been offered a new contract so early in the season,' he said. 'I'm disappointed with how the season has gone for us so far but I'm doing my best to help us improve.'

Manager Mick McCarthy was also trying everything and anything to get the best out of his troops. A Boxing Day point from a home goalless draw with Bolton coincided with the first time the team came out at half-time to run through a series of fitness drills with new fitness coach Alan Pearson. The Lads looked like they had done enough to earn another goalless draw five days later only for Everton's Tim Cahill to score a winner three minutes into injury time to flatten everyone's New Year's Eve spirits. Whitehead's big pal Liam Lawrence scored Sunderland's first ever BBC Goal of the Month winner at Fulham in the first game of the New Year but it was not enough to prevent another reverse.

With 12 defeats and a home goalless draw from the last 13 games, Sunderland's form was such that non-League Northwich Victoria publicly fancied their chances when coming to the North East in the FA Cup, where Whitehead's only goal from open play all season contributed to a 3–0 win. Duly boosted by remembering the taste of victory, an improved performance brought a narrow defeat at the hands of League leaders and eventual champions Chelsea followed by a much needed win at West Brom.

Sunderland by this time were so far adrift and so clearly not up to the standard required that there was no hope of survival even from ardent optimists but after the post-Christmas improvement there was a glimmer of hope that at least the Lads might have a better second half of the season. Those hopes were quickly dashed when Sunderland deservedly lost at third-level

Brentford to quash hopes of at least some FA Cup respite away from the miseries of the League. Over 3,000 fans followed Sunderland to Brentford despite all that had gone before. How many other clubs could command such support at a time when the team were doing so badly, and for a game involving a round trip of well over 500 miles?

Three days later Middlesbrough failed to bring as many fans 25 miles to Sunderland but rewarded those who travelled with a 3–0 win over their Wearside rivals, and Sunderland's misery continued at West Ham where two late goals saw spirited resistance again come to nothing. A fifth yellow card of the season in that game resulted in Deano missing his only game of the season. The following month the board dismissed manager McCarthy with former captain Kevin Ball taking over as caretaker manager.

Bally began with three defeats before a trip to Everton where one point was scant reward for an excellent performance where striker Stead finally got his only goal of the season. Rory Delap scored and hit the woodwork with a spectacular late shot at Goodison, only to break his nose and rule himself out for the rest of the season a week later in the home game with Fulham, which was abandoned due to snow after only 21 minutes.

For the next match away to Manchester United all the pre-match talk was about how many goals the home side would win by as they looked to strengthen their position in the leading pack. Sunderland's inevitable relegation was mathematically confirmed at Old Trafford but they left with some dignity after earning a point and respect from a goalless draw. Goalkeeper Kelvin Davis enjoyed a blinder that night. Nicknamed 'Calamity Kelvin' as he had dropped more clangers than a 1970s TV executive looking to modernise children's programming, Davis had had a terrible season right from the 11th minute of the opening game when he had got his angles all wrong and given Darren Bent a gaping hole to aim at and put newly-promoted Sunderland straight on the back foot. However, to Davis' immense credit he never hid. When he was finally dropped in favour of youngster Ben Alnwick he clamoured to get his place back, which he quickly did. A lesser man would have been glad to be taken out of the firing line and quietly continue to pick up his money. It was consistent with Davis' attitude that years later, when he had the chance to leave League One Southampton to become back-up 'keeper at top-flight West Ham, he chose to stay with the Saints,

Dean Whitehead in action on Sunderland's only visit to Brighton's Withdean Stadium.

where he would play every week. Such commitment was typical of Sunderland in 2005–06 – there is no arguing that the team were not good enough, but they were a set of lads proud to pull on the shirt and give everything they had.

Sadly Kelvin kept his most costly calamity for the next game at home to Newcastle. Caretaker Bally had his men well and truly wound up for the visit of the Magpies and with an hour gone the Black Cats deservedly led thanks to a goal from on-loan full-back Justin Hoyte. Disastrously, though, the 'keeper appeared to lose concentration as future Sunderland man Michael Chopra came on as sub and within seconds Chopra capitalised on a Davis howler to equalise. Within six minutes Sunderland trailed 3–1 with another conceded late on. It was a harsh scoreline but one in keeping with the season supporters were enduring.

Defeat to a rashly-conceded late penalty at Portsmouth and a 3–0 home reverse at the hands of a Thierry Henry-inspired Arsenal preceded a rearranged fixture with Fulham. Sunderland could claim four draws and 14 defeats from their home programme and had trailed to Fulham when the original game was abandoned. The Lads were long since relegated but victory was important. No one wanted the tag of going through an entire season without a home League win. Goals from Anthony le Tallec and Chris Brown brought a 2–1 win amid scenes of relief and even a lap of appreciation if not honour from the players.

A final-day trip to Villa brought another defeat but another huge turnout of travelling support, this time in fancy dress. Rumours had surfaced that former Player of the Year Niall Quinn was pulling together a consortium to take over the club and bring happier times back to Wearside.

This awful season was at last at an end. For the second time in four seasons the Supporters' Association did not give a Player of the Year award but Deano took the official club honour. 'We've dominated so many games and then conceded goals or not put chances away,' said Dean. 'I lie awake at night thinking how on earth have we lost some of the games we have lost but all we can do is pick ourselves up.'

The fact that Whitehead was the joint-top League goalscorer with a meagre three League goals shows where the team was most lacking. Sunderland were outclassed in 2005–06 but they were never outfought. Every regular member of that team commands respect for the fight that they showed. It was not their fault that they were not good enough. All you can ever ask is that players give their level best and that is what this team did with Whitehead chief among them in the most trying of circumstances. He would deserve the better days that were to come.

Dean Whitehead at Sunderland
Debut: 7 August 2004: Coventry City 2–0 Sunderland
Last game: 24 May 2009: Sunderland 2–3 Chelsea
Total appearances: 188+12 as sub / 14 goals

Season by season
2004–05	42+4 / 5 goals	
2005–06	39+2 games / 4 goals	
2006–07	45+2 games / 4 goals	
2007–08	28 games / 1 goal	
2008–09	34+4 games / 0 goals	

Other clubs
Oxford United 1999–2004
Stoke City 2009–

Nyron Nosworthy

Coca-Cola Football League Championship: First out of 24, promoted
FA Cup: Third round, lost to Preston North End
League Cup: First round, lost to Bury
Top scorer: David Connolly, 13 goals, all League
Ever present: No one
Player of the Year: Nyron Nosworthy
SAFCSA Player of the Year: Nyron Nosworthy

Maybe more changes were made between the end of the previous season and the start of this one than in any other summer since the Player of the Year award began. More possibly even than in 1997 when Roker Park was bade farewell and the Stadium of Light era began; more than 2003 when there was an exodus of talent following the record low 19-point season. What made the summer of 2006 so important was that Bob Murray CBE, the longest-serving chairman in the club's history, sold SAFC to the Drumaville Consortium, a mainly Irish group of backers fronted by 1998–99 Player of the Year Niall Quinn, who became chairman.

This did not just signal a change of ownership – it brought about renewed vision and appetite for success. The previous chairman, now Sir Bob, and vice chairman John Fickling were fans made good who had the best interests of the club at heart. After all, when they came on board Sunderland were still at Roker Park with a training ground that consisted of three pitches and a couple of ramshackle buildings. They left Quinn literally with solid foundations in a top-class stadium and training facility but the team was about as much use as the buildings at the former training base – simply not good enough. A meagre 15 points had been accrued in an entire season as Sunderland had set a lowest ever Premier League points tally for the second time in their last two top-flight seasons. Supporters were punch drunk at being on the receiving end of jibes; the time had arrived for a new beginning.

Niall Quinn says he never described Sunderland's forthcoming journey under his guidance as a magic carpet ride but the fans were ready for one with all the turbulence and excitement you might expect from such a mode of transport. Fittingly for a fan base prepared to accept entertainment that might put the wind up them, the Player of the Year in the first year under the new owners was Nyron Nosworthy.

'Nugsy' as he was known ('Because when I was a kid my dad said I had a head shaped like a nugget,' Nosworthy explains), was a player who divided fans. For some he was a trier they could not dislike but simply did not rate. For others the Londoner had a heart the size of the centre circle and for that they would forgive him not being at the front of the queue when raw talent was given out. If a nugget has rough edges then maybe Nosworthy Senior was mistaken and it was Nyron's feet that were like nuggets. Sometimes the ball would leave his feet in a direction that would make 'Spot the Ball' competitions impossible to predict. Notoriously in a match at Middlesbrough, Nugsy had tried to pass back to his 'keeper from the halfway line only to almost hit the corner flag as he put his team unnecessarily under pressure.

He had been signed following promotion a year earlier. Being a free transfer from Gillingham, who had been relegated to the third tier, he did not fill Wearsiders with glee as re-entry into the big League was pondered. On the bench on the opening day and considered to be a squad player, Nyron was suddenly thrust into the action when regular right-back Stephen Wright was injured. The first time the ball came to him, Nosworthy let a gently-weighted pass

Nyron Nosworthy in action in 2008.

slip under his foot and out for a throw-in. Almost 35,000 sets of eyes rolled to the heavens as people wondered, 'What have we signed here?' And yet within seconds the newcomer had shown power and indeed finesse to win and come away with the ball.

Watching Nyron was like watching a comedy duo – only he was the slapstick guy and the straight man rolled into one and while you never knew which one you would get, you always knew you would get both within the same game. Given that Nugsy was as strong as an ox and as quick as a whippet and that he could not have put more effort in if he had been born and raised in Monkwearmouth, he had serious attributes, but there was always likely to be a simple task that turned out to be anything but straightforward. Nonetheless, the lad's pace and power more often than not helped him rectify anything he did wrong. One such occasion was when he made an immaculately timed tackle in the box in a late season game against Stoke. 'What happened was that Parkin, I think it was, was about to receive the ball. He's not the quickest and I tried to read him but on that occasion he decided to go the other way to what I was expecting and got away from me. I managed to catch him up though and get a tackle in,' recalls Nyron of what was pure Nugsy – a mistake immediately followed by a piece of magic. There was more than a touch of the Tommy Cooper about him and he was just as loveable as the legendary comic magician.

Man of the Match in the last home game of the previous campaign – when the only home League win of the season had very belatedly been managed – Nugsy had been the last player to leave the pitch as he saluted the fans who had magnificently stood by a team who had put their hearts and souls into a season where the team simply were not good enough. If you have to have a special character to play for Sunderland, as more than one manager has asserted, then Nosworthy had that character in abundance.

As the new era kicked-off with Niall Quinn initially managing the team as well as being chairman, Nosworthy was out of contention, having been injured at Carlisle in pre-season. Sunderland had ditched their 'Ready to Go' run-out music in favour of U2's 'Elevation' but after five games they had lost four out of four in the League and been dumped out of the Carling Cup by Bury, who were propping up all four divisions.

Back to fitness, Nosworthy got a brief taste of action as a sub in Quinn's last game as manager as West Bromwich Albion were beaten 24 hours ahead of Roy Keane taking over as manager. The Manchester United legend wasted no time in signing half a dozen players as the transfer deadline approached but Nyron was out of the picture, not even making the bench in the new manager's first four games.

Called-up by Keane for the first time at the end of September, Nyron kept his place for four games before being dropped and not even making the squad for the next two fixtures before being recalled, at least to the bench. Occasional appearances followed, including one at left-back, by the middle of January the man who would be voted Player of the Year in a Championship-winning campaign had managed a mere eight starts, had seen more than twice as many fixtures played without him even being on the bench, and was yet to play in the position that propelled him to his individual award.

All that changed with a home game against Ipswich. Roy Keane named a team with Nosworthy at centre-back. Nugsy had reportedly been reluctant to play in that position when Mick McCarthy had suggested it but Nyron was not being given any options by Keane; he had simply named him in the side at centre-half. Sunderland had tried numerous people at the heart of the defence up to this point. Kenny Cunningham had proved a disappointment, Stan Varga was strong but had a turning circle comparative with the QE2, Danny Collins had done okay but had reverted to left-back before being dropped and Steve Caldwell had played his last game when being subbed the previous week.

Making his Sunderland debut at centre-back in that Deepdale Cup tie was a youngster on loan from Keane's old club Manchester United – Jonny Evans. And so it was that Evans' League debut was alongside Nosworthy.

The pair were a perfect blend. Nosworthy – big, powerful and brave – complemented by Evans, a man with an old head on young shoulders; calm, composed and able to read the game a step ahead as you would expect of a Manchester United player operating in the Championship. The pair's first outing brought a clean sheet and with it a 1–0 win.

Applauding the fans with the rest of the team at the end of the 2007–08 season.

Nosworthy would play every minute of the rest of the season and Evans would miss just one match. Only one of those games – the third from last – was lost and only three drawn as with a solid base at the heart of defence Sunderland got into their stride. Still in the bottom half of the table at the turn of the year, the Lads hit the top on Easter Monday with less than a month to go.

A thrilling home game with Burnley was won with the latest in an awesome collection of goals from right-winger Carlos Edwards, meaning that when Derby lost at Crystal Palace a couple of days later Sunderland's promotion was made mathematically certain.

The final day of the season saw Sunderland thrash already-relegated Luton 5–0 on their own patch to snatch the title away from Steve Bruce's Birmingham City, who slipped up at Preston. Despite Luton's relegation Kenilworth Road was packed to the rafters and beyond. Many a Hatters fan had cashed in by selling their season ticket seat to visiting supporters so that wherever you looked the Red and White Army were there with the greatest centre-half of them all in the directors' box, Charlie Hurley having travelled from his home in Hertfordshire.

Amid incredible scenes of joy from supporters who had seen as many points won in the past month as their side had managed in all of the season before, one player stood out among the celebrations. It was the same man who had been last to leave after the last home game of the previous year: Nugsy. Having always had a song for him that simply went 'Come on Nyron' to the tune of Gary Glitter's 'Do You Want To Be In My Gang' the fans now routinely serenaded their cult hero with a version of the Amy Winehouse song 'Rehab', singing: 'They tried to take the ball off Nyron but he said No, No No!' Shirt discarded, hat acquired, Nugsy was just about in with the fans. They were great scenes. In this day and age when players and supporters seem worlds apart this was an example of player and fans as one. Nyron Nosworthy may never be England's answer to Pelé but he is the heart and soul of what can be good in football and for that fans adored him. Nugsy laughs his deep laugh at the memory.

'That was such a good time and it goes past so quickly it's like a dream. Winning in the way we did by playing the most relaxed football you could think of and beating a team so well to win the League was just great. You have to remember those things by photography and I've got a copy of the picture in my archives but more than that the memory is always in my head.'

Winning both the official and the SAFCSA Player of the Year awards, Nosworthy polled almost 70,000 points on the club website which employed its normal system of 20 points for being first choice and 10 points for being second choice. Later in the year Nyron would share the North East Player of the Year award with skipper Dean Whitehead, who with 50,000 points was runner-up in the club Player of the Year voting ahead of Carlos Edwards with 25,000 points with top scorer and 'keeper David Connolly and Darren Ward in fourth and fifth positions.

Over the years a regular feature of the Player of the Year award has been that partnerships have been rewarded. Shaun Elliott and Jeff Clarke won in successive years in 1979 and '80, Eric Gates and Marco Gabbiadini dominated the late eighties, Kevin Phillips and Niall Quinn alternated in the late nineties and Julio Arca and George McCartney's left-flank partnership was recognised in 2004 and 2005. Similarly, as Nosworthy won the senior award in 2006–07, so his central defensive partner Jonny Evans was a runaway winner of the Young Player of the Year.

Manager Roy Keane declined an open-topped bus parade, reckoning for a club like Sunderland to get promoted was no big deal. He was right that supporters were sick of the sight of the trophy won for the fourth time in 12 seasons. To compete for it you have to be relegated and Sunderland hopefully will not suffer that fate again for many years to come. Nonetheless, under Quinn and Keane the Lads had got out of the second tier at the first time of asking and in Nyron Nosworthy had a player who will always treasure the esteem in which he is held by Sunderland supporters:

'The fans have always been great with me from day one,' he says. 'If you go to a club that's what you really want and I've always really appreciated the way Sunderland supporters have helped me. It's a part of me and a part of my history. Being Player of the Year puts a different step in your walk because you feel much better about yourself and you just want to do even more for the team. It is a terrific feeling as a professional footballer to get that recognition from the fans. It was a real highlight of my career, especially in respect of the fact that the season didn't start too well and a lot of changes happened. It was nice because I felt I proved a point to myself and showed everyone my capabilities. Winning the Player of the Year topped that off for me. It was fantastic.'

Nyron Nosworthy at Sunderland
Debut: 13 August 2005: Sunderland 1–3 Charlton Athletic
Last game: 27 January 2010: Everton 2–0 Sunderland (to date)
Total appearances: 113+12 as sub / 0 goals (to summer 2011)

Season by season
2005–06	26+6 games / 0 goals
2006–07	27+2 games / 0 goals
2007–08	31 games / 0 goals
2008–09	20 games / 0 goals
2009–10	9+4 games / 0 goals
2010–11	0 games

Other clubs
Gillingham 1998–2005
Sheffield United (loan) 2010–11

FA Barclaycard Premiership: 15th out of 20
FA Cup: Third round, lost to Wigan Athletic
League Cup: Second round, lost to Luton Town
Top scorer: Kenwyne Jones, 7 goals, all League
Ever present: No one
Player of the Year: Kenwyne Jones
SAFCSA Player of the Year: Danny Collins

Kenwyne Jones was part of the Red and White revolution under Niall Quinn and Roy Keane. Debuting a year after Keane made his own bow as boss, Jones did more than anyone to make sure that unlike their previous sojourn to the top flight, newly-promoted Sunderland did not slip straight back down.

Sometimes good footballing combinations come together more by luck than judgement. Marco Gabbiadini was signed to partner Keith Bertschin only for injury to Bertschin to quickly allow Gabbiadini and Eric Gates to blossom. In the 1986 World Cup it was Bryan Robson's injury and Ray Wilkins' sending-off after England had one point and no goals from two games that forced Bobby Robson into a rejigged team that brought in Peters Reid and Beardsley after which Gary Lineker sparkled as England were eliminated only due to Maradona's 'Hand of God'.

Similarly, Kenwyne Jones became a star at Sunderland only after other targets had been missed. Prior to Jones' arrival the Black Cats were linked with the Egyptian Mido. He went to Boro, where he joined future and former SAFC men Lee Cattermole and Julio Arca on the score sheet in his first two games. They would be his only two goals of what would be a season restricted to eight League starts. Had Mido become a Mackem, Sunderland's important first season after stepping up might have been a lot harder than it was.

Arriving for a reported £6 million from Southampton (where he had played under Roker old boy George Burley) just as the summer transfer window closed, Jones would end the season having either scored or contributed to 50 per cent of Sunderland's goals total. Rather than register record low points tallies as they had on their last two top-flight campaigns, Sunderland secured safety with the luxury of two games to go…against Boro.

'Everyone has their part to play in the team and I'm glad that my part is helping,' said Kenwyne upon becoming Player of the Year. 'Whether it is scoring, helping to make a goal or defending, it is all about teamwork and I'm glad I can fit into that profile and work for the team. Everyone has a part to play. Football is all about 11 players on the pitch as well as the people on the bench who could be on the pitch at any time. No player can go out there and make magic and play all positions so you have to give credit where it is due and I think everyone who has played and every staff member has played their part and deserves their share of credit.'

Jones was, in fact, an overwhelming winner of the club's Player of the Year. Nearly 8,000 people voted on the club's official website safc.com, which employed a points system whereby a voter's first choice was awarded 20 points with their second choice acquiring 10 points. Kenwyne romped home with just under 97,000 points with SAFC Supporters' Association Player of the Year Danny Collins coming second in the official count with almost 70,000 points, followed a long way back by Nyron Nosworthy, Craig Gordon and mid-season signing Andy Reid.

Kenwyne Jones stepping out against Reading, September 2007.

'Kenwyne has had a great season for us,' noted manager Keane – not one to be overexcited by individual awards, but it was not just the fans who were captivated. England centre-half John Terry was fulsome in his praise. 'He was fantastic and I've played against him twice now. He's a very good player, very hard working and probably the best in the air in the Premier League. He really is that good. All the lads were talking about him afterwards and saying how good he was.' Terry, in fact, got the only goal of the game when the Londoners came to Sunderland a couple of months before the end of the season to complete the double over the Lads, but throughout the season Kenwyne was the main man in Sunderland's attack.

His debut against Manchester United at Old Trafford, on a day when Sunderland played in front of what up to then was the biggest League gate they had ever played in front of, saw Jones not simply be the main man in Sunderland's attack but the only man as a 4–5–1 was employed. Nonetheless, a month before his 24th birthday Kenwyne demonstrated a boundless energy that was the hallmark of his first season as he combined the mobility of a jeep with the power of a tank.

An international break delayed his home debut during which time 1973 FA Cup-winning goalscorer Ian Porterfield passed away. Consequently the rest of the Cup-winning greats were at the Stadium of Light to pay tribute to 'Porter' and witness Kenwyne make a classic debut as he scored one and made one in a 2–1 win. 'It was great to see the crowd take straight to him when he scored a first-class goal and created another,' said Roy Keane, who was in danger of being delighted.

Jones was soon capturing the headlines as three headers in as many games starting away to Arsenal made him the first Sunderland player since Super Kevin Phillips five years earlier to score in three Premiership games in a row.

In fact the goals dried up for the Trinidadian at this point with only one coming his way in the following five months, in the last game of the calendar year against Bolton. It helped Sunderland to only their second win since his home debut. Despite the drought, Jones' contribution remained important. He continued to be Sunderland's best chance of a goal.

Ross Wallace sneaks a look at KJ's programme during a photoshoot, 2007.

Other strikers were tried: Michael Chopra, Daryl Murphy, Anthony Stokes, Roy O'Donovan, youngster Martyn Waghorn, veteran Andy Cole and January purchase Rade Prica all had opportunities. Second-top scorer Chopra managed six goals and the rest scored just five between them.

Only five players in the country managed more assists than Jones, three of them just one ahead of the Sunderland man, who as someone who spent much of his early international career for Trinidad and Tobago operating as a central defender proved invaluable for the team in defending set-pieces. Sunderland benefitted from the experienced old head of Kenwyne's hero Dwight Yorke in midfield but had Kenwyne's old schoolmate and winger Carlos Edwards been fit for more of the season in order to supply him with a stream of crosses perhaps opponents may have had even more difficulty keeping up with the Joneses.

Ironically Sunderland won their first away game of the season at the 16th time of asking as Kenwyne missed his first Barclays Premier League game since his arrival, Chopra grabbing a vital winner at Villa. Having not scored since the turn of the year, Jones returned to score in successive matches as a season-defining run of three successive victories lifted the team away from the danger zone at just the right time.

Receiving his award prior to the final game of the season at home to Arsenal, Kenwyne

Kenwyne Jones receiving the Player of the Year award, 11 May 2008.

Kenwyne Jones at the training camp in Portugal, August 2009.

modestly commented, 'I feel very happy, it's a great moment, it's an honour. I feel good but it is not just my award, my teammates have helped a lot this season. When you work all season to play well, to do something good for the team and then at the end the supporters give you this award it is a great motivation to carry on, to work more and to get better.'

They were exciting times at the Stadium of Light. After a period in the doldrums, Sunderland under Niall Quinn's chairmanship had stormed to the Championship a year earlier and now had gained a foothold in the top flight. Wearside was re-energised with the fans officially recognised as the loudest in the country. Needing a hero, the fans latched on to the talismanic target man. Able to dominate in the air as John Terry recognised, Jones was no slouch on the deck either and possessed the star quality to excite. Greeting his goals with a flamboyant somersault once the trademark of his uncle Philbet Jones, a former Trinidad and Tobago player, Kenwyne in 2007–08 was Wearside's own Caribbean King.

Kenwyne Jones at Sunderland
Debut: 1 September 2007: Manchester United 1–0 Sunderland
Last game: 9 May 2010: Wolves 2–1 Sunderland (scored)
Total appearances: 88+13 as sub / 28 goals

Season by season
2007–08   33 games / 7 goals
2008–09   27+5 games / 12 goals
2009–10   28+8 games / 9 goals

Other clubs
Joe Public 2002
West Connection 2002–04
Southampton 2004–07
Sheffield Wednesday (loan) 2004–05
Stoke City (loan) 2005
Stoke City 2010–

FA Barclaycard Premiership: 16th out of 20
FA Cup: Fourth round, lost to Blackburn Rovers in a replay
League Cup: Fourth round, lost to Blackburn Rovers
Top scorer: Kenwyne Jones, 12 goals, 10 League, 1 FA Cup and 1 League Cup
Ever present: No one
Player of the Year: Danny Collins
SAFCSA Player of the Year: Danny Collins

Danny Collins had been SAFCSA Player of the Year the previous season when Kenwyne Jones took the club's official award but cult hero Collins ensured his chapter in this book by making sure of the award in 2008–9 when he did the double – winning the official club award while retaining the Supporters' Association trophy.

Over 10,000 people voted in the Player of the Year poll on the club's official website safc.com, 2,685 of them for Collins who, in a system whereby a first choice earned 20 points and being a voter's second choice earned 10 points, Danny's tally of 46,670 was over twice the 23,210 earned by runner-up Anton Ferdinand.

Ironically Collins lost his place to Ferdinand when the latter was bought by manager Roy Keane from West Ham just as the summer transfer window drew to a close. Despite a cracking start on the road with a League win at Spurs and a Cup victory at Keane's first English club Nottingham Forest, the opening two home games had brought defeats for a side using Collins and Nyron Nosworthy as a central defensive partnership. 'We both knew that with Anton coming and us getting beat by Man City around that time that one of us was likely to miss out,' remembered Danny, who was the man to be dropped. 'Obviously I was gutted to miss out but all you can do is get on with it in training, sit tight and hope for another chance. Unfortunately for Nugsy [Nosworthy] he got an injury which helped me to come straight back in, which I was delighted to do.'

Manager Roy Keane found talk cheap. For him it was all about what you did rather than what you said you were going to do so Danny's professionalism in not sulking at being given the chop, but instead single-mindedly buckling down to win his place back was the perfect way to ensure he earned another opportunity by a manager known to be demanding.

For the notoriously difficult second season after promotion, Keane had invested heavily in the squad. Signings included an expensive trio from Tottenham in Steed Malbranque, Teemu Tainio and Pascal Chimbonda, former Liverpool and Bolton forward El-Hadji Diouf, the flamboyant Djibril Cisse and Northern Ireland's record goalscorer David Healy. Keane's pricey purchases of former Sunderland full-back George McCartney and Ferdinand from West Ham reputedly led to Alan Curbishley – manager of Charlton when they beat the Lads in the 1998 Play-off Final – leaving his post as manager of the Hammers.

Ferdinand walked straight into the Sunderland side, debuting at Wigan, where McCartney played the first game of his second spell. Collins and another future Player of the Year, Phil Bardsley, were the men to make way. Collins, in fact, returned to the side alongside Nosworthy, Danny operating at left-back in a Carling Cup tie against Northampton. It was a night Keane described as the worst of his career although his side won. Not unusually for Sunderland they did it the hard way, eventually scraping through against their League One opponents on penalties after coming back from two down with

Danny Collins with the SAFCSA Player of the Year trophy.

five minutes of normal time to play and a man short following the withdrawal of the injured Nosworthy after all the subs had been used.

Four days later Collins was restored to the Barclays Premier League side in central defence at Villa. Like all versatile players, Danny's ability to play equally well in more than one position simultaneously proved to be both a strength and a weakness. It was a strength in that there were two routes into the team open to him but a weakness in that no matter how well he did in one position or another, injuries and suspensions to other players meant that he would frequently have his role changed rather than being allowed to blossom from a long spell in a settled position. The Player of the Year award came Collins' way after a season in which, while he played over 40 games, until the run-in when he finished the final seven games at left-back, he had never played more than five games in a row without swapping position. 'My favourite position is centre-half but I don't mind playing left-back and I suppose in my time at the club I've played roughly half the time in each position. Its part and parcel of football and you just get on with it,' he says of his dual role.

But regardless of which role he was asked to play, Danny Collins, like so many Players of the Year, was first and foremost a wholly committed footballer. It is what Sunderland supporters like to see. Right from the first Player of the Year in Joe Bolton to the most recent in Phil Bardsley, to the man who won the most (Kevin Ball – one 'official' award and four SAFCSA wins), the first requirement for popularity in the eyes of the Red and White Army is that you have to get stuck in. Sunderland supporters spend an incredible amount of time between fixtures reflecting on the last game and keenly anticipating the next. If scientists reckon the average man thinks about sex every eight minutes then possibly the average Sunderland supporter thinks about football twice as often! These are the fans players have to impress but if they do then they are lionised.

Danny Collins receiving the official Player of the Year trophy, 24 May 2009.

A dozen years before Collins won the official Player of the Year award, Richard Ord – like Collins a man comfortable at centre-back or left-back – had a chant in his honour that included: 'Who needs Cantona when we've got Dickie Ord', while for Collins the fans came up with the following: 'For Brazil he should play up front, For Brazil he should play Danny Collins, 'Cos Danny Collins is a skilful ****!'

Collins also had the advantage of coming across as a decent lad. The press loved him because even on the darkest days when things did not go well for the team and the journos were desperate for an interview, Danny was the man who would always help them out and never let them down – exactly the same character trait that made him so dependable on the pitch.

'I got an elbow against Villa when big Carew caught me early on. The doc was a bit worried about me playing but I said I'd give it a go,' was Collins' recollection of his return to League action, itself indicative of his attitude. Although Sunderland narrowly lost on that trip to the Midlands, progress was being made. Manager Keane had a penchant for taking the squad away on bonding exercises be they go-karting, cycling across the Dales, warm weather training in Portugal or army assault courses and everything Sunderland had been seeking came together in late October.

While there had been some fabulous wins over Newcastle in the intervening period, it had astonishingly been 28 years since the local rivals had been beaten on Wearside. That was put right with a 2–1 win featuring a rocket-fuelled free-kick from Kieran Richardson. 'I've been up here a few seasons now and I've certainly grown into just how much the derby means to the fans. To beat them here was a great day because it's what the supporters had wanted for a long time,' noted Danny of one of the highlights of his time at Sunderland.

Football fortunes can change even quicker than political ones, however, and incredibly, just five weeks after derby delight, the Roy Keane era was over. A case of 'After the Lord Mayor's Show' following the high of beating the Magpies ushered in a run of mainly poor results that came to a head with an awful display as Bolton inflicted a 4–1 hammering at the Stadium of Light.

Chairman Niall Quinn installed coach Ricky Sbragia as Keane's successor. Highly respected and a former defender himself, Sbragia followed Keane's policy of using Collins interchangeably at centre-back or left-back. Masterminding a difficult first game away to Manchester United, the former United reserve-team coach saw his Sunderland side beaten only by a last-minute goal. Sbragia got a positive reaction. Previously Sunderland had not scored more than twice in a game all season and they had never managed more than three since promotion 18 months earlier, but back-to-back four-goal romps provided a post-Keane boost.

Barely a month after trouncing Sunderland on Wearside in Roy Keane's last game, Bolton returned in the FA Cup and Sbragia's transformed team beat another of his former clubs. But it was the next home game against Villa that provided a special memory for Danny Collins even though Sunderland lost. Once a goalscoring midfielder in his younger days, Danny had never scored at the Stadium of Light but headed home a Carlos Edwards cross for his big moment. One of the two goals he had previously scored away from home had come against Villa, who he had most controversially had a 'goal' disallowed against at home a year earlier.

While goals are always a pleasant bonus for defenders, when they receive their pay packets they have earned their thousands if they have prevented goals rather than scored them. In an effort to bolster his defence, the new manager added two defenders in the January transfer window. Dispensing with the services of Chimbonda and his former Bolton charge Diouf, Sbragia brought in another player he knew from Bolton, Israeli defender Tal Ben-Haim, and West Ham centre-half Calum Davenport, both on loan.

Despite their arrivals, Collins kept his place in central defence, Ben Haim starting at right-back and Davenport on the bench. When February ended with Sunderland 10th following a well-organised and fully-deserved goalless draw at Arsenal, the 'second season syndrome' seemed not to be a problem for Sunderland. A run of one point from five games quickly got rid of any feelings of being in a comfort zone.

Sbragia made five changes of personnel for the next game as well as switching Collins back to full-back, where Danny would remain for the rest of the season. Despite another poor run of just a single point from the final five games Sunderland had done enough to avoid the drop, although they were four points shy of the generally accepted 40-point safety target.

Having taken less than a point a game, it had been far from an exciting season, although there had been some real high points along the way. The final whistle of the last-day home

defeat to a Chelsea team with the best away record in the top flight signalled scenes of wild joy. Had a combination of results gone the wrong way it would have been possible for Sunderland to be relegated. As the final scores were confirmed, though, not only were Sunderland safe but local rivals Newcastle, along with near neighbours Middlesbrough, had plummeted through the trapdoor to the

Receiving the North East Player of the Year award following his move to Stoke.

Championship. Sunderland could look forward to being the North East's only top-flight representatives and the fans could celebrate being the undoubted holders of the regional bragging rights.

It had been a long and at times tough and troubled season. Throughout it all Danny Collins had been a stalwart of the side. It was no coincidence that the heaviest defeat of the season – at Chelsea – came in the only game when he was not named even as a substitute. 'I've been pretty happy with it carrying on from last year, where I thought I did pretty well,' reflected Danny. The fans were certainly happy with Collins, who had won three of the four Player of the Year awards spread over the last two seasons. Football is a strange game though, and by the end of the next transfer window he was sold by new boss Steve Bruce after starting the season as captain.

Danny Collins at Sunderland
Debut: 25 October 2004: Rotherham United 0–1 Sunderland
Last game: 22 August 2009: Sunderland 2–1 Blackburn Rovers
Total appearances: 146+17 as sub / 3 goals

Season by season
2004–05	7+8 games / 0 goals
2005–06	26+1 games / 1 goal
2006–07	36+4 games / 0 goals
2007–08	33+4 games / 1 goal
2008–09	41 games / 1 goal
2009–10	3 games / 0 goals

Other clubs
Buckley Town 1999–2001
Chester City 2001–04
Vauxhall Motors (loan) 2002–03
Stoke City 2010–

Darren Bent

Barclays Premier League: 13th out of 20
FA Cup: Fourth round, lost to Portsmouth
League Cup: Fourth round, lost to Aston Villa on penalties
Top scorer: Darren Bent, 25 goals, 24 League, 1 FA Cup
Ever present: Darren Bent, 38 out of 38 League games. (Played in both FA Cup ties but did not appear in the League Cup)
Player of the Year: Darren Bent
SAFCSA Player of the Year: Darren Bent

A minute from time in the penultimate pre-season friendly, a young French striker by the name of Oumare Tounkara came on for his first brief taste of senior action for Sunderland. The journey home from that night match at Peterborough saw Sunderland's top officials juggle phone call after phone call as they sought to tie up the loose ends of what would be a record transfer for SAFC with the purchase of Spurs striker Darren Bent. The following morning saw the i's dotted and the t's crossed on an initial £10 million deal that eventually reached £16 million. It was money well spent.

Playing for a Sunderland team who finished 13th, Bent scored 25 goals, all but one of them in the Barclays Premier League. No other player outside the top eight clubs managed even half as many as Bent, who was only outscored by Didier Drogba and Wayne Rooney – players in teams who produce chances by the bucketload. Bent scored exactly half of Sunderland's 48 League goals. Sadly, after seeming as happy as a sandboy in the North East, he became the fourth Sunderland footballer to become Player of the Year in his first season at the club who failed to complete a second successive season, joining Paul Bracewell, John Byrne and Don Hutchison in that list. In January of the following campaign Bent stunned an adoring public reeling from a second disappointing derby of the season with a shock transfer request and within a couple of days he had departed for Aston Villa for a fee reputedly worth up to 50 per cent more than the total of £16 million shelled out for him. While he only played half a season in his second year, significantly he still ended the season as Sunderland's joint top scorer.

Having captured Darren's signature following that return trip from Peterborough, Bent instantly showed his goal poaching ability, gobbling up a half-chance to win the final warm-up match at Hearts. Only Wayne Rooney, narrowly, had outscored Bent in the top flight since 2005, when Darren had returned to the Premier League with Charlton. Sunderland had secured a goal machine and manager Steve Bruce, who had played a leading role in the negotiations, was delighted: 'Darren's goal record speaks for itself. He has 50 goals in 100 Premier League games. He's a fantastic player so I'm thrilled to have him at our football club. He has pace and is a natural finisher so he will be a great addition to our strike force.'

Bent wasted no time in getting off the mark once the serious stuff started, becoming the quickest away debut scorer in 54 years as he tucked away what would be the only goal of the game just five minutes into his debut at Bolton. Following that up with what was the 100th League goal of his career on his home debut against Chelsea, Bent immediately had the fans toasting a new hero.

The first game of September began a run for Darren which saw him become the first man since Neil Martin in the 1960s to score in five consecutive top-flight games, a run that ended with him hitting the post from his only sight of goal at Birmingham. It already felt like a shock

Darren Bent with the hat-trick ball from the Bolton game, 9 March 2010.

to see him hit the woodwork as the man who had the Midas touch – the previous week he had scored a winner against Liverpool with a scuffed shot that infamously went into the net via a beach ball.

Never slow to serenade their heroes, the Red and White Army came up with a chant: 'Darren Bent is fast as lightning, Darren Bent is red and white. When he gets the ball he scores a goal, he's ****ing dynamite.' Benty lapped it up. 'I love the song. At Charlton they used to sing Darren Bent Bent Bent which I liked because it was after the Ian Wright song and he's one of my heroes. They didn't have a song for me at Spurs and at Ipswich it was just Darren Bent Bent Bent as well. The dynamite song is my favourite though because it's taken a bit of imagination, but the fans up here are just brilliant.'

While the Wearside crowd adored him, Darren still had plenty to prove. He had suffered public criticism from his Tottenham boss Harry Redknapp and lacked admirers in the national media, coming in for criticism for an England performance against the might of Brazil in the heat of Qatar where he became the first Sunderland player to win a full England cap since Gavin McCann in 2001. Shrugging off the same critics who hammered 20-year-old Jordan Henderson on his England debut a year later, Darren declared: 'Whatever people write about me, so be it. They can't take away my Sunderland goals or my Sunderland form and I know the way to be a success with England is to be a success with Sunderland.'

In the North East he was happy playing alongside the towering Kenwyne Jones. 'Kenwyne's a great partner for me up front and we have hit it off very well,' he claimed. Like Kenwyne, Darren had played under ex-Sunderland defender George Burley, in Bent's case at Ipswich, while Jones had been tutored by the Scottish international at Southampton. Bent was a Burley fan. Asked which of the 14 managers he had played under up to this point in his career he had liked the most, he showed as little hesitation as he did in the box. 'Definitely George Burley, 100 per cent. He had a big influence on me. He had me training with the Ipswich first team when I was just 16.'

Bent's formative years at Portman Road had seen him also benefit from working with two forwards with SAFC connections – 1960s star Colin Suggett and Marcus Stewart, who fired the lads to promotion in 2005. 'Colin always used to give me bits of advice about how to get into the first team. He was a good help and a good guy,' recalled Darren. 'I learned loads off Stewy. I used to watch him a lot when we were at Ipswich.' Good as Suggett and Stewart were, only Super Kevin Phillips could better Bent's goalscoring feats at Sunderland in the years since Suggett's era.

Laughably, there were those who suggested Bent did not do much outside the box. That was like saying Jimmy Montgomery was not much use up front. Great goalscorers like Jimmy Greaves and Gary Lineker never worried about chasing all over the pitch. They focused their energies in making sure they were in the right place at the right time to do what most find the hardest thing in the game. Bent was there to score and score is what he did. He was far from a lazy player and his work rate impressed the crowd. His partner Kenwyne Jones sometimes looked like he would not run for the bus let alone the ball, but Bent's application was well illustrated in a home game with West Ham when, after Jones was harshly sent off, Darren's willingness to chase down what looked like a lost cause created an equaliser for Kieran Richardson.

Not everything went Bent's way, however. His return to White Hart Lane, where he was eager to impress, saw him have a penalty saved and for the first time he went three games without scoring. Three games – barely a drought. Indeed, when he scored against Portsmouth in mid-December, Darren became the first Sunderland player since Kevin Phillips in his season as Europe's top scorer to reach double figures in the top flight before Christmas.

He had hit three more before the turn of the year and commented: 'I never knew I'd score at the rate I have so far this season but I always knew that when I played games I'd get the goals

Darren Bent with Young Player of the Year Jordan Henderson.

Darren Bent on the NEFWA 30th Awards Dinner poster.

SUNDAY 12TH DECEMBER 2010

RAMSIDE HALL HOTEL & GOLF CLUB

North-East Football Writers' Association

Awards Dinner

Sponsored by

🏛 BARCLAYS

30th
ANNIVERSARY

IN AID OF The Sir *Bobby Robson* ⚽
Foundation

and I think this season is a reflection of that. It takes me back to my Charlton days when I scored a lot of goals in so many games.'

Even the best strikers cannot score regularly without a stream of chances and Bent benefitted especially from a man who knew his game from Tottenham, Steed Malbranque. 'I've known Benty for a while now so I know the places he likes the ball. If I play the ball in behind the back four I know he'll like that,' said the notoriously quiet Frenchman who, unlike Darren who could talk for England, preferred to do his talking solely with his feet, and teed up two of Benty's hat-trick against Bolton, the team that Darren had scored more against than any other in his career.

The biggest win of the season against the Trotters ended a slump of 14 games without a win, Darren netting the first top-flight hat-trick by a Sunderland player on Wearside in a quarter of a century. Although it was his only hat-trick in a Sunderland shirt, within a month Bent twice bagged braces in match-winning home performances. Two goals in the first 11 minutes set the Lads en route to a fine win over Birmingham. The goals took Bent to 20 goals by mid-March with perhaps the most significant statistic being that 10 of those goals had come in the first 20 minutes of the games. In modern football the first goal is so important and right from day one at Bolton Darren had regularly put Sunderland in the driving seat.

The Easter Saturday visit of his former club Spurs proved to be the most eventful match of the season. Just 36 seconds into the game, Bent was celebrating a goal in front of his former fans. It was the quickest Barclays Premier League goal of the season and the sixth-fastest in SAFC history. Doubling the lead from a penalty, Darren then passed up two further opportunities to complete a hat-trick as Spurs 'keeper Heurelho Gomes twice saved from the spot in the first game in the club's entire history in which Sunderland had been awarded three penalties. Sunderland pulverised the Londoners but did not secure the three points until late on. Giant Peter Crouch – who had turned down Steve Bruce's attempts to sign him – halved the deficit, while the ref, who had given the Lads three penalties, took it upon himself to disallow a 'goal' from Anton Ferdinand, whose Michael Jackson tribute celebration was stopped in its tracks. It took a spectacular volley from Bolo Zenden to finish Tottenham off, Bent having scored two but spurned two. Disappointed to only score twice? There have not been many Sunderland strikers down the years good enough to be in that calibre as the brace left Bent with seven from his last six games.

Not surprisingly, the fans loved him. A signing session in one of the club shops scheduled to last 90 minutes lasted fully three and a half hours as thousands queued to get close to their hero. Despite impressive seasons by new signing Lorik Cana, Kenwyne Jones (who got a creditable nine goals) and midfielder Malbranque, there could only be one winner of the Player of the Year award and inevitably Darren did the double of the official club award and also the SAFCSA trophy. 'It caps off a great season for me,' he said upon being named Player of the Year. 'It really shows that the fans are 100 per cent behind you and that they've really appreciated what I've done. There's no bigger honour than when your club's fans vote you Player of the Year and I really do thank them for that.'

Had he stayed at Sunderland, Darren Bent would have had the chance to become the idol of a generation. As it is the modern footballer so often moves on as if changing clubs is as easy as changing cars. Darren Bent may have been a Ferrari of a forward but while being flash may turn heads supporters are about hearts and ultimately, in prematurely leaving a place where he was loved, Darren Bent lost something he will never gain elsewhere. To be idolised in the North East is to be put on a pedestal like no other.

Darren Bent at Sunderland
Debut: 15 August 2009: Bolton Wanderers 0–1 Sunderland (scored)
Last game: 16 January 2011: Sunderland 1–1 Newcastle United
Total appearances: 63+1 as sub / 36 goals

Season by season
2009–10   40+1 games / 25 goals
2010–11   23 games / 11 goals

Other clubs
Ipswich Town 2001–05
Charlton Athletic 2005–07
Tottenham Hotspur 2007–09
Aston Villa 2011–

Phil Bardsley

Barclays Premier League: 10th out of 20
FA Cup: Third round, lost to Notts County
League Cup: Third round, lost to West Ham United
Top scorer: Asamoah Gyan, 11 goals, 10 League, 1 League Cup
Darren Bent, 11 goals, 9 League, 2 League Cup
Ever present: No one
Player of the Year: Phil Bardsley
SAFCSA Player of the Year: Phil Bardsley

On the second Saturday of the season Phil Bardsley sat alone in the Sunderland dressing room at the Hawthorns an hour after defeat by newly-promoted West Bromwich Albion. Surrounded by leftover pizza and the detritus of a Barclays Premier League fixture, Bardsley cut a forlorn figure. Waiting for a colleague who was in the drug testing room, hoping for nature to play its part and enable him to provide the urine specimen that would enable them to leave, Phil scoured the scene and perhaps wondered if he would be a part of it any more. The player he was waiting for was a colleague rather than a teammate simply because Bardsley was not in the team.

He had been the subject of transfer speculation throughout the summer, West Brom being one of the rumoured pursuers, and had been an unused sub in the first two fixtures. Moreover, he had seen Sunderland buy not one but two international players who played in his preferred right-back position and with 10 days left of the transfer window the chances of him remaining a Sunderland player, let alone Player of the Year, were far from guaranteed.

Fast forward 271 days to chairman and former Player of the Year Niall Quinn's words the day after the club's first own awards dinner: 'If any footballer was at that awards dinner and didn't go home thinking "Bardsley has shown us all" then they're not worth their salt. Where Phil came from in the previous 12 to 14 months in terms of where his career was going to where he wanted it to go just shows you what can be done with application and the right life choices. He showed the desire to be the best and the work rate to match it. If we had 11 players with Phil Bardsley's level of application every week, this club will get to be where it wants to be. For me he's a classic example of someone who was happy to flow along and then suddenly woke up one day and decided, "I've got to get the best out of my career", and that's exactly what he's doing. He's been a credit to the game; he's everything that's good about footballers.'

While many a modern player will head for Dubai, LA or Las Vegas during the close season, Bardsley decided to focus on fitness and spent much of his summer in the gym. Working with a close friend, fellow Salford lad and reigning European super featherweight and former English and WBU featherweight champion Steve Foster Junior, Bardsley dedicated himself to seeing how good he could be and found that determining to make the most of the talent you have been blessed with can take you a long way.

Although he got two games in the Carling Cup and came off the bench in a Barclays Premier League win over his first club Manchester United's rivals City, it was late September before 'Bardo' got a League start. Asked to replace the injured Kieran Richardson at left-back rather than operate in his familiar berth on the right, Phil excelled in a fine display that deserved more than a point at Anfield against Liverpool. It was only his fourth League start of 2011 but from then on he would play in every game, all but two of them from the start. Holding his place after

Phil Bardsley with his Player of the Season and Player's Player of the Season awards.

Anfield for a goalless draw with Manchester United, Bardo found himself called-up to a Scotland squad for the first time.

Debuting with an excellent display against world champions Spain after getting a close-up view on the bench against the Czech Republic, Phil suddenly found everything going for him. 'Spain were unbelievable. They are the best team in the world,' said Phil, who qualifies for Scotland through his father, could have also played for the Republic of Ireland and may well make England feel as if they should have given him a chance. 'I gave myself time to think about playing for Scotland when I was first asked by Sir Alex Ferguson and Walter Smith a few years back but didn't feel as if the time was right then. Now I'm playing for Sunderland I felt the chance was too good to turn down. When I was playing for Manchester United in the Premier League and Champions League when I was 19 and 20 I got a letter from England Under-21s saying I was on standby but I never played and just fell off the radar.'

The current Player of the Year Phil Bardsley, left, with his Supporters' Association Player of the Year trophy along with SAFCSA Young Player of the Year Simon Mignolet

With further caps coming his way throughout the season in his previously regular position of right-back, Bardsley made light of being asked to play on the opposite side to his natural one for Sunderland, for whom his consistently solid performances re-established him as a key member of the side. Throughout a campaign of ups and downs ranging from the worst derby defeat in half a century to the club's best ever victory over any reigning double holders when Chelsea were handsomely beaten on their own turf in November, Phil's form was steady and assured.

Steve Bruce's side spent over three months – from early November to late February – in the top seven. Bardsley's first concern as a full-back is to stop goals and by the time Sunderland won 1–0 at Aston Villa just past the turn of the year, he could claim to have been part of a side that had kept 12 clean sheets in the 20 games he had played in up to that point. As the coach pulled away from Villa Park that night though, it was not Phil's part in another shut-out that was the topic of conversation but the fact that he had scored the winner. It was Phil's first League goal in England, his only previous strikes being at Forest in the League Cup two and a half years earlier and one against Falkirk while on loan to Rangers. Whereas his only previous goal for Sunderland had been scuffed in from close range, his winner at Villa (another club he had played for on loan) was a howitzer of a shot from outside the box. 'The ball came out to me and I just took a touch and hit it. Fortunately for me, the team and everyone, it went in. It was a great feeling to score my first Barclays Premier League goal. It's been a long time coming and I was delighted to get the goal, especially as it helped us to get all three points.'

Bardsley would blast two more scorching goals before the season was over but unfortunately for Phil neither would give him the satisfaction of scoring a winner. Late in the season he would net a cracker from a short free-kick in the reverse game with West Brom, while against Chelsea his first goal at the Stadium of Light saw him cut in from the left and beat Petr Cech all ends up within four minutes of kick-off.

The programme for that 1 February fixture with the Stamford Bridge club laid down a marker for Bardsley to win the Player of the Year award, stating: 'With the season now more than halfway over, surely Phil Bardsley must be one of the candidates for this year's honour if he can maintain the standards he's set himself. Bardsley is a Sunderland supporter's kind of Sunderland player.'

Bardsley remained a constant presence in the side in what was a difficult run-in as the team was decimated by a horrendous run of injuries before a late flourish of three wins in the last five games enabled the Black Cats to squeeze into the top 10 of the top flight for only the third time in over fifty years.

Phil was an overwhelming winner of the Player of the Year award. Having already bagged the impressive SAFC Supporters' Association trophy by now in its 35th year, Phil was the proud recipient of the official Player of the Year award at what was the club's first ever awards dinner of its own. After receiving the Players' Player of the Year award from Mr Chris Johnson of CJ Ceilings, Bardo then stepped forward to receive the main award from Mr Allan Bramley of dentists Complete Smile. After the season Bardsley had had in re-establishing himself and hitting new heights, while becoming an international footballer of repute, a complete smile was more than in order.

'In my young days I won Player of the Year awards with my Sunday League club but I've never won anything like this at professional level before so it's a massive achievement for me and I'm proud to have done it. It's normally the boys who get the headlines who win the awards so it's nice for me to get the award as a defender and I'll try to do the same again in the future. I'll always look back on it proudly. To win the award is an achievement and it's all down to hard work and dedication. To be a Player of the Season at Sunderland is a highlight for me. Sunderland is a great club and a great place.'

For Phil Bardsley to win the club's individual award in 2011 brings this book of SAFC Players of the Year full circle. The first SAFC Supporters' Association winner having been the full-blooded full-back Joe Bolton in 1976, Bardsley is out of the same mould. A player who plays with his heart and maximises his ability is a guaranteed hero at a club whose ground now stands on the site of a former pit and adjacent to what was once the biggest shipbuilding river in the world.

There have been many tremendous Players of the Year at Sunderland. You can now look back through them and select what would be your best XI from the players to have achieved the accolade of being the man whose contribution to a season has been outstanding. Great names and great characters: these are the players who provided many of the memories that enable the Red and White Army to keep the faith.

Phil Bardsley at Sunderland
Debut: 29 January 2008: Sunderland 2–0 Birmingham City
Last game: –
Total appearances: 96+13 as sub / 4 goals (to summer 2011)

Season by season
2007–08   11 games / 0 goals
2008–09   31+2 games / 1 goals
2009–10   20+8 games / 0 goals
2010–11   34+3 games / 3 goals

Other clubs
Manchester United 2003–08
Burnley (loan) 2006
Glasgow Rangers (loan) 2006
Aston Villa (loan) 2007
Sheffield United (loan) 2007

Appendix

Additional Player of the Year Awards

As well as the official Player of the Year Award and SAFCSA Player of the Year award, most of the Supporters' Association's 40 plus branches also make their own award. In addition to such club Player of the Year awards, Sunderland players have won numerous national and other awards, especially since the move to the Stadium of Light. This co-incided with an increase in top overseas players, many of whom have received awards from overseas organisations while on Sunderland's books.
These include:

1964   Charlie Hurley, Football Writers' Association, Player of the Year runner-up to Bobby Moore.
1982   Bryan 'Pop' Robson, North East Football Writers' Association Player of the Year.
1989   Marco Gabbiadini, North East Football Writers' Association Player of the Year.
1999   Niall Quinn, North East Football Writers' Association Player of the Year.
2000   Kevin Phillips, North East Football Writers' Association Player of the Year.
        Kevin Phillips, Football Writers' Association Player of the Year runner-up to Roy Keane.
        Kevin Phillips, Professional Footballers' Association Player of the Year runner-up to Roy Keane.
2001   Thomas Sorensen, North East Football Writers' Association Player of the Year.
        Claudio Reyna, USA Player of the Year
        Thomas Sorensen, Denmark Player of the Year runner-up
2002   Niall Quinn, North East Personality of the Year.
        Claudio Reyna, FIFA 2002 World Cup All Star Team
2003   Mart Poom, Estonian Player of the Year.
2004   Mart Poom, Estonian representative for UEFA Golden Jubliee.
2007   Dean Whitehead & Nyron Nosworthy, Joint North East Football Writers' Association Player of the Year.
        Kenwyne Jones, Trinidad & Tobago Player of the Year.
2009   Danny Collins, North East Football Writers' Association Player of the Year.
2010   Asamoah Gyan, BBC African Player of the Year
        Asamoah Gyan, Ghanian Player of the Year
        Asamoah Gyan, Ghanaian Sports Personality of the Year.
        Asamoah Gyan, AIG award as 'Most outstanding player at 2010 World Cup'.
        Asamoah Gyan, African Cup of Nations All Star Team
        Asamoah Gyan, CAF African Player of the year runner-up to Samuel Eíto
        Asamoah Gyan, FIFA Ballon díor (World Player of the Year) shortlist.
        Darren Bent, North East Football Writers' Association Player of the Year.
        Ahmed Elmohamady, African Cup of Nations All Star Team

BV - #0083 - 280426 - C0 - 234/156/12 - PB - 9781780913407 - Gloss Lamination